PERSONNEL
DOCUMENTS
OF THE
SS

PERSONNEL DOCUMENTS OF THE SS

By

Charles J. Barger

&

J. A. Bowman

IMPERIAL PUBLICATIONS

PERSONNEL DOCUMENTS
OF THE SS

By
Charles J. Barger
&
J. A. Bowman

1st EDITION

ISBN 1 871498 04 X

© Copyright 1991 Imperial Publications

Artwork and cover design by Brian Molloy.

Typesetting and layout design by Findlay Martin at Lakeland Computer Services, Kendal, England.

Senior Editor, Gail A. Bowman.

Printed by Billing & Sons Ltd. Worcester, England.

Published by
IMPERIAL PUBLICATIONS
PO BOX 5, LANCASTER LA1 1BQ, ENGLAND.

TABLE OF CONTENTS

ACKNOWLEDGEMENTS

It would not be possible to gather together such a diverse collection of documents, photographs and information without the contributions and support of many collectors worldwide. The authors would like to express their appreciation to all those who generously donated time and material to this book, however we would especially like to recognise the contributions provided by Chris Alisby from his extensive archive and Stuart Russell for sharing his unrivalled knowledge of the SS and their documents, along with the following individuals and institutions:

INDIVIDUALS

Chris Ailsby
John R. Angolia, LTC (Ret).
Klaus Brase
Steve Brindley
Malcolm Bowers
Graham Chambers
Dave Johnson
Robert Johnston
James Keogh
Jess T. Lukens

Heinz Macher
Arthur Meyer
Donald Mills
Doug Nash
Brana Radovic
Stuart Russell
Jost Schneider
Brenda Shaw
Gundi Shaws
Arthur Thornton

INSTITUTIONS

Bundesarchive: Koblenz, Germany
Imperial War Museum: London, England
Imperial Publications Library & Archive: England
National Archives: Washington D.C., USA
Public Records Office: London, England
Royal Army Dental Corps Museum: Aldershot, England
Wallis & Wallis: Lewes, Sussex, England

AUTHORS REQUEST

In the course of compiling this work it soon became evident that the scope of the subject would go far beyond a single volume: as the range of documentation produced by the SS was so extensive. As is the case with all military reference books the authors must rely heavily upon the involvement of fellow collectors, therefore we would greatly appreciate any photographs or copies of any interesting SS related documents for inclusion in any subsequent work on the Personnel Documents of the SS. We are especially interested in documents relating to the SS Honour Sword, SS Dagger, Totenkopfring or Jullecter and associated artifacts. Full acknowledgement will be given for any photographs or information supplied, which will hopefully lead to expanding our knowledge of this seldom documented area of collecting. Any reference material for future publications should be sent in care of the publisher, -Imperial Publications, PO Box 5, Lancaster, LA1 1BQ, England.

THE FIRST 500 COPIES OF THIS VOLUME ARE A NUMBERED LIMITED EDITION

FOREWORD

The volume of paperwork and documentation generated by the SS during its short history was phenomenal. The SS were arguably the most prolific and meticulous compilers and recorders of information relating to every facet and function of their organisation. A substantial part of the SS's preoccupation with recording every detail of the SS-Mann's life emanated from the head of the organisation, Reichsführer-SS Heinrich Himmler, who was the quintessential bureaucrat. A veritable torrent of orders, directives, and correspondence was generated from Himmler's office on the Prinz Albrecht Strasse in Berlin. Although Himmler controlled an organisation eventually numbering millions he had in many respects the mentality of a small office clerk. It is astounding to read some of the trivial matters which Himmler busied himself with at times, even when the Third Reich was on the verge of collapse.

In addition to the standard clerical forms and documents which would be essential to the efficient administration of any large paramilitary organisation, the aspiring SS recruit was also required to fill out additional documents such as the Ahnenpass and Ahnentafel inorder to prove his racial background and suitability as a candidate for the SS. Indeed it was necessary for the SS applicant to prove his pure Aryan descent as far back as the year 1800. and for officers to the year 1750.

After negotiating the many hurdles to gain entry into the SS, the SS-Mann was then inducted into a system which meticulously controlled and documented every aspect of his life both professional and personal: he was even required to fill in specific SS forms inorder to marry to ascertain the suitability of his prospective bride and to prove her pure Aryan descent. Virtually every action and duty carried out by the SS-Mann was accompanied by some piece of paper - signed, counter-signed and stamped by innumerable clerks. Ultimately this obsession with recording every detail of their actions would serve as the SS's own indictment at the end of World War II.

However the documents appearing in this volume are not all strictly SS. Where groups of documents belonging to an individual have survived intact we have endeavoured to keep them as complete as possible inorder to better illustrate the whole career of that personality, or to show how service in other Third Reich organisations such as the Hitler Youth, SA or RAD fit in with his SS career thereby maintaining the continuity of the man's biography. This principle in some instances has been carried through even into the post war era to show the continuing fortunes of an individual. With close scrutiny it is possible to reconstruct quite a detailed picture of an SS soldier's service by combining information not only from his military service records such as his Soldbuch or Wehrpass but also from ancillary documents such as leave passes, hospital discharges, marriage application forms, etc. Therefore inorder to maintain the integrity of these personality groupings it has not always been possible to put specific documents into strict categories. It was also believed that innumerable examples of the same document although ascribed to different individual's would be repetitious and serve no useful purpose.

There will undoubtedly be omissions and shortcomings in this work due to the enormous scope of the subject. However it is intended that as other SS documents come to light this work will be updated and extended at some future date.

SS AHNENTAFEL
(SS Ancestors Chart)
&
AHNENPASS
(Family Tree of Aryan Descent)

The following set of six documents are excerpts from the SS ancestral chart of Georg Muller. Prior to being accepted into the SS a prospective candidate was required to produce evidence of his racial purity and also that of his direct descendants. Every SS applicant had to provide a family tree dating back to 1750 A.D. for officers and 1800 A.D. for other ranks: this was to prove the individual's Aryan descent or at the very least that he was descended from Nordic stock. The RUSHA (Rasse und Siedlungshauptamt/Race and Settlement Main Office) was directly responsible for evaluating the completed ancestral charts to determine their validity. In addition to the ancestral chart, the SS recruit/applicant was required to pass a general medical examination and was also required to provide evidence that his family was free from any hereditary disease or deformity.

Finally upon completion of these various conditions the applicant was required to appear in person before a RUSHA examination board who carried out a visual examination of the individual to determine his racial qualities based upon his physique, physiognomy as well as his general bearing and bodily development.

The SS Ahnentafel (SS Ancestors chart) was a document designed specifically for members of the SS, however prior to being accepted into the SS a prospective applicant was required to produce a valid Ahnenpass. The Ahnenpass had a similar format to the SS Ahnentafel showing Aryan descent, however it had a much more general application. Prior to World War II all German citizens were required to possess a completed and validated Ahnenpass and the document was compulsory for any individual wishing to join any NSDAP organisation, the civil service or any other Governmental department.

During the war years the issuing of the Ahnenpass virtually ceased, not only as a consequence of war restrictions, but also because a great deal of the credibility of the pass had been lost after numerous incidences of forgeries being used spawning from a lucrative market which had grown up during the late 1930's.

SS AHNENTAFEL

4

ᛋᛋ-Ahnentafel von

Name — Vorname

Anleitung.

1. Welche Angaben muß die Ahnentafel enthalten?

Die Ahnentafel muß alle Vorfahren des ᛋᛋ-Angehörigen bzw. seiner Frau oder Braut bis zu den Ahnen enthalten, die spätestens am 1. Januar 1800 geboren wurden. Bei ᛋᛋ-Führern sollen sich die Angaben möglichst bis 1750 erstrecken.

Für jeden Vorfahren ist anzugeben:

1. Name (bei Frauen nur Geburtsname) und sämtliche Vornamen.
2. Geburtsort, Geburtsjahr, Geburtsmonat, Geburtstag (hinter *).
3. Sterbeort, Sterbejahr, Sterbemonat, Sterbetag (hinter †).
4. Religion (hinter R.).
5. Beruf (hinter Ber.).
6. Heiratsort, Heiratsjahr, Heiratsmonat, Heiratstag (hinter ∞).

Für die Frau bzw. für die Braut ist eine besondere Ahnentafel einzusetzen. Kinder sind auf der Rückseite der Ahnentafel anzugeben.

2. Wie wird die Ahnentafel ausgefüllt?

Zunächst trägt der ᛋᛋ-Angehörige (bzw. seine Frau) — möglichst in Maschinenschrift, sonst mit Tinte — alle geforderten Angaben über sich selbst ein. Sodann werden in Feld Nr. 2 die Angaben über den Vater und in Feld Nr. 3 die Angaben über die Mutter eingelegt. Feld Nr. 4 ist für die Angaben über den Großvater väterlicherseits, Feld Nr. 5 für die Angaben über die Großmutter väterlicherseits bestimmt. Feld Nr. 6 und Nr. 7 dienen für die Eintragungen über die Großeltern mütterlicherseits. In gleicher Weise sind in den Feldern Nr. 8 bis Nr. 15 die Urgroßeltern zu verzeichnen, in den Feldern von Nr. 16 bis Nr. 31 die Ur-Urgroßeltern und in den Feldern Nr. 32 bis Nr. 63 die Ur-Ur-Urgroßeltern.

Dazu vergleiche folgendes Schema:

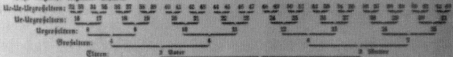

Aus den vorhandenen Urkunden sind sämtliche Angaben wie Namen, Beruf und Religion der Eltern des betr. Vorfahren einzutragen, auch wenn über diese Eltern keine besonderen Urkunden vorliegen oder die 1800-Grenze ihnen überschritten ist.

Es ist besonders darauf zu achten, daß die Eltern eines Vorfahren immer in den beiden unmittelbar darüber liegenden Feldern stehen müssen.

Sämtliche nicht urkundlich belegten Angaben (errechnet oder aus Familienüberlieferung) sind mit Bleistift einzutragen.

Begründung für fehlende Angaben oder Vermerke wie „nicht festzustellen" oder ähnlich gehören nicht in die Ahnentafel. Sie sind in den hierfür bestimmten Raum auf der Rückseite der Ahnentafel unter Angabe der Ahnennummer einzutragen.

3. Beschaffung von Urkunden für die Angaben in der Ahnentafel.

Für den ᛋᛋ-Angehörigen selbst (bzw. seine Frau) und für alle Vorfahren sind folgende Urkunden als Beleg für die Richtigkeit der Ahnentafel erwendig:

1. Geburtsurkunde oder Taufschein, 2. Heiratsurkunde oder Trauschein. Erwünscht ist die Sterbe-Urkunde.

Der ᛋᛋ-Angehörige stellt zunächst alle Angaben, die er in der Familie erfahren kann, auf einem besonderen Bogen zusammen. Er fordert dann die entsprechenden Urkunden an unter ausdrücklichem Hinweis darauf, daß die Urkunden zum Nachweis der arischen Abstammung für die Reichsführung ᛋᛋ benötigt werden. Für die Zeit nach 1876 die Standesämter zuständig, für die Zeit vorher die Pfarrämter. Urkunden aus dem Auslande vermitteln die jeweiligen Deutschen Konsulate, sind bei dem Sippenkanzlei-Amt, Berlin W 5, Wilhelmstraße 74, zu erfahren.

Alle besonderen Daten sind bei der Anforderung genau anzugeben. Ist ein Datum nicht genau bekannt, so ist die Hilfe des örtlichen Schulungsleiters zu erbitten.

Die Gebühr für jede Urkunde beträgt RM –.60. Bei nachweisbarem und von der zuständigen Dienststelle bestätigtem Unvermögen kann die Gebühr erlassen werden.

4. Beifügen von Urkunden.

Urkunden und Belege über die Angaben in der Ahnentafel sind bei Einreichung der Ahnentafel beizufügen. Die Urkunden sind für jede Ahnentafel getrennt in einer besonderen Briefsichtung zu ordnen. Auf dieser Briefsichtung sind Name, Wohnort, Dienstgrad, ᛋᛋ-Nr., ᛋᛋ-Einheit, gegebenenfalls VB-Nr. zu vermerken. Auf über Urkunde ist in der für Ahnen oben rechts die Nummer, unter der der betreffende Vorfahr in der Ahnentafel gehört ist, mit Bleistift anzugeben, zum Beispiel Geburtsurkunde der Großmutter mütterlicherseits „7". Trauschein der Großeltern und der Großvater mütterlicherseits „6/7". Die Ahnentafel ist von der Abteilung an das Kasse- und Sippungs-Bureau dem zuständigen Schulungsleiter vorzulegen. Dieser hat die Eintragungen in der Ahnentafel mit den vorgelegten Urkunden zu vergleichen. Nicht anzuerkennen ist eine anerkannte (1. 1. 1800) und geprüfte Ahnentafel sind nur dem Schulungsleiter von der Abteilung an das Kasse- und Sippungs-Bureau zurückzusenden. Die Urkunden erhält der Antragsteller nach Prüfung vom Kasse- und Sippungs-Bureau zurück.

ᛋᛋV R 1 mit Nachnachverlag M. S. Manz, München (Genf. Original)

65	66	67	68	69	70	71	72	73	74	75	76	77	78	79
	33		34		35		36		37		38		39	

Geburtsname / Name / Geburtsname / Name / Geburtsname / Name / Geburtsname

Vornamen / Vornamen / Vornamen / Vornamen / Vornamen / Vornamen / Vornamen

* Ort / * Ort / * Ort / * Ort / * Ort / * Ort / * Ort

Datum / Datum / Datum / Datum / Datum / Datum / Datum

† Ort / † Ort / † Ort / † Ort / † Ort / † Ort / † Ort

Datum / Datum / Datum / Datum / Datum / Datum / Datum

R: / R: / R: / R: / R: / R: / R:

Ber: / Ber: / Ber:

∞ / ∞ / ∞

Ort / Datum / Ort / Datum / Ort / Datum / Ort / Datum

17 Fundas
Lüttgens (Vandermann) Geburtsname
Peter Duncken, Anno Vornamen
Emmesheim * Ort
6.2.1757 Datum
Emmesheim † Friemersheim 7.8.1830
C.3.1809
evangl. R: evangl.
Friemersheim 16.4.1738

18
Mispohr Name
Heinrich Vornamen
Wardheim * Ort
14. März 1765 Datum
Friemersheim † 15.3.1829
∞ evangl.
Friemersheim

19
Lüttgens Erkes Geburtsname
Prüttgen Chertm Vornamen
Filier Leim * Ort
26.2.1776 Datum
Filier Leim † 11.4.1868
evangl. R:
∞ 10.5.1804

8 Lüttgens, Peter Vornamen
Ödenhausen 18.10.1798 Datum
Friemersheim 26.1.1867 Datum
Ber:
∞
Friemersheim Ort
4. 7. 1824 Datum

9 Mispohr, Vornamen
Mliersheim 1.9.1801 Datum
† Friemersheim 9.11.180 Datum
Ort
R: evangl.

Lüttgens Name
Peter Vornamen
Friemersheim 26.11.1830 Ort Datum
∞ * Friemersheim 4.9.1899 Ort Datum
evangl. Ber:
6.
Datum

Lüttgens Name
Hermann Vornamen
Mliersheim 29.11 Ort Datum

4

81	82	83	84	85	86	87	88	89	90	91	92	93	94	95
	41		42		43		44		45		46		47	

21	22	23
Hufen	Bergmann	Enokstein
Gerhard	Dietrich	(Sophia) Feiser
Friemersheim	Friemersheim	Hochemmerich
14.49	6.6.1769	13.5.1787	16.10.1784
Homberg	Homberg	Friemersheim	Friemersdorf
30.12.18..	11.9.1826	17.7.1854	5.4.1856
R: evangl	R: evangl.	R: evangl.	R: evangl.
...Wirt	22.3.1795.	Weber Friemersdorf	18.7.18..

10 Hufen, Johann — Homberg 28.6.1801 — Friemersheim 24.3.1840 — evangl.
∞ Friemersheim 28.12.1833

11 Bergmann, Catharina — Rumeln 7.11.18.. — Rumeln 27.3.18.. — evangl.

5 Hufen — Sophia — Rumeln 22.11.1835 — Friemersheim 29.3.1833
1858

⚭ Friemersheim 10.10.1924 — R: evgl. — Ber: Schlosser — Friemersheim

1 Lüttgens — Sophia — Friemersheim — .3.9.18..

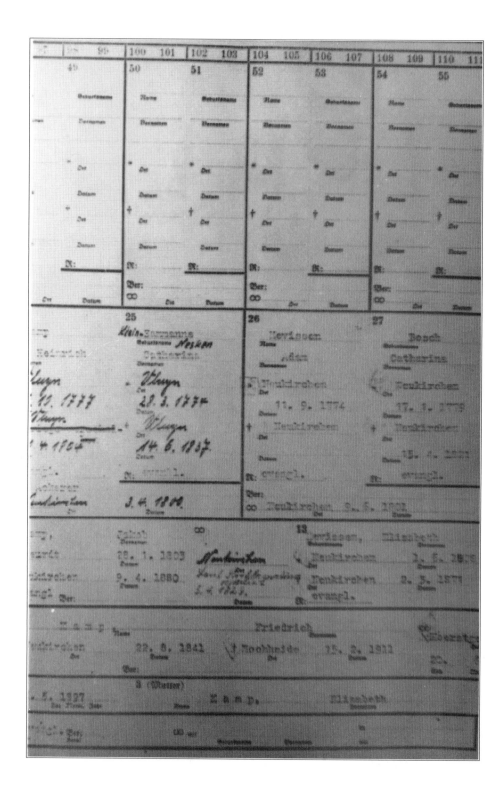

113	114	115	116	117	118	119	120	121	122	123	124	125	126	127
57		58		59			60		61		62		63	

29	30	31
Ellers(Müllers)	Thielen(Brenders)	Weirhaus
Letgen	Hermann	Sybilla
Neukirchen	Rheurdt	Bayen
9. 10. 1768	1o. 1. 1768	12. 12. 1771
Neukirchen	Rheurdt	Bayen
1. 1o. 1845	22. 1. 1844	28. 8. 1843
evangl.	evangl.	evangl.
Neukirchen 29. 11. 1798	Rheurdt 10. 4. 1806	

Einhorst	Jakob	15 Thielen(Brenders) Margarethe
Neukirchen 27. 7. 1809	Neukirchen	Bayen 20. 5. 1813
Neukirchen 2. 1o. 1894	12. 4. 1854	Neukirchen 5. 1o. 1858
evangl.		evangl.

7 Einhorst	Sybilla
Neukirchen 30. 9. 1842	Hochheide 18. 5. 1908
evangl.	
Hochheide 2. 7. 1870	evangl.

Bemerkungen auf die Rückseite der Ahnentafel!

AHNENPASS

Ahnenpaß

**Family tree of
Aryan descent**

Nr. 142

Ahnennachweis

Family tree

des/der

of

Name: Name

Ort: Place

Wohnung: Address

Verlag für Sippenforschung und Wappenkunde C. A. Starke, Görlitz

Bestell-Nr. 140 (in Umschlag), Nr. 142 (Halbleinen)

[Beliebig erweiterungsfähige Zusammenstellung „Ahnenpaß Unendlich" mit 6 Beilagen im Ziehdeckel. Nr. 146]

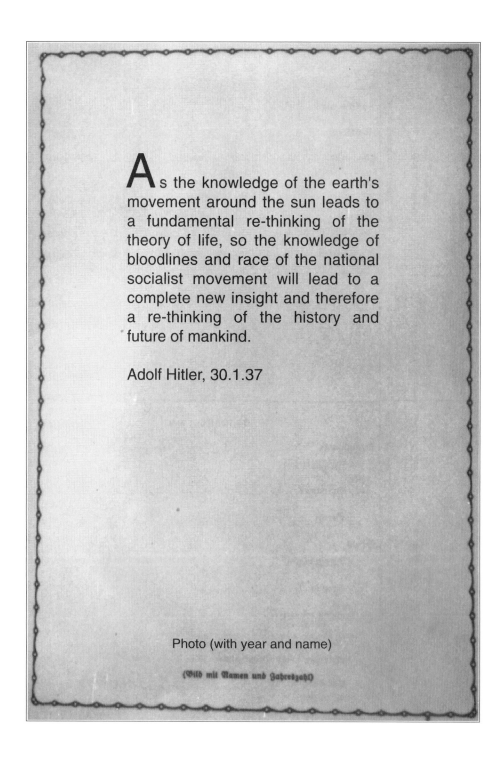

As the knowledge of the earth's movement around the sun leads to a fundamental re-thinking of the theory of life, so the knowledge of bloodlines and race of the national socialist movement will lead to a complete new insight and therefore a re-thinking of the history and future of mankind.

Adolf Hitler, 30.1.37

Photo (with year and name)

(Bild mit Namen und Jahreszahl)

So wie die Erkenntnis des
Umlaufes der Erde um die Sonne
zu einer umwälzenden Neugestaltung
des allgemeinen Weltbildes führte, so
wird sich aus der Blut und Rassenlehre
der nationalsozialistischen Bewegung
eine Umwälzung der Erkenntnisse und
damit des Bildes der Geschichte der
menschlichen Vergangenheit und ihrer
Zukunft ergeben

Adolf Hitler, am 30. Januar 19

①

Familienname:

Vornamen:

geboren in _____ am _____ Bekenntnis:

getauft in _____ am

Standesamt: _____ Register-Nr.

Pfarramt:

Kind des

und der

Die Richtigkeit der Ausfüllung entspricht den vorgelegten Urkunden

_____ Worte weggelassen

_____ „ eingefügt

Standesbeamter
Kirchenbuchführer

Stempel

Die Richtigkeit der Ausfüllung entspricht den vorgelegten Urkunden

_____ Worte weggelassen

_____ „ eingefügt

Standesbeamter
Kirchenbuchführer

Stempel

Eheschließung von ①

Bräutigam:

Familienname:

Vornamen:

Beruf:

Braut:

Geburtsname:

Vornamen:

Die Trauung erfolgte:

in _____ am

Bekenntnis des Bräutigams: _____ der Braut:

Standesamt: _____ Register-Nr.

Pfarramt:

Die Richtigkeit der Ausfüllung entspricht den vorgelegten Urkunden

_____ Worte weggelassen

_____ „ eingefügt

Standesbeamter
Kirchenbuchführer

Stempel

(Ehegatte von 1)

Familienname:

Vornamen

geboren in _____ am _____ | Bekenntnis:

getauft in _____ am _____

Standesamt:
Pfarramt: _____ Register-Nr.

Kind des

und der

gestorben in

am _____ Bekenntnis:

Beruf:

Standesamt:
Pfarramt: _____ Register-Nr.

Sonstige Nachweise der Abstammung oder des Bekenntnisses, falls pfarramtliche

Register nicht vorhanden. Genaue Angabe, wo und wie beurkundet:

Die Richtigkeit der Ausfüllung entspricht den vorgelegten Urkunden

Worte weggelassen
eingefügt

Standesbeamter
Kirchenbuchführer

Stempel

Die Richtigkeit der Ausfüllung entspricht den vorgelegten Urkunden

Worte weggelassen
eingefügt

Standesbeamter
Kirchenbuchführer

Stempel

Die Richtigkeit der Ausfüllung entspricht den vorgelegten Urkunden

Worte weggelassen
eingefügt

Standesbeamter
Kirchenbuchführer

Stempel

2 (Vater von 1)

Familienname:

Vornamen:

geboren in   am   Bekenntnis:

getauft in   am

Standesamt: Register-Nr.
Pfarramt:

Sohn des   **4**

und der   **5**

gestorben in

am   Bekenntnis:

Beruf:

Standesamt: Register-Nr.
Pfarramt:

Eheschließung von 2 mit 3

Bräutigam:

    Familienname:

    Vornamen:

    Beruf:

Braut:

    Geburtsname:

    Vornamen:

Die Trauung erfolgte:

    in   am

    Bekenntnis des Bräutigams: der Braut:

    Standesamt: Register-Nr.
    Pfarramt:

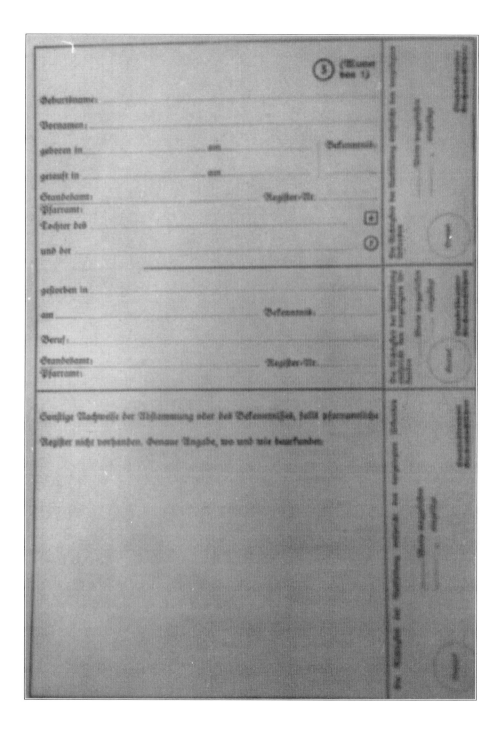

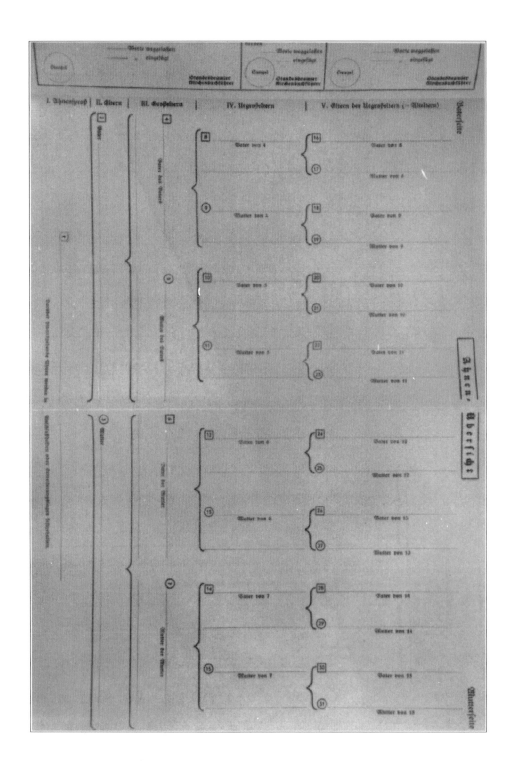

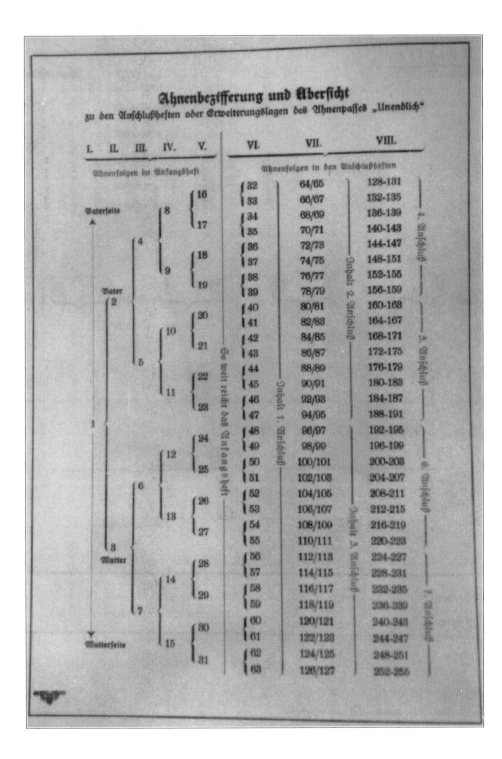

Durch die Gesetzgebung des Reiches und das Programm der NSDAP. wird es jedem Deutschen zur Pflicht gemacht, nachzuweisen, daß er deutschen Blutes (arischer Abstammung), also frei von artfremder Blutbeimischung ist. Dieser Nachweis wird durch Vorlage von Geburts- und Heiratsurkunden der Ausgangsperson und ihrer Ahnen oder, wo diese Urkunden nicht mehr zu beschaffen sind, ausnahmsweise auch durch die Sterbeurkunden erbracht. Um einen Verlust dieser Belegstücke zu vermeiden und das Mitführen und Einreichen der Urkunden zu erleichtern, dazu dient der „Ahnennachweis", der bei sorgfältiger Ausfüllung durch die Ausgangsperson und nach Beglaubigung durch den zuständigen Standesbeamten oder Kirchenbuchführer eine Urkunde im Sinne des Gesetzes darstellt und laut Erlaß des Reichs- und Preuß. Ministeriums des Innern als vollgültiger Ersatz für die darin verzeichneten Einzelurkunden gilt.

Bei der Übertragung der Urkunden in die Vordrucke des „Ahnennachweises" ist zu beachten, daß beide übereinstimmen müssen. Es ist also unzulässig, etwa die Schreibweise eines Namens oder eine Berufsangabe zu ändern, in der Einzelurkunde etwa fehlende Angaben (z. B. den Namen der Mutter) zu ergänzen u. dgl.

Die für das Beschaffen der Urkunden entstehenden Gebühren sind aus dem Erlaß des Reichs- und Preuß. Ministeriums des Innern vom 4. III. 1935 – IB 3/39 – zu ersehen. Sie betragen im allgemeinen, falls keine Suchgebühren in Frage kommen, innerhalb des Deutschen Reiches 60 Rpf. je Urkunde. Für die Beglaubigung im „Ahnennachweis" werden bei vorheriger genauer Ausfüllung durch den Antragsteller von dem Standesbeamten oder Kirchenbuchführer je Beglaubigung 10 Rpf., für 10 oder mehr Beglaubigungen in einem Ahnennachweis nicht mehr als 1 RM erhoben.

Die Anordnung des „Ahnennachweises" beginnt mit der Ausgangsperson, welche die Ziffer 1 bekommt und männlich oder weiblich sein kann. Der Vater erhält die Ziffer 2, die Mutter die Ziffer 3, die väterlichen Großeltern die Ziffern 4 und 5, die mütterlichen Großeltern die Ziffern 6 und 7, die Urgroßeltern 8 bis 15 und so fort (vgl. Übersicht). Jede männliche Person bekommt also eine gerade, jede weibliche eine ungerade Ziffer, ausgenommen die Ausgangsperson, die männlich oder weiblich sein kann.

Bei der Eintragung erscheint stets zuerst der Familienname, dann die Vornamen, der Geburtsort, das Geburtsdatum usw.

Für jede Ausgangsperson ist ein Ahnennachweis anzulegen.

Im allgemeinen ist für staatliche Zwecke (für Beamte, Angehörige der Wehrmacht und des Arbeitsdienstes, Ärzte, Rechtsanwälte, Notare, Mitglieder der Pressekammer, der Reichsschrifttumskammer, des Theaters, des Films usw.) der Nachweis bis zu den Großeltern einschließlich, für Parteizwecke bis zu allen am 1. Januar 1800 bereits geborenen Personen zu erbringen. Die Deutsche Adelsgenossenschaft und teilweise die ﬀ fordern den Nachweis bis 1750. — Die vorliegende Buchausgabe dürfte bis zum Jahre 1800 ausreichen. Sonst ist sie durch Erweiterungslage 146 G leicht zu ergänzen und auch jederzeit auf den „Ahnenpaß Unendlich" umzustellen. (Darüber vergleiche den Hinweis auf dem letzten Einbanddeckel.)

Über die Beschaffung der Urkunden unterrichtet Sie das Fachschrifttum, z. B. das im Verlage C. A. Starke in Görlitz erschienene Heft 2 der „Schriftenreihe" von Erich Waßmansdorff „Die Ahnentafel, Wege zu ihrer Aufstellung" (Preis 60 Rpf.).

Diese Schnittlinie bei Kürzung der Deckel nicht überschreiten!

Die Fortsetzung

dieses Ahnenpasses geschieht zweckmäßig durch Umwandlung zum „Ahnenpaß Unendlich". Er besteht aus Heftlagen, die in beliebiger Anzahl im praktischen Ziehdeckel vereinigt werden. Als 1. Lage würde dieses Heft gelten (Preis 60 Rpf.). Erweiterungslagen, reichend für 32 Ahnen (Preis 50 Rpf.), Leerlagen für Sondervermerke (unbedruckt, Preis 25 Rpf.), Registerlage A—Z zur Namen-, Sach- und Ortsfindung (Preis 50 Rpf.), sowie ein Ziehdeckel (Preis 1,25 RM) als Einband bilden die beliebig erweiterungsfähige Zusammenstellung.

Wen der Kartonumschlag bzw. Einband stört, kann ihn bis an die bezeichnete Schnittlinie kürzen. (Etwa 7,5 mm entfernt von der Sicherungs-Nahtheftung.) Nur nicht mehr wegschneiden, damit sich die Nähte nicht auflösen und der Paß zerstört sein würde.
Die beiden Drahtklammern im Rücken zum Durchzug der Heftbänder des Ziehdeckels lasse man sich vom Buchbinder nachheften. Um die richtige Klammer-Entfernung zu finden, ist der Ziehdeckel vorzulegen.

Ahnenpaß Unendlich (Bestell-Nr. 146)

Sein Vorzug liegt in der beliebigen Erweiterungsfähigkeit, da der Inhalt lagenweise aufgeteilt wurde. Die Erstfüllung besteht aus der Anfangslage, d. i. der Ahnenpaß mit den Ahnen 1—31, 3 Erweiterungslagen, reichend für 3×32 Ahnen, der Leerlage (unbedruckt) für Sondervermerke, der Registerlage A—Z zur Namen-, Sach- und Ortsfindung und dem Einband in ansprechender Ziehdeckelarbeit; zusammenfassend ausreichend zunächst bis zur VII. Ahnenfolge (= Ahnen 1—127). Durch Nachbezug von Erweiterungslagen Nr. 146 E für jedesmal 32 Ahnen kann der Umfang für die größten Forschungsergebnisse erreicht werden. (Preis dieser Gesamtausgabe 4 RM.)

The legislation of the German Reich demands of every German citizen to prove he is of Aryan descent and therefore free of alien blood. This proof will be given by presenting the birth and wedding certificates of the citizen and his (her) ancestors, or if those documents are unobtainable, through presentation of the death certificate . To avoid loss of these documents and for easier use, the ancestral book may be used, which has to be filled in very carefully by the bearer and verified by the appropriate registrar or parish officer. It then becomes a legal document and replaces all individual documents .

When transcribing any document into the ancestry book, it is forbidden to alter anything at all, i.e. old spellings of family names, profession, etc.

The fee for the procurement of the documents is in general 60 Pfenning per document, (1 Reichsmark) for 10 and over) is payable.

The order of persons in the ancestry book is as follows:

The bearer is number 1, male or female. The father is number 2, mother number 3, fathers parents 4 & 5, mothers parents 6 & 7. and so on. Always the male will have an even number, the female an odd number , excepting number 1, which can be either male or female.

The order of entries is: Surname, Christian names, places of birth, date of birth, etc.

Every citizen is to have an ancestry book.

In general the ancestry book has to be completed for official use (i.e. for doctors, civil servants, lawyers, members of the press, theatre, films, etc) up to and including the grandparents, for Party use up to and including all persons born after 1 Jan. 1800, for members of the aristocracy and members of the SS up to 1750.

This book should be sufficient for all persons up to 1800, but additional pages can be easily obtained.

SS AUSWEIS
(SS Identity Cards)

In the period 1933 to 1945 the SS utilised six main categories of identity card. The cards in each category varied slightly in size, colour, print and paper quality depending on the period in which they were printed or issued. Anomalies also occurred in the method of issuing SS Ausweis, for example a specific identity card was introduced for NCOs (Unterfuhrerausweis) yet some NCOs, especially the junior grades, were issued with the Schutzstaffel der NSDAP Ausweis (SS Ausweis) though this occurred mainly in the early days of the Third Reich.

SS personnel employed in Concentration Camps were initially issued with the SS Dienstausweis Totenkopf Verbande (SS Deaths Head Companies) although later on a specific card for SS Camp guards was introduced, the Lager Ausweis. These two categories of SS identity card are probably the most difficult to locate, as they specifically identified the holder as a Concentration Camp guard, and most of them were consequently destroyed by their owners prior to the individual's capture.

Members of the SS-VT (SS-Verfügungstruppe/Armed Special Purpose Troops) were issued with the SS Truppenausweis. In 1940 the "SS-VT" was redesignated at the "Waffen-SS".

SS officers were issued with the Führer Ausweis which maintained a similar format until the end of World War II.

The six main categories of SS Identity Card were issued at various times to the following:

SS-FÜHRERAUSWEIS: Officers, SS-VT, Waffen-SS and Allgemeine SS

SS-UNTERFÜHRERAUSWEIS: NCOs, SS-VT, Waffen-SS and Allgemeine SS

SS-TRUPPENAUSWEIS: NCO and enlisted, SS-VT and Waffen-SS

SS-AUSWEIS: NCO and enlisted, Allgemeine SS and Waffen-SS

SS-DIENSTAUSWEIS: NCO and enlisted, Totenkopf Verbande, Allgemeine SS

SS-LAGERAUSWEIS: NCO and enlisted Concentration Camp guards

Obverse view of a Truppenausweis for SS-Verfugungstruppe. This card is printed on green oilcloth and has a red validation stamp affixed. The card measures 10.5 cm X 15 cm. Entries include the holder's name, details of his facial features and physique such as height and weight, and date and place of birth. The photograph of the holder SS-Funker/Radio Operator Kurt Sauerbier is rivited in place in the bottom lefthand corner and overstamped with an SS inked rubber stamp. The card was issued on the 1st of April, 1939 and was validated by an SS-Sturmbannfuhrer/Major. The holder's signature appears on the 3rd line above the photograph.

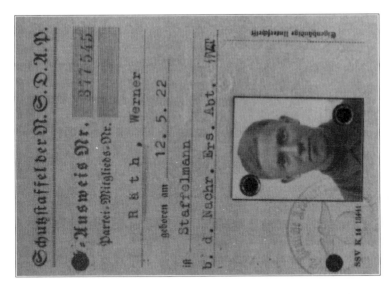

Obverse and reverse of SS Ausweis Nr. 377545, an example of the commonest and most frequently encountered type of SS ID card, although this particular Ausweis is interesting in that the reverse date stamp is for the 1st of November, 1940 and yet the holder of the card Werner Rath has been designated as belonging to an Abteilung of the SS VT rather than by its new title of Waffen-SS. These cards were printed on card stock measuring 9 cm X 12 cm. A pale yellow or light grey watermark with an eagle and swastika design was printed into both sides of the card to make forgery difficult. The photograph of the holder is rivited into place and overstamped.

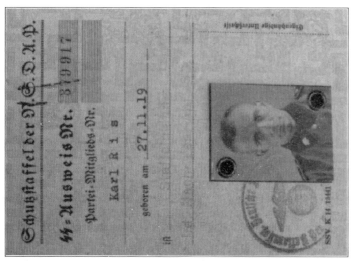

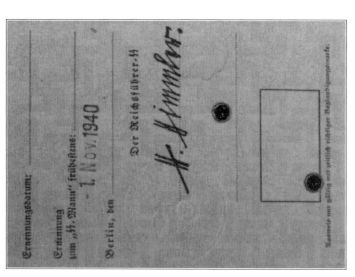

Obverse and reverse sides of another SS Ausweis Nr. 379917 made out to a Karl Ris. This card carries the same details as the previous example, however the holder's rank and unit have been rubber stamped onto the card in purple ink rather than' being typed as the previous one was. The reverse of this card bears the issue date and a fascimile H. Himmler signature. In addition to the inked stamps which are visible there is also a round SS stamp embossed into the middle of the card next to Himmler's signature. The form number of this type of card was SSV K 14 13441, which appears on all cards of this period and type. The card colour is a very light grey with a mottled mustard colour pattern in the background. The printing at the bottom of the reverse side of the card states that "This ID card is only valid with the proper stamps affixed."

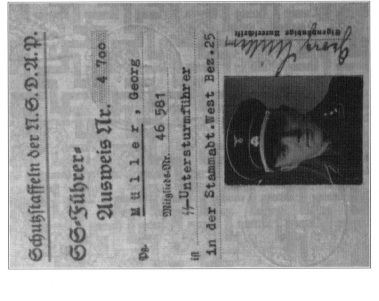

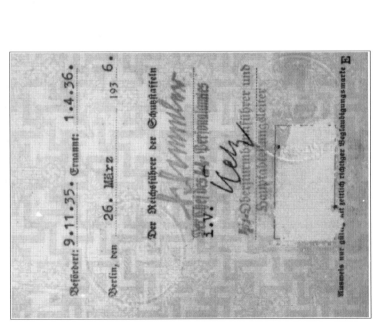

Obverse and reverse of an SS-Fuhrer Ausweis (SS Officer's ID Card). This card measures 9 cm X 12 cm and is printed almost exactly the same as the SS Ausweis for other ranks. In this example the holder in Allgemeine SS uniform is wearing his service hat. This has been mentioned due to its being an uncommon occurrence, as most Ausweis photographs were taken with the holder bareheaded. A raised embossed stamp has been applied over the photograph as opposed to an ink stamp. The data entries include Muller's ID number, Nazi Party Number, name, rank and organisation. Unlike the SS Ausweis the Fuhrer's ID card has no entry block for the holder's date of birth. The reverse side of the SS-Fuhrer Ausweis has entries showing the holder's date of commission and the date the card was issued. Himmler's fascimile signature appears on the reverse along with the issuing authority title, signature and location of validation stamp (removed).

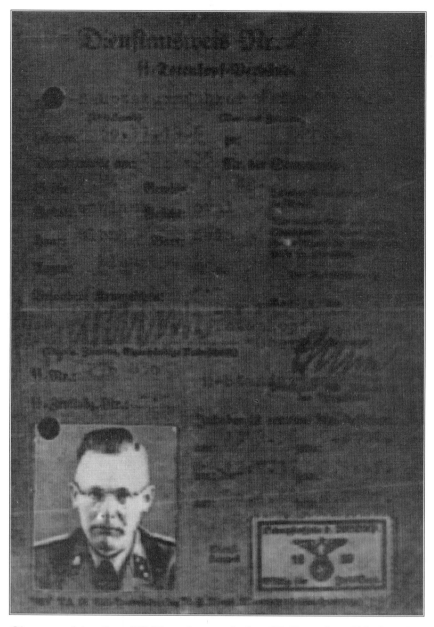

Obverse side of an SS Dienstausweis for SS-Totenkopf Verbande. This type of Service ID card was for Death's Head Companies and is printed exactly as the Truppenausweis ID card except the title is different. This type of ID card was also printed on green oilcloth and bears the same type of validation stamp. The holder of this card was an SS-Haupsturmfuhrer assigned to SS Totenkopf Standarte Ober Bayern (Upper Bavaria) which was stationed at Dachau Concentration Camp.

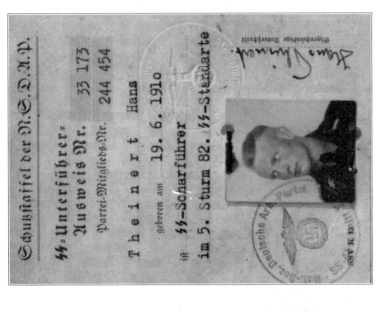

SS-UNTERFUHRER AUSWEIS (SS NCO Identity Card) (Form Nr. SSv K 15) of SS-Scharfuhrer Hans Theinert. The obverse side of the card bears Theinert's photograph stapeled into position, along with his SS rank, Ausweis Number, NSDAP Party Number and his unit details. The reverse of the card bears at the top of the page the date 20.4.1939 which was his "Beforderungsdatum" (Promotion Date). As was customary in the SS, Theinert's promotion took place on Hitler's birthday (20th of April), however 1939 was a special anniversary being Hitler's 50th birthday - an occession for more than the usual number of annual SS promotions. The Ausweis bears a Himmler signature in black ink and purple ink block stamp for Theinert's unit and commander. A red SS gummed stamp has ben applied in the appropriate box on the foot of the reverse page.

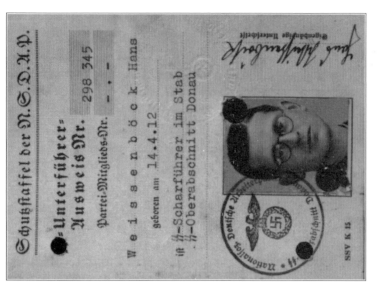

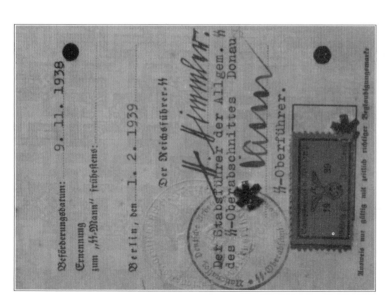

SS-UNTERFUHRER AUSWESS (SS NCO Identity Card) (From Nr. SSV K 15) of SS-Scharfuhrer Hans Weissenbock. The obverse side of the card carries a photograph of Weissenbock rivited into position, and is over stamped with an SS unit validation stamp. The card gives details of his SS Ausweis number, date of birth, and unit which indicated that he was an SS-Scharfuhrer attached to the staff of SS-Oberabschnitt Donnau (SS District Headquaters, Danube). The reverse of Weissenbock's Ausweis carries his Beforderungsdatum (Promotion Date) 9.11.1938 indicating he was promoted on the anniversary of the Munich Putsch at the Feldherrnhalle in Munich. The issue date for the Ausweis is 1.2.1939 and carries a fascimile signature of the RFSS and an ink signature of Weissenbeck's unit commander, an SS-Oberfuhrer. Note the detail of the watermark on this card which is made up of interlocking swastikas and early SS/NSDAP eagles.

SS-TRUPPENAUSWEIS (SS Enlisted Rank Identity Card) of SS-Mann Erich Mohr. The card is printed on a dark green oilcloth and bears a photograph of Mohr along with an ink unit validation stamp and a gummed SS stamp valid for July/September, 1939. This type of card was issued in the late 1930's to enlisted personnel of the SS-Verfugungstruppe, the forerunner of the Waffen-SS. The card carries Mohr's: date of birth of 26.3.1921, his date of induction into the SS as 1.11.38 followed by his Muster Roll number, height, weight, physique and facial features, etc. The card bears an ink stamp and signature of the holder's commanding officer, an SS-Hauptsturmfuhrer. The reverse of the card specifies Mohr's date of assignment (1.12.1938) to SS-''Deutschland'', 4th Kradschutzen-Battalion. The reverse of the card also bears the unit validation stamp and the unit commander's stamp and signature.

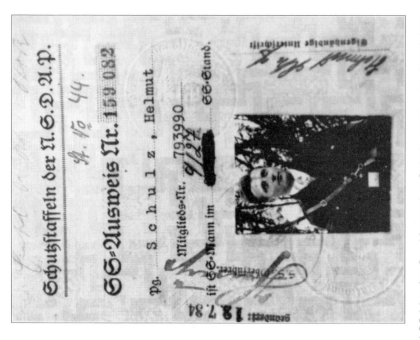

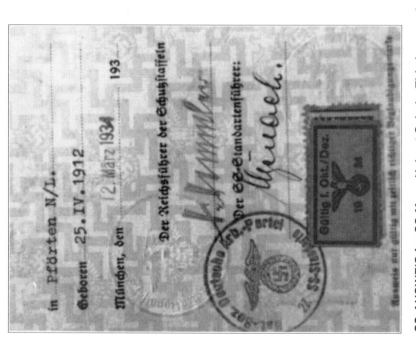

SS-AUSWEIS for SS-Mann Helmut Schulz. This is an early enlisted SS Identity Card issued to Schulz on 12.7.34. Provision for entering details on these cards was not as extensive as on later examples, mainly confining them to: the holder's photograph, Ausweis Number, SS Number, date of birth, unit number, and place and date of issue. The ink validation stamp on the reverse side is the early NSDAP type with the SS-Standarte 27 number included within the circle of the stamp. Schulz's regimental commander's signature has been entered in ink underneath his rank, SS-Standartenfuhrer. The card also bears a machine embossed SS validation stamp.

FRAU HIMMLER

The following photographs are extracts from the Reispass (Passport) of Frau Margarete Himmler. Although not strictly an SS document Frau Himmler's passport has been included because of her status as the wife of Reichsführer-SS Heinrich Himmler. The passport was issued in 1940, however the passport bears no exit or entry stamps. Undoubtedly due to the war even Himmler's wife would have been somewhat restricted in foreign travel.

The inside page bears the passport no. and holder's name.

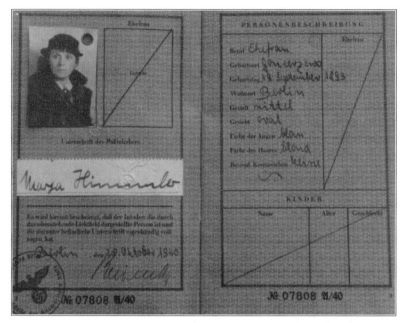

Pages 2 and 3 show that the passport was issued on the 25th of October, 1940. Other entries show Frau Himmler's photograph, signature and personal data. She is a housewife, born on the 19th of September, 1893 in Berlin. She has an oval shaped face, blond hair, blue eyes and no distinguishing scars or other marks.

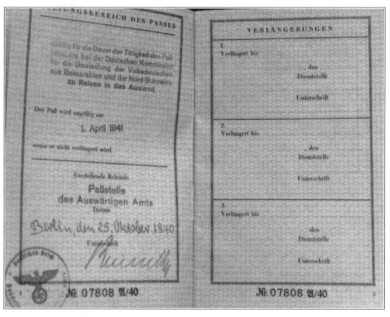

Pages 4 and 5 show that the passport was up to the 1st of April, 1941 for travel into Bessarebien and Nord Bukowine. The passport contains no entry or exit stamps which should not be viewed as unusual in view of the period for which it was issued.

AUFENTHALTS-AUSWEIS
fur GROSS-BUDAPEST
(Entry Permit for Greater Budapest)

Issued to Feldwebel Fritz Schulze on the 7th of July, 1944, this permit authorises the bearer to enter Budapest for an unspecified purpose restricted to the months of July and August as is indicated by the two month validation stamps on the reverse of the card. At the time this permit was issued in mid-1944 there were a large number of German troops stationed in Hungary helping to prop up Germany's shaky alliance with Hungary. Hungary under her leader Admiral Horthy was coming under mounting pressure to leave the Axis camp, and with Russian Armies advancing over her eastern frontiers the political situation was extremely unpredictable. In addition to fighting the Russians the SS were endeavouring to keep the civilian population of Budapest under control, and were also in the process of rounding up several hundred thousand Hungarian Jews under the direction of Adolf Eichmann for transportation to labour camps in Germany and Poland. Therefore this type of permit would have been essential in order to pass through the many SS control points surrounding and within the city of Budapest.

VORLAUFIGER AUSWEIS
(Temporary Permit)

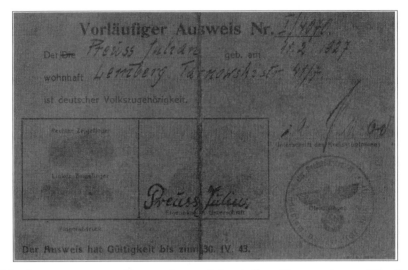

This temporary permit was issued to Julian Preuss to certify that Preuss was of ethnic German descent. The document bears the holder's signature along with fingerprints of his left and right forefingers. The permit is validated by an SS Police official in Lemberg with SS stamps over the individual's photograph. The front of the permit carries the Ausweis number along with the bearer's name, date of birth and address. This type of permit was issued by the SS to civilians of ethnic Germanic descent often in occupied countries to allow the individual to travel outside the environs of his home town or city. The expiry date of this permit was the 31st of August, 1943.

SS-AUSWEIS
(SS Special Identity Pass)

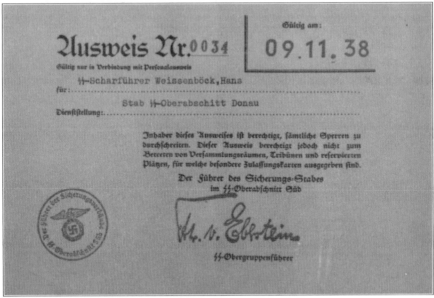

This was a special identity Pass issued to SS-Scharführer Hans Wissenbock enabling him to participate in the 9th of November Feldherrnhalle Celebrations in Munich. The Pass was valid for 9.11.38 and was issued by the SS-Oberschnitt Sud with the validation stamp and signature of the head of the SS security, SS-Obergruppenführer Ebbstein. The Pass authorises the holder to enter the restricted area, but not the collection room, or other reserved places where special permission was required. This type of pass was required in addition to the regular SS ID Card for men attending the annual gatherings commemorating the Munich Putsch of 1923.

SS-SOLDBUCH
(SS-Soldiers Paybook - ID Papers)

The Soldbuch (paybook - ID Papers) consisted of 28 pages and was broken down into the following categories:

Personal profile and characteristics
Previous military training
Address of immediate family
Individual clothing and equipment record
Vaccinations
Prescription eyeglasses
Hospital entries
Dental entries
Finance records
Awards and accommodations

Page 1. Personal profile.
Page 1 recorded the following information: rank (entered when book was originally started) and rank updates, payroll signature, ID tag number, blood group, gas mask size, and service number.

Page 2. Personal profile.
Page 2 recorded the following information: Date-of-birth, location of birth, religion, and civilian occupation. The centre of the page contained places for entering the holders height, build, shape of face, hair, eye colour, special features, shoe size and width. The bottom of the page was used by the approving authority and contained his title, rank and signature. The unit stamp was placed adjacent to the signature block for validation

Page 3. Certifications and amendments.
Page 3 recorded the following information: Changes (normally promotions and transfers to other units) the effective date, the organisation, and signature and rank of the person entering data.

Page 4. Previous Army reserve/training installations.
Page 4 was broken down into 4 sub-paragraphs A-D respectively. Paragraph A recorded the previous Army Reserve station, sub-paragraph A-C of para B recorded the name of the Reserve unit, company and roster number.

Paragraph C and its corresponding subparagraphs pertained to active duty units and was filled in and amended when the soldier was transferred.

Paragraph D pertained to the new responsible Reserve unit. Soldier was required to requisition from his field commander or military hospital commander. The soldier was responsible to organise his own replacement uniform and equipment.

Page 5. Address of immediate family.

Page 5. blocks 1-3, recorded the name and address of the next-of-kin. Other relations or a fianceé was to be filled in if no immediate family member existed.

Pages 6-11. Individual clothing and equipment record. Entries were to be made when transferred from Reserve unit to active unit, and when on leave, except during enquiry or sudden illness. Entry blocks included organisation, day, month and year or issue. Standard items of clothing and equipment were as follows:

Steel helmet	**Gloves**	**Rucksack**
Field-cap	**Coatstraps**	**A-frame**
Tunic	**Mess kit straps**	**Overcoat**
Underjacket	**Shelter quarter**	**Camouflage**
Trousers	**Tent poles**	**Pullover/Uniform**
Boots	**Tent pegs**	**Mess kit**
Brown Shirt	**Clothing bag**	**Shelter quarter**
Underpants	**Chin strap (steel helmet)**	**Accessory items**
Pullover	**Rifle sling**	**Belt Buckle**
Ear muffs	**Ammunition pouches**	**Bread bag**
Socks	**Shoulder strap**	**Canteen**
Necktie	**Belt hooks**	**Fatigue uniform**
Undershirt (white)		

Page 12. Special remarks on clothing and equipment.

Application of field unit for exchange, re-issue, statement of charges etc.

Page 13. Vaccinations.

Entries were as follows: Paragraph a: Smallpox; Para b: Typhoid, Paratyphoid, Para C: Dysentery; Para D: Cholera and Para D: Typhoid or Paratyphoid.

Page 14 and 15 pertained to measurement, issue, and re-issue of prescription eye glasses.

Page 16-17. Details of admission to military hospitals (stationary, field, war or Reserve).

Entries record the hospital, day, month and year and reason for stay. Entries were made by and signed by an officer and record the date of release, comments and final approving authority by the discharging officer/doctor.

Page 18-19. Disposition of personal property.

Entries recorded papers, money, valuables etc. taken to the hospital.

Page 20. Dental records.

Entries pertained to false, missing or replaced teeth. Treatment on dental station and remarks.

Page 21.

Same as page 4.

Page 22-23. Finance records.

These pages were filled in by the appropriate paymaster. The pay masters rank, signature, duty station, and official validation stamp were required on all entries. Entry blocks record validation period, pay grade and paymaster entries.

Page 24-25. Finance records.

Entries on these pages were filled in by any paymaster other than that of the current organisation.

Page 26. Awards and accommodations.

Page 27-28. Leaves and Passes.

These Pages were used to record leave for periods longer than 5 days. Entry blocks recorded leave address, beginning date of leave and company commanders signature, with validation stamp.

The Soldbuch of SS Panzer Grenadier Friedrich Pajonzecki. He was trained at the SS Panzer Grenadier A.u.E Battalion 1 in Berlin. Upon completion of his training on 23rd of June 1943 Pajonzecki was posted to the newly formed, 12th SS Panzer Division "Hitler Jugend."

MAX HANSEN

This SS Soldbuch was officially reissued to its owner SS Standartenführer/Colonel Max Hansen on the 1st of May, 1945 whilst Hansen was recovering from wounds in a Field Hospital. This book is made up of a series of one line entries which were entered by the Adjutant of the 1st SS Panzer Corps and chronicles Hansen's 12 year career in the SS. The reason for Hansen having his Soldbuch reissued is not known at this time, but all of the entries are contemporary with the period and the word "Zweitschrift!"/Reissues appears above the word "Soldbuch" in the same hand as the other entries.

Standartenführer Max Hansen was an outstanding officer who served with the Leibstandarte throughout the war beginning his service as a Platoon Leader in the 3rd Battalion and going on to become Company Commander of the Heavy Machine Gun Company of the 3rd Battalion. As the war progressed Hansen went on to become Commander of the 1st Battalion of 1st Panzer Grenadier Regiment, LAH, and finally took over command of the 1st Panzer Grenadier Regiment, LAH. Max Hansen saw service in Poland, France, Greece, Russia and Hungary and finally in Germany. In all the actions he was involved in Hansen proved himself to be one of the bravest soldiers in his Regiment risking his life on many occasions. Max Hansen died in March, 1990 having spent his last remaining years in a coma.

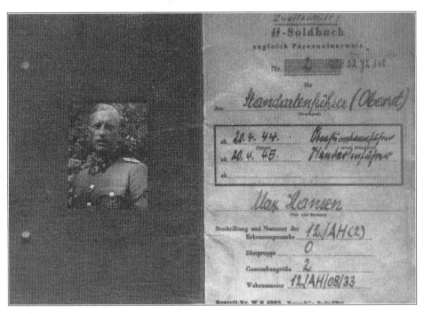

The inside cover of this Soldbuch has an excellent photograph of Hansen wearing the rank insignia of an Obersturmbannfuhrer. The first page contains his current rank of Standartenfuhrer (Oberst), name, blood group, gas mask size and service number. Note the entry "Zweitschrift"/Reissue at the top of the page.

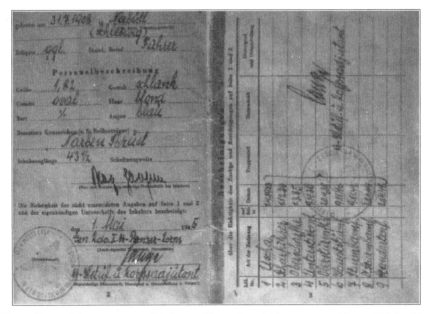

Page 2 contains personal information about Hansen and is validated by the Adjutant of 1st SS Panzer Corps Hauptsturmbannfuhrer. The first page contains his current rank of Standartenführer (Oberst), name, blood group, gas mask size and service number. Note the entry "Zweitschrift"/Reissue at the top of the page.

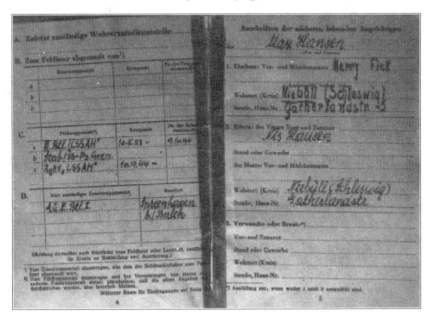

Page 4 of Hansen's Soldbuch contains entries identifying the units in which Hansen had served ending with his appointment as Commander of Regiment 1 of "Leibstandarte Adolf Hitler". Page 5 gives details of Hansen's home address and next-of-kin.

Lazarett	Tag und Monat	Jahr	Krankheit	Unterschrift der abaendenden Truppenteils	Tag und Monat	Jahr		
Verwundungen:								
	15.5.41		*a.g. Wade*	*Griechenland*				
	15.4.41		*a.g. li. Ellenbogen*	*Griechenland*				
	15.10.41		*a.g. li. Arm*	*Soltskoje/Russland*				
	19.11.41		*a.g. re. Bein*	*Rostow/Russland*				
	24.1.43		*a.g. Kopf*	*Belaschi/Russland*				
	13.3.43		*a.g. li. Oberschenkel*	*Petrewskoje/Russland*				
	15.9.43		*a.g. Kopf*	*Monte-Sosino/Italien*				
	22.1.45		*a.g. Rücken*	*bei Stadtkyll/Eifel*				
	28.6.44		*a.g. Brust*	*Person*				
	04.1.45		*Minen Ohren*	*Kemenca/Ungarn*				
	12.1.45		*Explos. Gesch. Kopf*	*Sitar/Ungarn*				
	16.2.45		*a.G. Kpf, Brust*	*Kemenca/Ungarn*				

Pages 20 and 21 list Hansen's various wounds. In a four year period from 1941-1945 Max Hansen was wounded no less than 12 times. Two of the wounds were received in Greece, five in Russia, one in the Eifel, three in Hungary and one unspecified. As can be seen from the details Hansen was wounded in every conceivable part of his body: with ten of the wounds received resulting from shrapnel, the remainder being attributed to a mine explosion causing damage to his hearing and a head wound he suffered from an explosive bullet. The entries have been stamped and validated by Adjutant Meyer.

Pages 22 and 23 of the Soldbuch list Hansen's various Awards:

Iron Cross 2nd Class	9.11.39
Knight's Cross of Iron Cross	27.4.43
Iron Cross 1st Class	7.5.41
Oakleaves to Knight's Cross	17.4.45
General Assault Badge	3.10.40
Gold Close Combat Clasp	17.4.45
Infantry Assault Badge	11.3.42
Bulgarian Bravery Order 4th C.	31.5.42
German Cross in Gold	26.12.41
Rumanian Crown for Valour	3.9.42
Silver Wound Badge	25.8.42

Of particular note are the two foreign Awards and also the Close Combat Clasp in Gold of which Hansen was one of only 75 recipients within the Waffen-SS. Also the number and variety of Hansen's awards attest to his courage and skill as an officer.

SS SOLDBUCH
(Green Oilcloth Type)

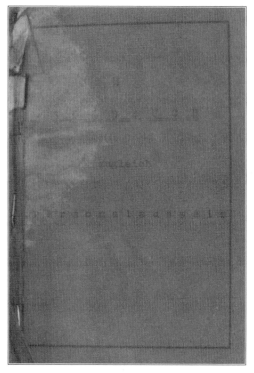

Obverse and reverse views of the SS Soldbuch with Green Oilcloth Cover.

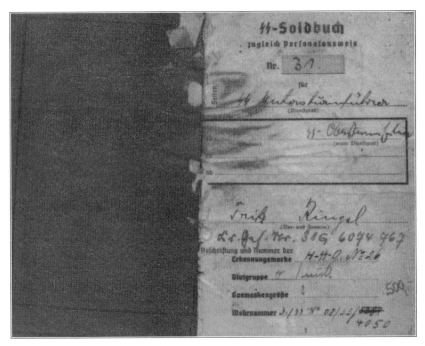

SS-Unterstürmfuhrer Fritz Ringel, most current rank: Oberstürmfuhrer, ID tag: H-SS-g No. 26, Blood group: O, Gas Mask size: 2, Service No: 3/SS "N" 08/35/4050

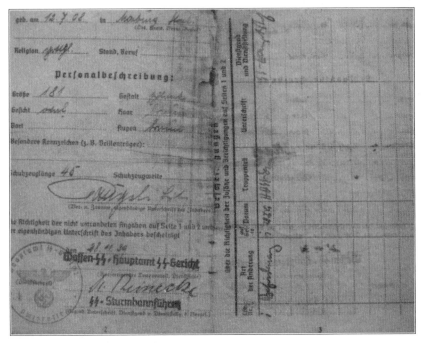

Born: 12 July 1906, Marburg Steiermark (Austria), height: 181 cm, build: slim, face: oval, hair: brown, eyes: brown. Validated by the Waffen-SS headquarters, SS Legal affairs.

Assigned: (a) Ps Jgd KDO 8. (b) Corps group Bork, 96th Company.

Straf. 8 SS Pol (8th Penal Company, Poland)

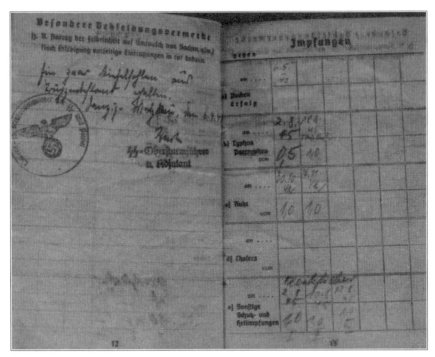

Page 12, received one pair of wool socks from unit supply. Page 13, inoculated for: Smallpox, Typhoid, Paratyphoid and Dysentry.

Glasses reissued September 1944 at Danzig.

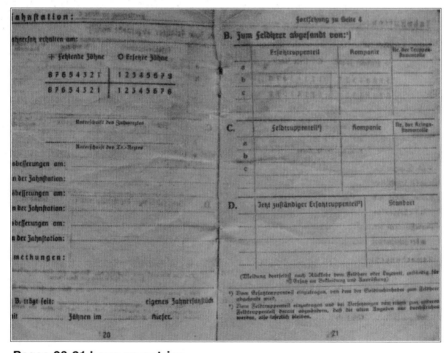

Page 16 shows no specific details apart from Field Hospital names and dates.

Pages 20-21 have no entries.

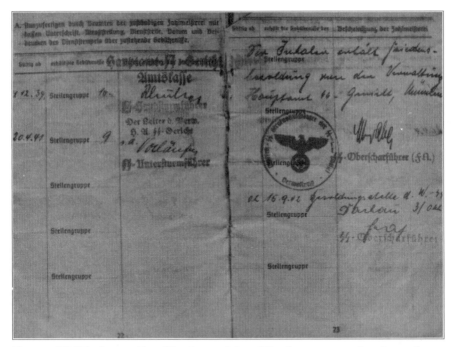

Pages 22-23 shows Pay Master entries. The bearer received pay from the SS-Administration main office 44 Munich. (no date).

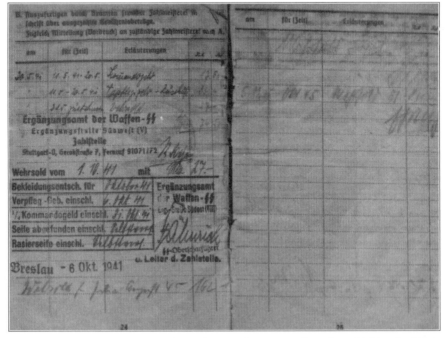

Page 24 shows the bearers basic pay from 1st October 1941, clothing allowance, ration allowance, quarter hazardous duty pay, soap purchased himself and shaving soap purchased himself.

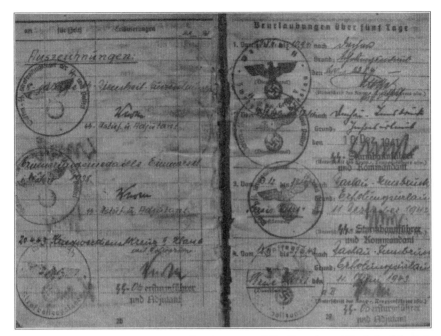

Page 26 shows the award of 8 years SS Service Medal, Medal of remembrance Annex of Austria 1938 and War Service Cross, 2nd Class 20th April 1943.

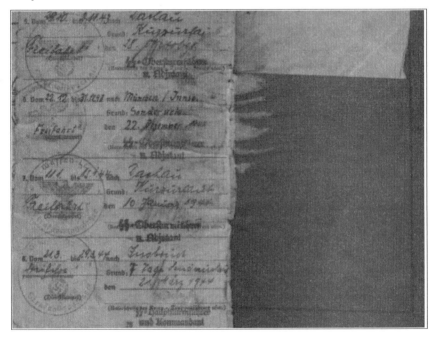

Page 28 has the following entries: (5) 29.10 - 2.11.43 Dachau (short leave), (6) 22.12 - 31.12.43 Munich/Innsbruck (Special leave), (7) 11.1 - 15.1.44 Dachau (short leave), (8) 21.3 - 29.3.44 Innsbruck (7 days special leave).

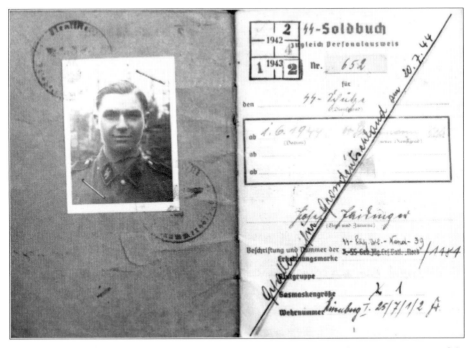

The Soldbuch of Joseph Jadinger has the card stock type covers with the holders photograph stapled onto the inside front cover. The photograph of Jadinger bears two Waffen-SS validation stamps at the top and bottom corners. Joseph Jadinger was an ethnic German from the South Tyrol who was killed in action on July 20th 1944. Page one of the Soldbuch has a red line drawn diagonally across the page on which is handwritten "Gefallen Fur Grossdeutschland 20.7.44" - died for Greater Germany. This was a common inscription written on page one of the SS Soldbuch of Ethnic German volunteers killed in action.

Entries on pages 2 and 3 of the Jadinger Soldbuch record details of his physique, date of birth, payroll signature and his assigned unit - SS Mountain Troops Training Battalion "Nord" the unit validation stamp and commanders signature have been applied to the bottom of page 2.

Page 4 and 5 indicate that Jadinger served with the 3rd Company, 6th SS Motorised Battalion of SS Division "Nord". This unit saw considerable action in North Russia and FInland as part of Army Group North.

Inside cover of the Soldbuch of SS Funker (Radio Operator) Nikolaus Schmatz. This gives the details of the Soldbuch number, the holder's rank, blood group, gas mask size, etc. along with a photograph of Schmatz on the opposing cover.

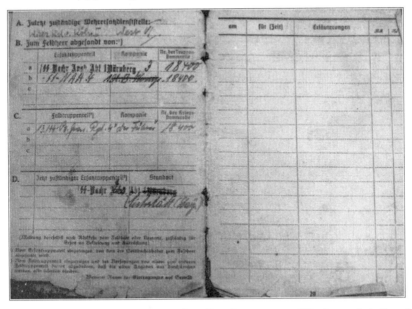

Entries in the rear of Schmatz's Soldbuch on page 28 show details of the training he received at the SS Nachtrichtung Ausbildungs Abtiellung (Signal Training Detachment) in Nurnberg. The entries go on to document his posting to the 13th Company of Regiment "Der Fuhrer". Schmatz saw service in Normandy, the Ardennes and Austria-Hungary where he was captured by the US Army in May, 1945.

The two documents illustrated are discharge papers given to Schmatz upon his release by the Americans on the 15th of May, 1946 from the US 4th Armoured Division Discharge Centre. The discharge documents represent a Certificate of Discharge which Schmatz would have been required to produce upon request by civil or military authorities within post-war Germany. Also included on the discharge form in section 2 (on following page) is a medical certificate signed by a Captain in the US Medical Corps giving the details of Schmatz's health status at the time of release. The second document represents the particulars of discharge which bear Schmatz's thumb print and brief service details. In addition to the discharge stamp for May, 1946 there is also a later stamp from the Reichsbank in Koln dated December, 1947. Both of these documents were part of the de-Nazification program instituted by the Allies at the conclusion of World War II.

Inside cover and page 1 of SS Sturmann Edmund Schaleks's, Soldbuch. Page 1 has the Soldbuch number 961, the bearer's name, rank and unit, however Schaleks's blood group and Wehr number have not been recorded.

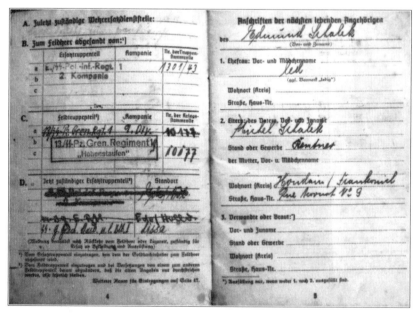

Pages 4 and 5 of this Soldbuch indicate that Schaleks's served briefly with the SS Police Division, and that he was then transferred to the 13th SS Panzer Grenadier Regiment 1 "Hohenstaufen": this unit was deployed on several Fronts during the war seeing action in Russia, Normandy, Arnhem, Ardennes and finally in the Spring 1945 offensive in Hungary. The entries on page 5 of the Soldbuch give details of Schaleks's next-of-kin.

SOLDBUCH FOR RUSSIAN VOLUNTEERS

This type of Soldbuch was issued to Russian Volunteers of the POA and consisted of 20 pages printed in bi-lingual text: Russian on the lefthand pages and German on the right. The Soldbuch has a box at the foot of page 2 which states that the holder "is a Russian Volunteer fighting against Stalin and not the Russian people and that the Russian and German peoples have formed a union to rid their homeland of the scourge of Bolshevism".

The POA Soldbuch bears no photograph of the holder but does carry the same personal details found in the German Army Soldbuch. An interesting innovation on this book is the inclusion of several charts showing comparative rank structures between the German and Soviet Armies. The middle pages of the book feature a foldout sheet for recording clothing and equipment issued to the holder.

The Russian Volunteers who were issued this type of Soldbuch served with both the SS and the German Army during World War II and usually had some prior military experience in the Soviet Army. The young men who were members of the POA had invariably found themselves Prisoners of War following the massive encirclements of Russian Armies in 1941 and 1942 when millions of Soviet prisoners were taken by the German Army.

Many of the men volunteering to serve with the German forces originated from the formerly independent states of Georgia and the Ukraine and preferred to fight Stalin and the Red Army rather than spend the war in a German POW camp where their life expectancy could often be measured in weeks especially in the long and cruel Russian winter.

A considerable number of Russian Volunteers fought in the Normandy Campaign and were captured there by the British Army who transferred them to Internment Camps in England. Most of these men were de-briefed at the Intelligence Unit at Ely near Cambridge where they were interrogated and had items such as their Soldbuchs confiscated.

The fate of these Soviet Volunteers was sealed by the Allied leaders at the Yalta Conference (January, 1945) where it was agreed by Churchill, Roosevelt and Stalin that all Soviet prisoners held in British and American hands would be returned to Stalin's clutches as soon as the war ended. This agreement for forced repatriation was duly adhered to by the Western Allies and tens of thousands of these former German Army Volunteers ("The victims of Yalta") were handed over to the soviets along with their German Army Soldbuchs which were sufficient grounds to incriminate them and might just as well have been death warrants.

The only soldbuchs which have survived had belonged to men who had either evaded capture at the end of the war or were lucky enough to "hang on" in British captivity until the forced repatriation was ended in 1947.

For all the reasons previously stated the Russian Volunteers Soldbuch can be regarded as one of the scarcest of the Wehrmacht Soldbuchs.

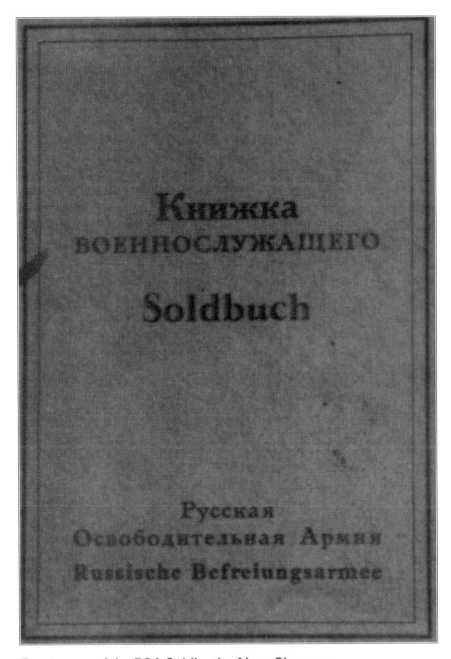

Front cover of the POA Soldbuch of Ivan Simonov.

Page 1 of the POA Soldbuch has a text in Russian Cyrillic script on the left and the German text on the right of the page. It has a preamble which states the aims and aspirations of the Volunteers joining the POA, however ironically most of these Russian Volunteers were barely semi-literate and were unlikely to even be able to read the text, let alone understand the muddled ideology and propaganda it espoused. Briefly the text states the following: "Land for the peasants. Freemen with well paid work for the workers. National independence for the Russian people, equality for the families of the new Europe. A new Russia without Bolshevists or Capitalists."

Page 2 of the POA Soldbuch documents the personal details of Freiwilliger (Volunteer) Ivan Simonov.

Page 3 has family details, date of enlistment (22-2-1943) and Simonov's unit "Ost-Stamm Regt. 4".

Page 4 shows Simonov's physical and facial characteristics. Both the Russian and German pages carry an official validation stamp countersigned by Simonov's battalion commander.

Присвоение звания

Чин. Звание	Время производство, присв	Войсковая часть	Кем присвоено	Подпись
а.*)				
б.				

*а) Последнее звание и последняя занимаемая должность в Кр. Армии
б.) Чин или звание полученное в Р. О. А.

Награда

Дата	Чем награжден	Кем награжден	Подпись

Page 5 was for entering details of the holder's rank and promotions if any, including a section for any rank attained during service in the Red Army.

Beförderungen

Dienstgrad	Datum	Truppenteil	Durch wen befördert	Unterschrift
*a)				
b)				

*a) Letzter Dienstgrad und Dienststellung in der Roten Armee
b) Dienstgrad in der R. B. A.

Auszeichnungen

Datum	Art	Verleihender	Unterschrift

Прохождение службы

Дата	Войсков. часть	Должность	Ком.части(подраздел) подраз	Должность Звание
1-12-1942	Д.Б.I сар		Кав. н клн. дивн.	

Versetzungen

Datum	Truppenteil	Dienststellung	Vorgesetzter	
			Unterschrift	Dienstgrad
1-12-1942	6ct.6II.I.ин.		Krh u. Off.Bat.	

Бытность в отпуску (более пяти суток)

1. От: _____ до: _____ Куда: _____
   Причина: _____
   подпись ком. части

2. От: _____ до: _____ Куда: _____
   Причина: _____
   подпись ком. части

3. От: _____ до: _____ Куда: _____
   Причина: _____
   подпись ком. части

4. От: _____ до: _____ Куда: _____
   Причина: _____
   подпись ком. части

Beurlaubungen über fünf Tage

1. Vom: _____ Bis: _____ Nach: _____
   Grund: _____
   Unterschrift des Truppenführers u.a.w.

2. Vom: _____ Bis: _____ Nach: _____
   Grund: _____
   Unterschrift des Truppenführers u.a.w.

3. Vom: _____ Bis: _____ Nach: _____
   Grund: _____
   Unterschrift des Truppenführers u.a.w.

4. Vom: _____ Bis: _____ Nach: _____
   Grund: _____
   Unterschrift des Truppenführers u.a.w.

The top section of Page 6 gives details of transfers with the lower portion of the page reserved for any leave time over 5 days duration.

Nachweisung über etwaige Aufnahme in ein Пребываниев					Standort-, Feld-, Kriegs- od. Reservelazarett госпиталях и лазаретах			
Lazarett Лазарет	Datum der Laz.-Aufnahme Дата поступления	Krankheit Болезнь			Unterschrift des absendenden Truppenteils Отметка отсылавшей воинской части	Datum der Entlassung aus dem Lazarett Дата выписки	Etwaige Bemerkungen in bezug auf die Entlassung aus dem Lazarett Отметка о переводе в часть	Unterschrift des die Entlassung bewirkenden Lazarettbeamten Подпись

Состоящее на руках оружие и снаряжение					Besitznachweis über Waffen und Gerät			
Род оружия	№	Система	День получения или сдачи	Кем выдано Кому сдано	Waffen oder Gerät	Fertigungs- Zeichen / Nummer	Tag des Empfanges	Nummerzeichen des Gerätverwalters
					Jewicka	3	13-8-44	October L.R.B.
					Gasmaske, Gasplane, Waffenreinigungs-...			
					Hautentzstoffe, Ersatzmittel			

Page 7 itemises weapons and equipment issued to Simonov.

Four members of the POA relaxing on the Eastern Front in 1944. Ivan Simonov is the second soldier on the left cradling the 98K rifle.

Выдача вещевого
Mitgegebene Bekleidungs-

Выдача вещевого имущества
Mitgegebene Bekleidungs- und Ausrüstungsstücke

Page 8 folds out into 3 sections to record clothing and uniform items issued to Simonov.

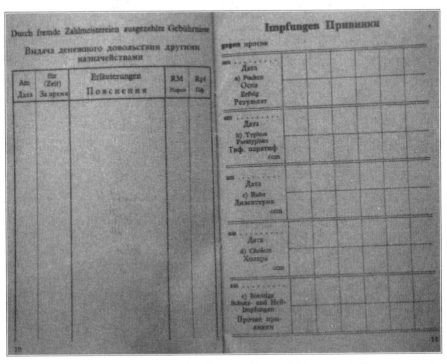

Page 9 is for pay details.

Page 10 has space for pay details: on Page 11 innoculations were to be entered.

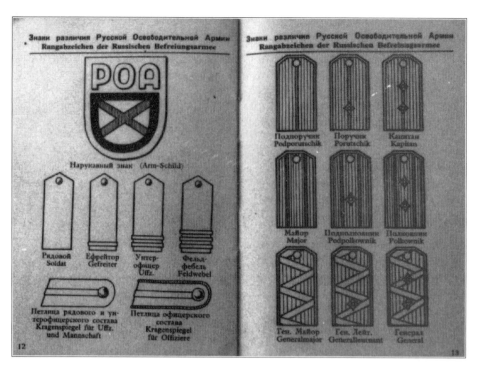

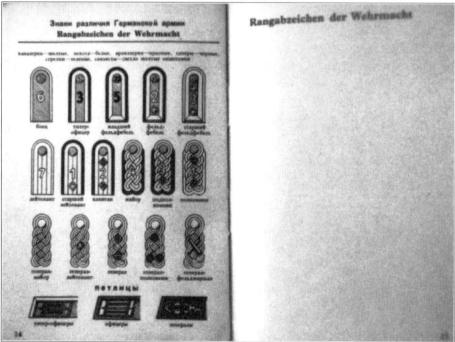

Pages 12-15 show illustrated rank charts with comparative rank structures of the German Army and Red Army.

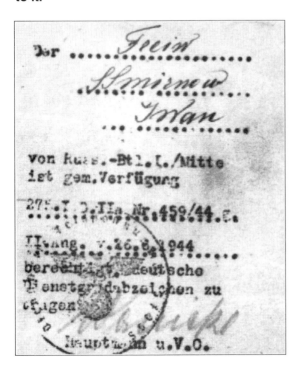

The Russian text on page 20 is repeated on the inside of the back cover in German. The five points listed inform the holder about the functions of the Soldbuch and also the soldier's duty and responsibilities with regard to it.

This small and very flimsy document is a leave pass granted to Freiwilliger Ivan Simonov in August, 1944. It measures approximately 50mm x 75mm and has just been typed on to a piece of coarse typing paper of the type used by the Wehrmacht in the latter part of World War II. It bears an official validation stamp and is countersigned by an officer.

SS-WEHRPASS
(SS Service Record Book)

The Wehrpass consisted of 58 pages and was broken down into five sections. Section I was for details. Section II pertained to enlistment and discharges. Section III pertained to Reichs Arbiets-Dienst (RAD) or Labour service. Section VI pertained to military service while in Reserve status. The final section was used to record additions. Printed on the inside back cover was for the regulations and governing use, disposition and transportation of the document procedures.

Page 1. Personal information:
Name of the bearer both Christian and surname. Service record book number and ID tag number. The bottom of the page contained the signature and rank of the approving authority. The page was also over stamped with the unit validation stamp. This was usually the Defence District Command where the soldier was inducted into service.

Page 2. Personal Characteristics:
This page contained the official photo and records, the bearers payroll, signature, his height, build, eye colour, hair colour, distinguishing features and blood group.

Page 3. Personal Characteristics:

Blocks 1-9:
1.	Surname	6.	Religion
2.	Christian Name	7.	Married, Single, No. of Children
3.	Date of Birth	8.	Civilian occupation
4.	Place of Birth	9.	Name of parents
5.	Nationality		

Page 4. Personal Characteristics, Blocks 10-13:
10. Education
11. Knowledge of foreign languages
12. Certifications and qualifications
13. Address of next-of-kin
13a. Additions

Page 5. Enlistment:
Blocks I-III were for entries pertaining to area commanders, and

induction decision, as to whether the medically examined individual was fit for service in the Army or SS. Block 14 I-III recorded grade of fitness and type of service.

Page 6. Induction and Discharge:
Blocks 15-16. Block 15 contained entries on the decision regarding labour service. Block 16 recorded information or discharge from the RAD or transition to active duty.

Page 7. Discharge and additions:
Blocks 16-17. Block 16 recorded the information as page 6. Block 17 was used for additional remarks.

Page 8. RAD service:
Entries included career, position starting as, date and duty station, RAD roll number, date and duty.

Page 9. RAD service:
Blocks D-G, contained further details on discharge. Block D categories were as follows:

B = Promoted
Ern = Nominated
K = Commended
V = Transferred

Block D, stated that the bearer had been given briefings on sabotage, treason, and operational security (procedures for handling classified material). Block F recorded comments on suitability and Block G, reasons for discharge.

Page 10. RAD Service:
Block G recorded special notes and Block H recorded discharge date, rank and remarks.

Page 11. Active Duty Service.
Block 18 recorded the following: Enlistment examination date, unit, station and medical decision. The bottom section of this page contained blocks for entries in the event of a failed medical examination.

Page 12 & 13. Active Duty Service - Army or Air Force.
This page recorded all active duty units in chronological order to which the individual had been assigned. Block 19 was used to enter the date

of assignment, the unit and roster number.

Page 14 & 15.
Same as previous page.

Page 16-17. Active Service, Land Commando, Navy.
This page consisted of block 20, which recorded similar information as in block 19, date, division, station, and all military exercises, and operations.

Page 18-19. Active Service - Navy or Air Force.
This page consisted of block 21 and recorded the ship, from and to, and how many days in foreign waters. All exercises the individual had taken part in were recorded.

Page 20-21. Active Service Training.
Block 22 recorded the type of weapons the individual was qualified on. Block 22a recorded special training on duty related equipment; block 22b was an ID card for medics and recorded issue date.

Page 22-23. Active Duty Promotions, Nominations, and Awards.
Block 23 was used to record confirmation of promotions, awards and nominations. Any entry required a validation stamp and approving authority signature.

Page 24-25. Active Duty orders, merits, mentions in the honour list during active service and during leave.
Block 24 recorded type of award, date and approving signature.

Page 26-27. Discharge.
Block 26 recorded the date, rank, location of personnel residence from (duty station) promotion or nominations, characterisation of discharge, final medical report and details to registration home registration office.
The top half of page 27, was used to record details if the individual was entitled to preferential treatment for finding employment.

Page 28-29. Active Service.
This page block 41b and 26 were used to record details of fulfilment of active duties from - to -.

Page 30-31. Active Service - Combat Engagements.
Block 28 recorded the date, name of location of battle or deployment.

Page 32-33.
Same as page 30-31.

Page 34-35. Illnesses, injuries and Hospitalisation.
Block 29 recorded date, description of injury and location, if with unit or at hospital.

Do not record venereal diseases or mental illness here. If a soldier is killed record the time and place, but not the cause of death.

Page 36-37. Service during reserve status.
Blocks 31 and 32, recorded location of transfer, date and approving authority signature.

Page 38-39. Service during reserve status.
Blocks 36 recorded meetings and briefings, relating to espionage, sabotage, treason, and operational security.

Page 40-41.
same as page 38-39.

Page 42-43. Service during reserve status.
Block 38 recorded information on eye glasses, gas mask size, helmet, shoe size and width and hat size. Block 38a, recorded the date, testing and duty station.

Page 47-53. Additions to Sections I-V.
Entries are recorded in block 39.

Pages 54 & 55. Service record book.

1. The service record book was the identification document for conscripts during the duration of the military service including the Reichs Labour (RAD) service duty.

2. The service record book had to be carefully looked after. It was to be shown only at the offices of Army, SS, Reichs Labour Service and county together with call-up papers or conscription papers. without these papers it would only by shown to Party officials and officers of technical aid (TENO) services. It could not be taken to other countries. If abroad for longer than 60 days, the record book had to be handed to the appropriate Army Reserve Station.

3. The record book had to be shown when called up, attending a lecture or attending a military exercise.

4. The service record book was a public document. Any forgeries or misuse would be punished. Entries were only to be made by officials of the Army, SS, Reichs Labour Service, police and embassy.

5. The loss of the service record book had to be notified immediately in writing or in person. If the book was not recovered within 4 weeks a new service book had to be applied for. If it can be proved that the bearer was of no fault regarding the loss, the replacement book would not be charged against the individual.

6. The bearer of a service record book had to be reachable by post. Therefore he had to notify his Army area command regarding the following:

a. Any change of address.

b. Start and finish date of any travel, holiday, etc. which was no longer than 14 days.

These notifications had to be made within 1 week during peace times and within 48 hours during war.

FREIDRICH KURTZ

Front cover of Freidrich Kurtz's Wehrpass which bears the German Army eagle insignia printed on the cover with the word "Wehrpass". It was not unusual for SS personnel to be issued with this type of Army Wehrpass, especially when serving with Frontline units or where a Wehrpass had been reissued after being lost or destroyed. Kurtz's Wehrpass is extremely interesting as the entries within it are quite comprehensive spanning his service with the Waffen-SS over virtually all of World War II.

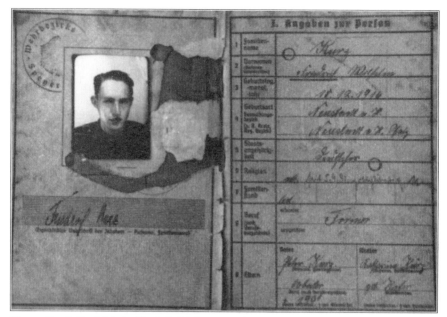

Page 2 of Freidrich **Kurtz'** Wehrpass has a photograph of him in SS uniform and carries his payroll signature beneath. Page 3 documents his personal details such as: name, date and place of birth, his civilian occupation (farmer), religion etc. At the foot of the page are the names and occupations of his mother and father.

Page 4 of the Kurtz Wehrpass gives details of his schooling and qualifications. Two of the categories, 11 and 12, carry the word "Keine" (None). Page 5 carries details of his enlistment (Musterung). This section indicates that Kurtz was a "Dienstpflichtiger" (Conscript) who was inducted on the 30.4.36.

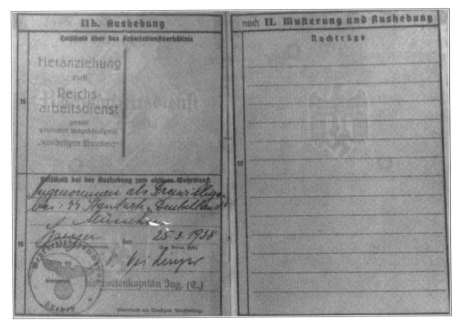

Page 6 records details of any service in the RAD in section 15. The bottom portion of page 6 (section 16) shows that Kurtz joined the SS-Standarte Deutschland in Munich as a "Freiwilliger" (Volunteer) on 25.3.1938. Interestingly this entry has been validated and signed by a Kreigsmarine officer (Korvettenkapitan).

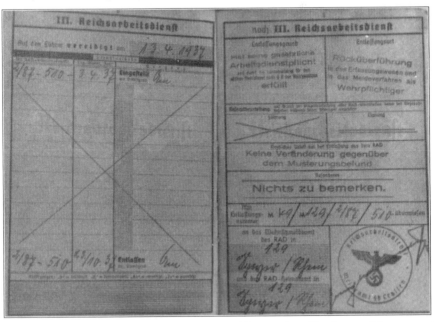

Pages 8 and 9 record further details of RAD service. Kurtz would appear to have only spent a very short period of time in the RAD in 1937 before being released to do compulsory military service as a "Wehrpflichtiger" (Conscript).

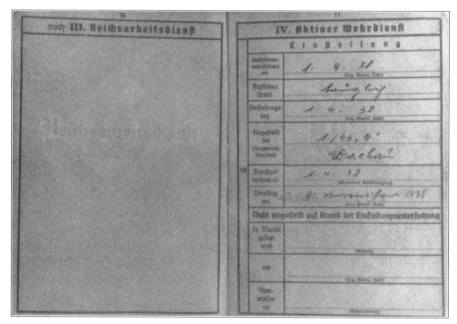

Page 11 records the dates of active service wit the SS including an entry for Dachau 1.4.38. At that time Dachau was a training camp for SS recruits as well as being a Concentration Camp. The bottom entry on this document indicates that Kurtz did graduate from his training on the 9th of November, 1938.

Page 12 documents the active service postings of Freidrich Kurtz dating from his service at Dachau in 1938 through service with "Das Reich". The final entry shows that Kurtz was serving in the Baltic at Riga.

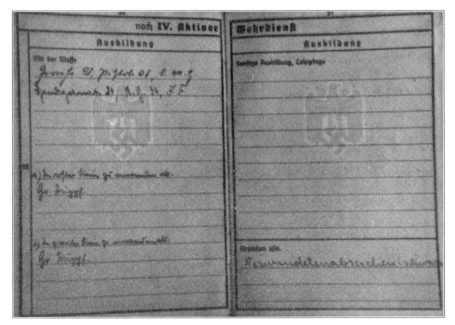

Pages 20 and 21 are pen and ink entries of further active service assignments in which Kurtz participated. The foot of page 21 notes that Kurtz had received the "Verwundetenabzeichen (Silber)" (The Wound Badge in Silver).

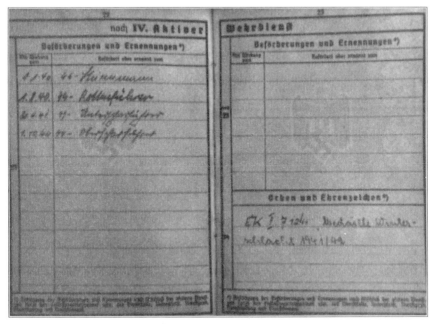

Page 22 details four separate promotions which Kurtz received between 1940-1944 raising him up through SS-Sturmann, SS-Rottenfuhrer, SS-Unterscharfuhrer and finally to the rank of SS-Oberscharfuhrer. Page 23 has entries for awards which include: the Iron Cross 1st Class 7.12.41, and the Winter War Medal 1941/42.

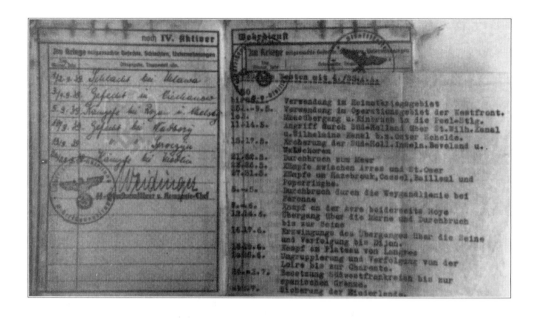

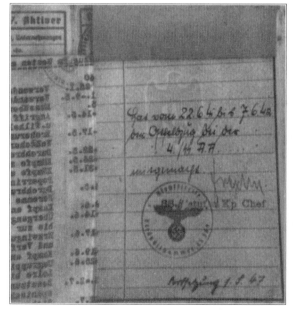

Pages 32 and 33 of Kurtz's Wehrpass carry entries for Kurtz wartime service: of special interest are the entries on page 32 detailing no less than 6 actions which Kurtz was involved in during the Polish Campaign of 1939. The unit validation stamp on this page is countersigned by then Company Commander <u>SS-Obersturmfuhrer</u> <u>Otto Weidinger</u>. The entries of page 33 were so numerous that they required typing on a separate sheet of paper. These 16 entries record Kurtz war service on the Western Front in Belgium, Holland and France where he was involved with his unit the 4th SS-Aufklarungs Abteilung (4th Reconnaissance Company) in all the major battles and ultimately to as far south as the Spanish border.

These entries have been typed onto a separate continuation sheet and stuck onto page 33 with Kurtz other wartime service entries. The 19 entries on this sheet document Kurtz battle deployments from 31.3.41 to 31.12.41 and mainly include details of the actions he was involved in during the invasion of Russia. As can be seen from the penultimate entry "Abwehrschlacht vor Moskau" (the Battle for Moscow), Kurtz was at the very cutting edge of the German invasion of Russia.

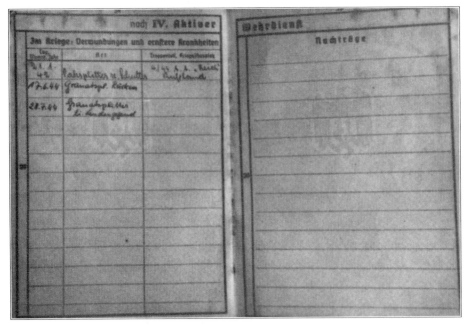

Page 34 bears pen and ink entries for 21.1.42 in Russia, and 17.6.44 and 28.7.44 - both for actions in France.

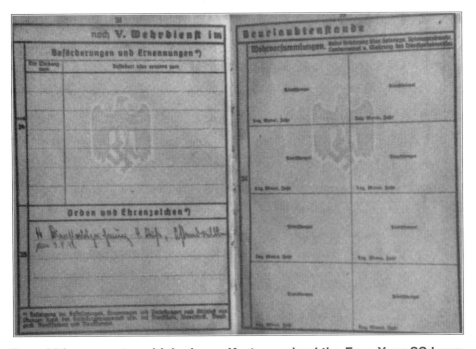

Page 38 has an entry which shows Kurtz received the Four Year SS Long Service Medal on 3.8.42.

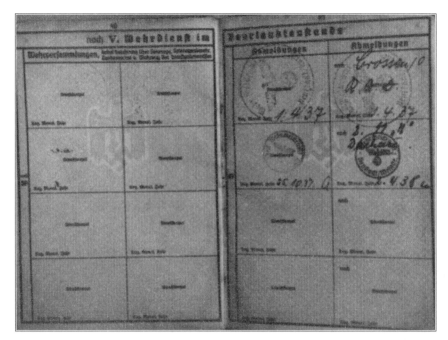

Page 41 has unit stamps and ink entries relating to Kurtz's service at Dachau in 1938.

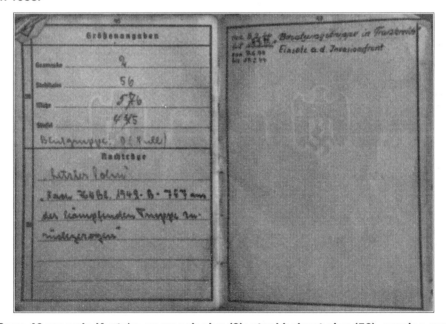

Page 46 records Kurtz's: gasmask size (2), steel helmet size (56), service cap size (56), boot size (45) and blood group (Type O Negative). The foot of page 46 contains ink written supplementary details. Page 47 carries ink entries covering the dates 3.2.44-17.8.44 indicating that in March, 1944 Kurtz and his unit were transferred to France, and that from the 7th of June, 1944 (the day after D-Day) to the 17th of August, 1944 Kurtz was stationed on the (Normandy) "Invasionsfront".

OTTO STIRNWEISS

Pages 2 and 3 of the Wehrpass of SS Unterscharfuhrer Otto Stirnweiss. Page 2 of the pass shows a photograph of Stirnweiss in civilian clothes; the photo is rivited to the page and is validated with two control stamps. Page 3 gives personal information about Stirnweiss: name, date and location of birth, religion and profession. Stirnweiss had been employed as a toolmaker.

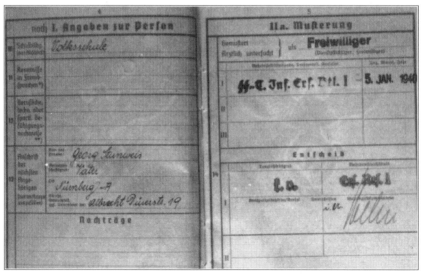

Pages 4 and 5 give details of the education Stirnweiss received and also his next-of-kin. Page 5 is headed with "Freiwillinger" indicating Stirnweiss was a volunteer and that he was inducted on the 5th of January, 1940 into the SS Infantry Ersatz (Training) Battalion 1.

Page 12 of the Wehrpass shows 8 service entries from the 1st of March, 1940 through to the 4th of November, 1943 indicating that Stirnweiss served in numerous units but all within the structure of the 3rd SS Panzer Grenadier Division "Totenkopf". The unit entries are as follows: 3rd Company, 1st Battalion, SS Totenkopf Infantry Regiment "E" (Eicke); 6th Company, 3rd Regiment; Headquarters Company, Totenkopf Infantry Regiment 3; 7th Company, SS Panzer Grenadier Regiment "E" (Eicke); SS Panzer Grenadier Replacement and Training Battalion 3.

The entries on these pages give details of Stirnweiss' postings and actions he was involved in between May, 1940 and September, 1943, and include service in the French Campaign and in Russia.

Page 22 gives details of Stirnweiss' promotions between 1.12.40 and 1.10.43 amounting to four different rank changes: 1.12.40 SS Mann; 1.9.41 SS Sturmann; 1.3.42 SS Rottenfuhrer; 1.10.43 SS Unterscharfuhrer. Page 23 lists the six Awards Stirnweiss was entitled to wear: 27.9.41 Black Wound Badge; 1.8.42 East Front Medal; 20.5.43 Bronze Driver's Badge; 31.6.43 Silver Wound Badge; 13.7.43 Iron Cross Second Class; 18.10.43 Bronze Close Combat Clasp.

SS General Josef (Sepp) Dietrich.

MEDICAL RECORD
(Front Page)

SS STAMP	Branch of the Armed Forces	Year of Birth 19 . . .	. . . . 2/3 letters of surname
Last section roll number			Service Number

Military Area Commando or Military Registration Office	Enlistment Date:	Active service counted from:
	Blood Group:	

HEALTH RECORD (G-Book)

of

Name

Date of Birth: . . . .

Rank: . . . .

Profession: . . . .

Birthplace: . . . .

Religion: . . . .

. . . .

(Last working as)

Responsible Authority: . . . .

Reichs Labour Service Office / Military Duty Station

INDEX

(Please refer to headings of pages)

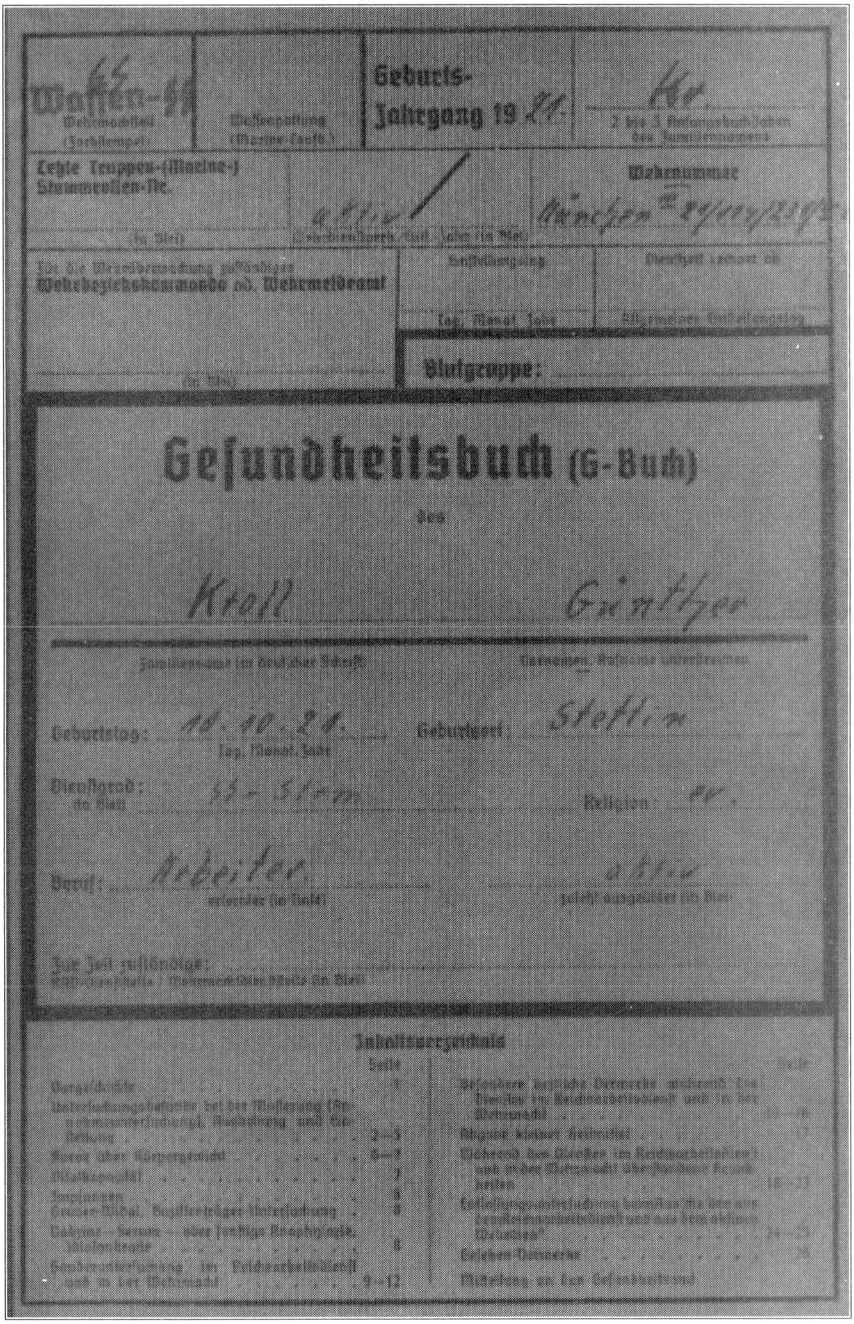

Waffen-SS
Wehrmachtteil (Farbstempel)
Waffengattung (Marine-Laufb.)
Geburts-Jahrgang 19 24
Kr
2 bis 3 Anfangsbuchstaben des Familiennamens

Letzte Truppen-(Marine-) Stammrollen-Nr.
(in Blei)
aktiv /
Wehrdienstverh./Entl.-Jahr (in Blei)
Wehrnummer
München [illegible]

Für die Wehrüberwachung zuständiges Wehrbezirkskommando od. Wehrmeldeamt
(in Blei)
Einstellungstag
Tag, Monat, Jahr
Dienstzeit rechnet ab
Allgemeiner Einstellungstag
Blutgruppe:

Gesundheitsbuch (G-Buch)

des

Kroll Günther

Familienname (in deutscher Schrift) — Vorname, Rufname unterstreichen

Geburtstag: 18.10.24. (Tag, Monat, Jahr) — Geburtsort: Stettin

Dienstgrad: (in Blei) SS-Sturm. — Religion: ev.

Beruf: Arbeiter — erlernter (in Tinte); aktiv — zuletzt ausgeübter (in Blei)

Zur Zeit zuständige: RAD-Dienststelle - Wehrmachtdienststelle (in Blei)

Inhaltsverzeichnis

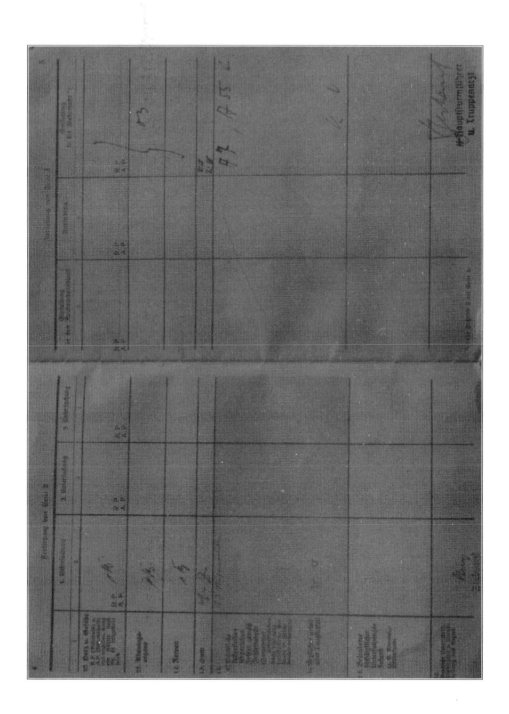

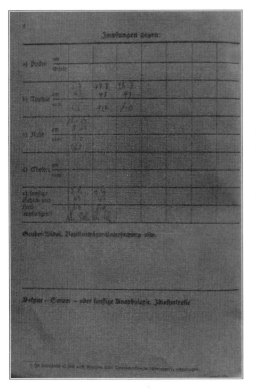

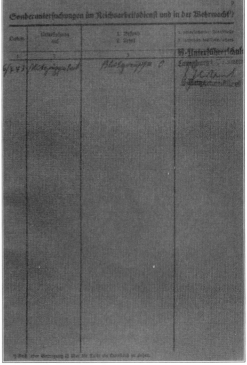

"G" BOOK ENTRY DETAILS

The responsibility for the G-Book lies with the military doctor of the section the conscript serves under.

The book is kept at the appropriate army medical service station and is transferred with the soldier. If a soldier is injured and taken to a military hospital the G-book follows him as soon as possible, where the doctor in charge has to sign. (see page 26).

If a soldier is discharged or leaves the service (i.e through injury) the G-book is sent to the appropriate registration office.

If social benefits are claimed, the G-book is to be kept with all other relevant documents. The roster book has to be marked accordingly with the entry of where the G-book is deposited (i.e. Department for War Invalids, etc.)

Para 6: The accuracy of the entries has to be confirmed by the responsible doctor through his signature.

Para 7: Explanation for entries:
Cover Page: The bloodgroup has to be completed by the section doctor here and again on pages 9-12.

Page 1: Later additions to hereditary diseases or earlier illnesses are to be entered in red ink and dated.

Pages 2-4: Entries, which have to be transferred to the rostercard have a tinted background. The transferral of this data is to be completed by the Duty Station requesting the examination.

Pages 9-12: These pages should hold all entries regarding examinations during active service for special reasons. i.e. special sports; state of fitness for duties such as diving, tropical, alpine, flying; marriage suitability, x-ray examinations, bloodgroups etc. BUT NOT the results of the examination for ability to be arrested.

Para 13-16: Exact data of any x-ray treatment has to be recorded here.

Folder: VD card and L-Book have to be kept here (and other relevant cards).

PAGE 1 - MEDICAL HISTORY

1) **Family:**
   a) Mental illnesses   b) Suicides and attempts   c) Alcoholism
   d) Epilepsy   e) Consumption   f) Other

2) **Personal History:**
   Any severe illnesses, operations, accidents, venereal diseases, vaccinations and whether a twin.
3) **Opinion of** a)Teacher and b) School Doctor regarding:-
   a) physical, mental psychological state, any permanent damages, signs of psychopathic or neurotic behaviour.
   c) general behaviour, character, exam results, talents.

4) Other important information: from the Dept. of Health, Doctor of the Hitler Youth etc.

Sporting Awards such as: (Date and place)
State Youth Athletics Award . . . .
State Athletics Award . . . .
Swimming Awards . . . .
German Riding & Driving Awards . . . .

PAGES 2 & 3 - MEDICAL EXAMINATION RECORDS

Page 2 - At time of Enlistment
1) Duty Station ordering the
medical examination.
2) Date
3) Height
4) Weight
5) Chest
6) Build
7) Eyes a) Strength
        b) Image definition
8) Ears a) Hearing test
        b) Eardrum state
9) Teeth @ Fillings
       / Damaged
       + Root problem
       o Missing
10) Heart & Arteries
      Heartbeat - resting
              - working
11) Lungs
12) Nerves
13) Urine
14) a) Any physical defects
    b) Medical verdict re.
     military fitness
15) Specialist examination
    results
16) Signature & rank of
    examining doctor

Page 3 - Upon passing out/posting.

Installment Into Reich Labour Service	Passing Out	Installment into the Army

PAGES 6 & 7 - WEIGHTCHART

(It seems if you served in the Reichs Labour Service you only got weighed upon starting, finishing and once in between. In the Army you got weighed once every month!)

PAGE 8 - VACCINATIONS

a) Smallpox b) Typhoid c) Dysentry d) Cholera e) any other i.e. Tetanus

Gruber-Widal Test (Bacillus carrier tests

Allergies, aversions etc.

PAGE 9 TO 12 - SPECIAL TESTS

i.e this soldier had a test for blood grouping. He is group o.

PAGES 13-15 - MEDICAL NOTES

Special medical observations during service in the Reichs Labour Service or in the army.

Anything worth noting which is not recorded anywhere else.

i.e observations during sports weeks, x-rays, follow up examinations, VD, blood donor information.

PAGE 17 - MEDICAL AIDS DISPENSATIONS

Dispensation of medical aids (i.e. glasses, rubber stockings, false teeth, insoles for flat feet, etc.

1) Which item(s) 2) Place of delivery 3) Date of receipt

PAGE 18-25 - SERVICE MEDICAL RECORDS

Illnesses whilst in the Reichs Labour Service or in the Army.
1) Year
2) & 3) Dates From/To of illness
4) Duty Station - ie regiment, detachment, company etc.
5) Where treated and notes on duties exempted
6) Manner of final release from medical treatment
7) Name of illness
8) Index number
9) 1) Cause of illness
   2) Observation Chart started?
10) Signature of doctor and remarks. (how long under observation and if a registration from been completed.

General Notes:
On leaving the Reichs Labour Service a line should be drawn underneath the last entry and should be drawn underneath the last entry and marked with "wehrdienst".
If transferred from the Army to the RLS, the line should be marked "Reichsarbeitsdienst".
After final dismissal from the RLS the book is to be handed in to the authority.

PAGE 24 & 25 - DISCHARGE EXAMINATION

Upon leaving the RLS and active military duties including military exercises (note any complaints).

Date | Test Result | Signature of examining doctor/duty station

PAGE 26 - ENDORSEMENTS

Duty Station | Date | Signature of doctor

Page 27 - On discharge from active military duty this page to be sent to the appropriate public health department by the Military Registration Office. If the conscript has registered for military surveillance

Surname/Christian Names
Address (after discharge)
Place of Birth   Country of Birth

Date of Birth	Religion at Birth	Legitimate / Illegitimate	Twin: Y/N Identical / Not Identical
Single, Married for the . . . time, widowed, divorced.	Age on Marriage	Own children: Total	Stillborn . . . . Still Living . . . . . .

Frame: slim, muscular, round.

Manner of discharge from military duty
(after . . . . year service fit or unfit for military service)

Report on discharge.

Blood Group.

Any physical defects

. . . .
Date, Place   Signature and rank of
doctor

page 28) To the Public Health Department in . . . .

page 29) Content of Folder (information regarding the health report)

1)
2)   . . . . . . .etc

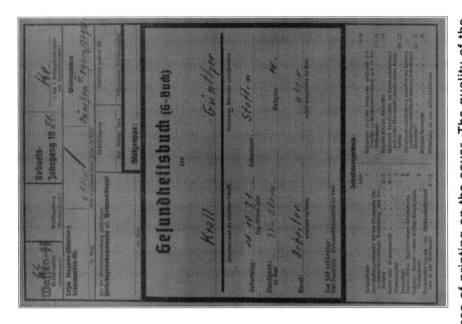

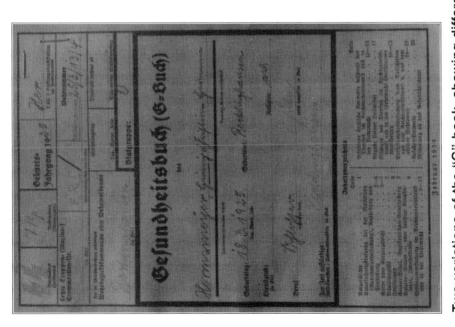

Two variations of the "G" book, showing different types of printing on the cover. The quality of the paper varied, as did the colour, ranging from light cream to a turquoise shade of blue.

SS FÜHRERSCHEIN
(SS Drivers Licence)

The following section illustrates four different examples of the SS Führerschein (Drivers Licence). The vehicle operators permits for the SS were relatively standard documents consisting of four pages in a folding card format. The SS Führerschein usually carried a photograph of the holder, overprinted with a validation stamp of the issuing authority. The licence holders personal details such as his name, rank. place and date of birth and his current unit were typewritten onto pages one, two and four of the document.

The usual format for the SS Führerschein was four pages each measuring 95mm x 140mm = $3\frac{3}{4}$ x $5\frac{1}{2}$ inches, printed on a grey cloth material with a light lamination applied over it.

The primary function of the SS drivers licence was to indicate that the holder had received proper training on the types of vehicles specified, and that he was proficient in their operation.

A qualified individual received his operators permit upon completion of the specified training course, which could be conducted at a drivers training centre or within his own unit. As can be seen from examples in this section. The early Waffen-SS drivers permits were overstamped on the front cover with letters VT, this was discontinued after 1940 when Waffen-SS licences had the formation details printed on the front cover.

It was customary to retain the same licence throughout the individuals military career, however the holders photograph was usually changed whenever he was promoted or demoted. Therefore it was not unusual to find an SS-Führerschein with the holder wearing a uniform with rank insignia different from the rank specified on the cover of the permit.

When an individual received his driving instruction from a branch of the Wehrmacht other than the SS he was often issued with the standard Wehrmacht Führerschein, this was especially so in the closing stages of World War II

The regulations regarding the holders photograph specified that it should show the holders head and shoulders pictured from his left side, and that the photograph should measure 52mm x 74mm. However licences issued in late 1944 and into 1945 were devoid of any photograph of the holder and carried a validation stamp in the photo box on page three of the licence. It can only be assumed that wartime shortages were responsible for the photograph being omitted on some SS Führerschein issued late in the war.

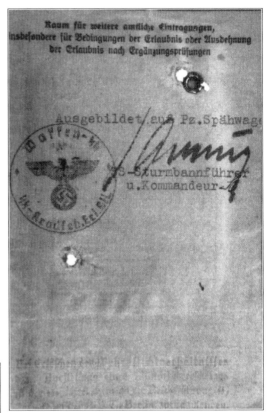

Front and back cover of the SS Führerschein (Driver's License) of Carl Heinz Fruhauf. Issued in April, 1939 this Führerschein is overstamped "SS VT" pre-dating the formation of the Waffen-SS in 1940.

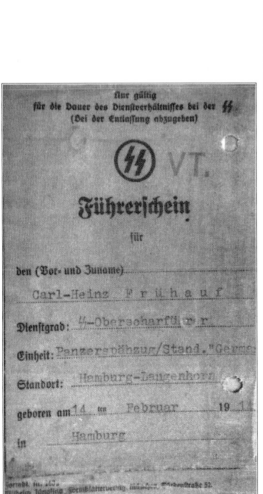

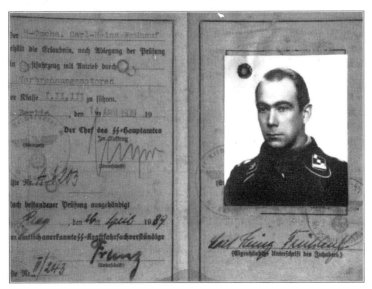

The Driver's Licence is made out to SS-Oberscharführer Fruhauf although the photo shows him wearing the rank insignia of an SS-Hauptsturmführer. This should not be viewed as unusual for SS driver's licenses and indeed ID cards tended to be updated with a new photograph of the holder, rather than issuing a completely new document following promotion. Note that the old validation stamp on the lower left of the photo is underneath whilst the most current stamp has been applied over the lower righthand corner of the updated photograph.

A photograph of Fruhauf taken in late 1939 following the Polish Campaign in which he was awarded the Iron Cross 2nd Class, the ribbon of which can be seen on his tunic.

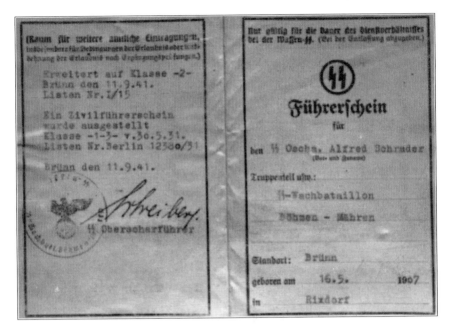

SS-Führerschein (Driver's Licence) of SS-Oscha (SS-Oberscharführer) Alfred Schrader. Schrader was a Senior NCO in the SS-Wachtbattalion (Watch Battalion) Bohemia-Mahren. The license and the holder's photograph bear the unit's validation stamps. The reverse of the licence indicates the class of vehicles Schrader was entitled to operate, it also gives details of Schrader's civilian driving licence issued in Berlin in 1931. The SS-Führerschein was printed on grey oilcloth with a light lamination, each of the four pages measured 95mm x 140mm = $3\frac{3}{4}$ x $5\frac{1}{2}$ inches.

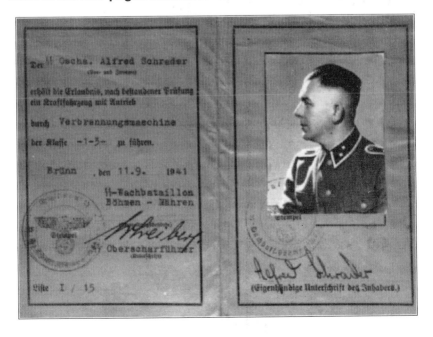

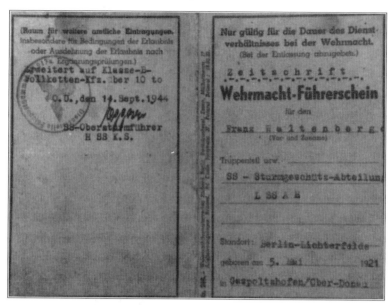

Front (right) and back cover (left) of SS-Rottenfuhrer Franz Waltenburger's Führerschein (Drivers Licence). This licence was issued relatively late in World War II (14.9.44) and is a regular Wehrmacht Drivers Licence adapted for the use of SS Personnel by the expedient of the inclusion of SS typing and SS validation ink stamps.

The two inside pages of Waltenburger's licence carry an SS validation stamp on each page, not the absence of a holders photograph, however the positioning and clarity of the stamp would indicate a photograph was never affixed to the appropriate pages. The lack of photo and the fact that this is a regular Wehrmacht rather than SS licence could indicate that the licence was issued as a temporary document.

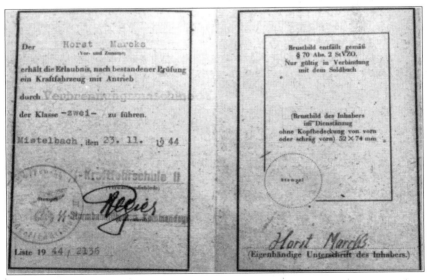

An SS Führerschein (Driver's Licence). The front cover of this Führerschein has the holder's name Horst Marcks, licence number and place and date of birth type written.

The inside pages of Marcks Führerschein indicate the types of vehicles he was qualified to operate, namely a Verbrennengsmachine (wheeled vehicle). The licence was issued to Marcks at the SS Driver's School at Mistelbach on the 23rd of November, 1944. The licence is overstamped with the official SS driving school stamp and bears the Commandant's signature and rank.

SPORTS AWARDS

Participation in sports activities and the pursuit of fitness were viewed as extremely important in the heirachy of the SS, this was especially true in its formative years during the early 1930's.

Although a specific SS sports award was planned to be introduced, initially during the early years of the SS, all SS members were required to train for the SA Wehrsportabzeichen (SA Military Sports Badge) and the (Reich Sports Badge).

The importance attached to sporting activities can be graphically illustrated by recounting what Reichsführer SS Himmler had to say about Sports Awards in a speech to the Hitler Youth on the 22nd of May 1936.

"I require that every SS man completes his bronze, silver and gold badges (National Sports Badge). Then I require the SA Sport Badge. I will build on these two awards from year to year with an SS performance badge. There are stipulations to this, namely that it must be sustained on an annual basis."

"I ask from men say 24 years old who are young, supple and quick, a performance level equal to the speed and capability, while on the other hand I ask for steady performances from a 40 year old. Every one of us is asked to do something which requires training and practice, but not for a sport badge that anybody from the masses can achieve, if this were the case the award would have no value. I always require something that one must train for. I would also like to add that in 1934/1935 we did not ask for this performance, each of us had mountains of paper work that kept us detained. The situation could no be altered no matter how much one complained about it. Therefore we did not take full part in physical training. Last year I instituted the requirement that the officer corps must achieve the SA Sports Badge in addition to the enlisted men. Today I estimate that 80% of all SS men hold the sports badge, Men over 30 years of age are exempt. By 1 July of this year I will require all of the SS officer corps to achieve the SA Sports Badge and by 1 October the Reichsport badge. The following year we will begin with a proficiency badge. We stand at the beginning of this growth and some things which will later be a foregone conclusion, are not possible today as with the SS men in the 20, 25 and 35 year groups. That doesn't matter. What is more important is that the generation that took part in the struggle lay the basis. Then everything will run its-self in the future."

"Why do I place such a value on the sports badge? First the sport and the badge select and recognise the elite and eliminates those who are weak. Second it requires all members to participate in some form of physical activity. I therefore avoid getting an officer corps where the age over 40 grows bellies. I direct that everyone must train in some form of sports and ask those who indulge in alcohol and nicotine to do so in moderation."

"We will raise ourselves to this, and I also see for the future the task of strengthening the sports program further, so may I repeat what I already said in Potsdam: That we must only have tough youths. but we also ensure hardness with age. It must not be, as in the last 100 years or so and as we experienced in the War (1914-1918) an age led through democracy, humanity, freemasonry and knee bending, which eventually says that the youth will do it. Instead we must, when people are back on an even keel, look today to create an age before which one can raise one's hat."

Inorder to qualify for the SA Sports Badge the individual was required to satisfactorily complete the various tasks and disciplines contained in the programme. During the course of fulfiling the various award criteria the individual had to have his completion of each discipline recorded and validated in his SA Sports Award Training Book. Award of the SA Sports Badge could not be made unless the Training Book was filled out and completed.

SA SPORTS AWARD
(Training Book)

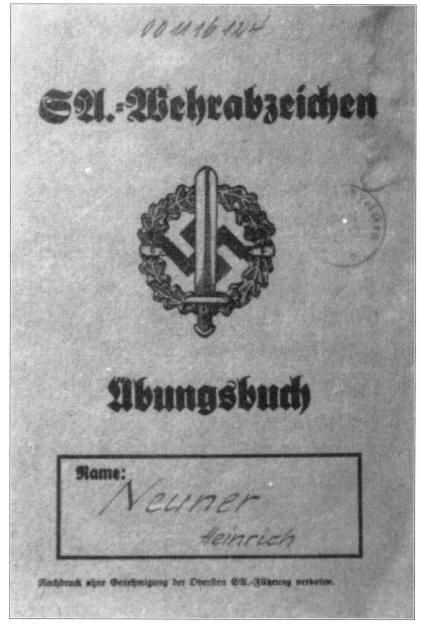

The SA Service Award training book of Heinrich Neuner. The various tasks and disciplines contained in this book had to be satisfactorily completed by the applicant before he was eligible for the award of the SA Service Badge.

Die Bestimmungen für den Erwerb des SA-Wehr-Abzeichens sind mir bekannt. Ich erkläre mich hiermit bereit, den
Pflichten, die mir bei der Vorbereitung und nach dem Erwerb
des Abzeichens auf Grund der Ausführungsbestimmungen er-
wachsen, gewissenhaft nachzukommen.

Vor- und Zuname _Heinrich Neiner_

Stand oder Beruf _Läufer_

Gliederung oder Verband _M-Bahnr_

*) Reichssportabzeichen: Bronze, Silber, Gold.
   HJ-Leistungsabzeichen: Eisen, Bronze, Silber.

Geboren am _5.2.21_ Geburtsort _Hall zr. Rhannl_

genaue Briefanschrift _Aulendorf_

Ort _Aulendorf_, den _26.5._ 19_40_

Neiner Heinrich

Eigenhändige Unterschrift

Der Inhaber dieses Übungsbuches hat die Bedingungen
der §§ 3—5 der Ausführungsbestimmungen erfüllt und die vor-
stehende Erklärung eigenhändig unterschrieben. Er wird deshalb
zur Ausbildung für den Erwerb des SA-Wehr-Abzeichens
zugelassen.

Ort _Aulendorf_, den _26.5._ 19_40_

SA-Sportabz.
Prüfer
Prüferstempel

Führer der Einheit

*) Nichtzutreffendes ist zu streichen.

The applicant was required to swear an oath that he agreed to abide by
the rules and regulations of the program during the period of preparation
and training. The applicant further swears to continue to uphold the
regulations if and when the award has been achieved. The program of
instruction and training was divided into 3 categories.

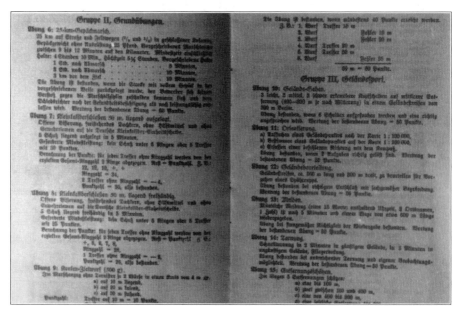

Part 1 of the program covered physical training in the following 5 events:- 100 Meter Run - Long Jump - Shot Putt (7 Kg Shot) - Discus - and 3,000 Meter Run. Various points could be attained by carrying out the 5 disciplines to the required standard.

Part 2 of the program required the completion of a 25 Kilometre Road March carrying a 25 Pound Field Pack. Points could be earned by completing the March within the specified time tables. The second part of this group included weapons training and marksmanship with a Small Bore rifle and dummy grenade.

Part 3 of the training program was the most complex of the 3 training groups; this involved:- Map Reading, Orienteering, Camouflage and Range Estimation. Integrated into these tasks was the deciphering of a coded message required to complete the course, and essential to attaining a satisfactory score.

SS TOTENKOPFRING

The SS Deathshead ring has been cloaked in secrecy and mystery for many years, much of which did not come about by accident, but was rather the deliberate design of Heinrich Himmler to endow the ring with a mystique shrouded in Nordic mythology. To this end there was even a prohibition on newspaper reporting of recipients of the ring, and upon the death of a bearer the ring had to be returned to Himmler whereupon it was given a place of honour at Wewelsburg Castle.

Himmler first introduced the ring as an SS Honour on the 9th of November, 1933, however the actual Order of Institution and laying down the conditions for award was not issued by the RFSS until some 6 months later on the 20th of April, 1934. In the 10 years following the date there were several Orders issued by Himmler changing the award criteria for bestowal of the ring. Each of these Orders and Amendments is quite lengthy and is reproduced in full elsewhere in this Chapter. However a brief resume of the award criteria is as follows. As will be seen the first requirement for award of the SS Honour ring was for holders of low SS ID card numbers: initially the qualifying number was 3,000, but in subsequent Orders this number was raised to 5,000 in 1936 and then raised once again to 10,000 in August, 1939 - a reflection of the dramatic increase in membership of the SS during this early period.

Officers who joined the SS prior to the 30th of January, 1933, the date of Hitler's accession to power as German Chancellor, and also officers who joined after that date could qualify for the ring after 3 year's service in the SS.

Officers who had served in the Reichswehr or had been members of the German Police who had been prevented from joining the SS could qualify for award of the ring after 2 year's service in the SS. This Order was also extended to include the Austrian Army and Police Force after Austria's annexation in 1938.

Membership in other National Socialist Party Organisations such as the SA, NSKK, HJ and the NSDAP itself was also taken into account if the individual's membership in the Nazi Party was uninterrupted when joining the SS. The qualification period for these officers transferring from other NSDAP organisations was 2 years.

SS holders of Party badges of honour entitled to apply for the Deathshead ring under the following conditions: an SS member holding the gold Party badge with a membership number lower than 10,000, or upon whom the badge had been especially conferred; and members holding the Coburg badge which was awarded to the street fighters of the Party in the early days also qualified for the ring, however NCOs and enlisted men were required to produce the award certificates of their badge when applying for the Totenkopfring.

Officers who had resided in Austria and had been members of the illegal SS in that country prior to the Anschluss were qualified to apply providing they had held their commissions for 2 years or longer. This regulation also applied to officers who had resided in the Sudetenland prior to its annexation in August, 1938. At a later date a similar 2 year membership qualification provision was also made for officers who had resided in the Memel DIstrict and who had joined the SS before the 1st of June, 1944 which was the official date of its annexation.

In addition to the qualifications required for the award of the Totenkopfring there were also a number of exclusions which could prevent an SS member applying for the ring for a specified time period. These ranged in severity from a formal reprimand up to actual expulsion from the SS. Commiting any of innumerable misdemeanours or more serious offenses carried a penalty of a three months to three years period of time during which the offender was not permitted to be eligible for award of the ring. Additionally these time penalties could be used where an offense was committed by a holder of the ring whereupon he would be required to relinquish his ring for a specified period.

Although the conditions for award of the Totenkopfring were quite wide ranging it was still only awarded to a relatively small number of SS members, and in 1936 Himmler also allowed exceptional individual cases to be presented to the SS Personnel Office for the personal consideration of the Reichsführer-SS.

Even the Totenkopfring was awarded to an individual, ownership of the ring always reverted back to the RFSS when the holder died, resigned or was expelled from the SS. Orders were also to be strictly adhered to where an SS member had been reprimanded: whereupon he had to return the ring along with the Investiture Citation to the main Personnel Office pending whatever period of exclusion had been prescribed. This same rule also applied to men who had been reduced in rank even if they still remained in the SS after demotion. In some minor cases of infringement or even a mere rebuke from a more senior officer the ring was looked upon as a punishment in itself. So strictly applied were the rules governing the Totenkopfring that an officer even on an authorised leave of absence from the RFSS was required to present his ring and papers to the Personnel Office.

After the start of WWII an Order was issued on the 6th of December, 1939 which was directed mainly at Waffen-SS members who had been killed in action which required Waffen-SS Commanders to ensure that the rings of members who had died should be taken from them before burial and be returned to the SS Personnel Office. This same Order also applied to Waffen-SS men who had subsequently died of war wounds in hospitals in Germany or any SS men serving with Army units. Local SS officers were even required to visit relatives of the deceased SS men to retrieve the Totenkopfring. The Order stressed that the officer should give tactful explanations as to why the ring should be returned to the Reichsführer-SS and to point out that in accordance with the Investiture Citation the ring reverted to the property of the SS Personnel Office upon the holder's death.

All of the rings which were retrieved from deceased, retired or expelled SS members ultimately found their way to Himmler's Wewelsburg Castle where they were displayed in a place of honour and remained until the Castle's virtual destruction in 1945.

Bestowal of the SS Totenkopfring was terminated on the 7th of October, 1944 by Heinrich Himmler: "The Reichsführer-SS has in consideration of the war efforts of all available forces, decided to discontinue the production and bestowal of the Totenkopfring. Applications of the bestowal are to cease from this date." It may or may not be significant but this is about the only Order pertaining to the SS Honour ring which was **not** signed by Himmler himself, but bore the signature of the Head of the SS Personnel Office, SS Obergruppenführer von Horff.

The SS-Totenkopfring was produced by the jewellry firm of Gahr of Marianen Strasse 3, Munich. This firm was the sole authorised manufacturer of the ring, a privilege which the firm had acquired from the SS due to the Party affiliations of the owner and his wife. Indeed after the death of Herr Gahr, Frau Gahr carried on the business. The Gahr firm produced many Nazi Party emblems including flag and standard pole emblems, as well as decorative jewellry bearing Nordic symbols for the SS.

The Award document for the SS-Totenkopfring was a most cherished possession for any SS recipient of the Award, almost as important as the Ring itself. Each document was signed by Heinrich Himmler and was presented to the recipient along with the Ring at a special ceremony which usually took place on a day or date of special significance to the SS (such as Hitler's birthday the 20th of April, or the Anniversary of the Munich Putsch at the Feldherrnhalle on the 9th of November).

Heinrich Himmler held the Totenkopfring and its Award document in especially high esteem: to the extent that he issued a special order instructing relatives of deceased Totenkopfring holders where they could purchase a frame approved by the Reichsführer-SS in which to display the Award certificate. The approved retailer of the Totenkopfring document frame was Georg Braun Markt Grafing, Markt Platz 14 Berlin. The cost of this frame was 1.45 Reichsmarks.

Upon the death of a holder of the Totenkopfring, the Ring had to be returned to the SS Personnel Office in Berlin. After being documented the ring was taken to Wewelsburg Castle where it was enshrined in a special vault of honour to commemorate fallen SS men. However the Award document could be retained by the family of a deceased holder of the Ring as a momento, and as proof of the honour bestowed on their loved one. This honour was also extended to include SS members who had honourably retired from service in the SS or were compelled to leave due to ill health. Where an SS man had been deprived of his ring as a consequence of some dishonourable act, or had ben expelled from the SS, the holder or his family were not then permitted to retain the Award document.

Reichsführer-SS Heinrich Himmler created a shrine to the deceased holders of the SS Totenkopfring at his Wewelsburg Castle near Paderborn, Germany. Himmler expressed his reasons for dedicating a shrine for the SS Totenkopfring to a group of SS Leaders in 1938 in which he said that by retaining the Rings in a place of honour they would instill strength, honour and ideology into future generations of SS officers.

The Wewelsburg Castle served as a centre for research into ancient Aryan culture as well as being a shrine to fallen SS officer's. Its other main function was to serve as scheduled retreat for high ranking SS officers. Within the walls of the Castle there was stored a vast treasure house of military and historical artifacts, and also a massive library.

In the closing days of World War II Himmler ordered one of his officers, Heinz Macher, to destroy Wewelsburg Castle to prevent it falling intact into the hands of the advancing US and British Armies. At the time Macher was assigned to destroy the Castle some of the artifacts had already been removed, however a considerable amount of material still remained within its walls when Macher ignited his demolition charges. The destruction of Wewelsburg Castle was only about 80% successful, and when Macher and his small Pioneer team had left Wewelsburg the residents of the village proceeded to help themselves to any articles remaining: including priceless Persian rugs which they had to cut down to fit into the tiny rooms of their small village houses!

The US Army arrived at Wewelsburg two days after Macher's demolition attempt, and proceeded to strip the Castle of anything of value which still remained. It was not only small portable objects which were removed from the Castle, surviving local residents have stated that US Army officers even stripped out the solid oak staircases and massive Medieval stone fireplaces to be shipped back to the USA. It is also recorded that a US Army Captain, Theodore M. Black of the counter-intelligence corps, was one of the first Americans to enter the Castle, and subsequently made a statement to the effect "I immediately went to the Wewelsburg to examine the facility. I found (and expropriated) a cigar box full of SS Silver Rings which were awarded to SS men upon their admission, and which had to be returned to Wewelsburg upon their deaths; there must have been 200 of the Rings." These 200 Rings along with many other artifacts including Heinrich Himmler's personal collection of Medieval weapons and firearms disappeared whilst the Castle was under Allied control, and have to date never been recovered.

The front entrance to Heinrich Himmler's castle at Wewelsburg where the Totenkopfrings of fallen SS men were sent for safe keeping.

The west tower of Wewelsburg Castle: this contained the living quarters for SS officers serving at the castle's research centre.

The main tower or keep of Wewelsburg Castle pictured from the inner courtyard. It was a special room in this tower that the returned SS Totenkopfrings were housed in a place of honour.

Although the main intention of this work is to explore the documentation of the SS rather than any particular artifact, it may be of interest to know a few facts about the SS-Totenkopfring itself. It is believed that somewhere between 16,000 and 20,000 Rings were awarded between 1934-1944 when Award of the Ring was terminated. The numbers of rings awarded between 1936-1944 are documented as being 14,752 in total for the period: with an average of 1,500 Rings being awarded each year. The high point for Awards of the Totenkopfring came in 1942 when no less than 2,240 Rings were awarded. The reason for the projected figure of 16,000 - 20,000 being given is that there is no accurate record for the actual number of Rings awarded for the years 1934 and 1935. Therefore it is necessary to use an estimated average for these two years.

However in view to the fact that the Totenkopfring only came into existence in 1934 it is safe to assume that as a new Award a substantial number of SS personnel would have qualified for the Award of the Ring. This is borne out by the SS-Dienstalterliste for 1935 which clearly indicates that almost all the officers above the rank of SS-Hauptsturmfuhrer had already been awarded the Ring, and that for lower ranks from SS-Hauptsturmfuhrer down to SS-Unsturmfuhrer a substantial majority of junior officers had also received the Ring by 1935.

The Totenkopfring was presented to the recipient in a small silver jewellry container with a black velvet lining. The lid of the container bore two SS Runes within a circle embossed in silver on black leather. This container is a considerably rarer artifact than the Rings themselves.

The focal point of the Totenkopfring was the Deathshead emblem which had long been a tradition Germanic military symbol: in particular it was used by Prussia as a cap badge on the Busbys of the 1st Leib-Hussar Regiment and also by the German State of Brunswick with their black Brunswicker contingent which served in the Napoleonic Wars. Later in the 19th Century Totenkopf was used as the helmet plate on the Picklehaube of the Bodyguard Battalion of the Brunswick 92nd Infantry Regiment. Around the edge of the Ring were four Runic symbols which were used to further decorate the Ring and imbue it with Nordic mysticism. Each of these symbols carried with it a specific significance in Nordic mythology and have been illustrated and explained elsewhere in this Chapter.

The SS-Totenkopfrings produced by the Jewellry firm of Frau Gahr in Munich were usually made from .835 silver and were constructed in such a way that the Deathshead symbol covered the joint where the two ends of the ring were joined together. The dimensions of the Ring were a 7mm wide band with a weight of approximately 11-12 grams. This variation in weight is accounted for by different ring size: a larger size ring obviously weighing more than a smaller one. The current reproductions of the Totenkopfring tend to be slightly underweight weighing approximately 10 grams and are between 5-10% wider in their dimensions.

The inside of the Totenkopfring carried several engraved inscriptions starting with: "S. Lb." meaning "Seine Leib"; then the engraved name of the recipient; the date of the Award; followed by a facsimile signature of Heinrich Himmler; finally a silver assay mark of .835 denoting the silver content of the Ring.

Reproductions of the SS-Totenkopfring have been in circulation for many years and vary considerably in their quality. However a master jeweller living in Germany today, Bertold Peicl, who worked on the original rings is still producing extremely high quality reproductions which are difficult to distinguish from originals due to his use of .835 silver and superb attention to detail. These good quality reproductions cost 150 DM each and could very easily pass for originals at many times the cost of their true reproduction value!

Award of the SS-Totenkopfring was suspended by Reichsführer-SS Heinrich Himmler in September, 1944. The Totenkopfring Award was not scrapped permanently by Himmler; he had stated that he intended to reintroduce the Award at some later date. The reasons he gave at the time for suspending the Award were: that there were not sufficient expert personnel available to process the applications for the Totenkopfring due to most of his staff being involved in war related work; another reason was that the Award Ceremony was also a drain on manpower, and also that the materials used in the Ring's production could be applied towards the war effort. To this end Himmler ordered Frau Gahr to stop production of the SS-Totenkopfring until further notice.

Apparently by September, 1944 there were just two SS staff officers (an SS-Hauptsturmfuhrer and SS-Untersturmfuhrer) working on the processing of Totenkopfring Award applications, and they were also required to perform other duties as well. There were a considerable number of applications already received by the SS Personnel Office when award of the Totenkopfring was suspended, and Himmler ordered that these applications would be given priority for processing when the production of the Ring was resumed. Frau Gahr was authorised by Himmler to produce a further small quantity of Rings in late 1944 to cover the Awards which had been processed and approved immediately prior to the time of the Suspension Order.

A considerable amount of time and effort was put into recovering SS-Totenkopfrings belonging to deceased, degraded, discharged or transferred SS recipients of the Ring. A strict accounting was kept of all the Rings, an SS staff officers went to often extreme lengths to recover Rings from relatives of deceased Ringholders and from the actual bodies of SS men killed in action. Th Rings of SS men who were killed in action were sent to Wewelsburg to be given a place of honour. However the Rings of any SS man who had his Ring withdrawn for any dishonourable reason or because he had left the SS were melted down and the silver used for other purposes.

Towards the end of the war Himmler and the SS although having suspended Award of the Totenkopfring were still expending a great deal of effort recovering Rings. The SS documented 2,431 SS men whose Rings had to be recovered for various reasons of which 1,562 were duly recovered and handed back to the Personnel Office. In a further 236 cases investigations by the SD showed that the Rings had been lost either as a result of enemy action or by being buried with the bearer. By 1945, 633 Rings had still not been returned, and of this number 350 cases were still under active investigation by the SD. Of the other 283 Rings, 170 could not be reclaimed as the men were listed as Missing in Action, and a further 105 cases were pending investigation when the appropriate amount of time had elapsed allowed for returning the ring. This left just 8 Rings unaccounted for which were put down to either an inability or refusal on the part of deceased families to surrender the cherished Ring to the SS Personnel Office.

The following numbers of Rings were awarded in the years 1936-1944:

1936 - 1,137	1939 - 1,257	1942 - 2,240
1937 - 1,873	1940 - 1,471	1943 - 1,798
1938 - 1,837	1941 - 1,184	1944 - 1,935

Note the high number of Awards in 1942: this was as a consequence of an Order by Himmler that the number of Awards be increased by speeding up the processing of applications. Although a higher total was attained in this particular year the processing of Awards could not be increased or even sustained due to subsequent manpower shortages. The Awards appearing in any particular year do not necessarily indicate that this was the only number of SS men entitled to the ring in that year, rather it reflects the annual number of Ring applications processed. At the time the Ring was suspended there were literally thousands of SS men eligible for Award of the Ring: some with applications dating back almost two years which the SS Personnel Office were never able to keep up with.

SS TOTENKOPFRINGS

Eight different views of a modern reproduction Totenkopfring. These superb quality rings are handcrafted and engraved (usually with a wartime award date) in Germany and are very difficult to detect without a direct comparison with an original specimen of the Ring. Note that compared to the genuine example this reproduction is noticeably thicker and has a wider band, although the detailing is excellent.

Eight different views of a genuine Totenkopfring awarded to Willi Raum on Hitler's birthday in 1937. Note the quality of the engraving.

TOTENKOPFRING SYMBOLS

TOTENKOPF (DEATH'S HEAD).

This was a traditional symbol used by the German military for hundreds of years as a form of insignia usually on headdress and was used to strike fear into the hearts of the enemy. The interpretation and meaning of the Death's Head was "absolute obedience even unto death".

TRIAG (TRIANGLE) & SIGRUNE (VICTORY).

The symbol of a triangle pointing upwards was the Nordic symbol of the processes of Life. Each of the three sides represented respectively: the beginning of Life, the development and living of Life, and the end of Life. The Nordic sign of victory used as an ancient German exhortation and greeting: This is the origin of the "Sieg Heil" (Hail Victory) salute.

HAGAL RUNE.

The Hagal rune is the basic symbol from which all 18 of the Nordic Runic symbols originate. It's sexagon shape can be used to form any other symbols in the Runic Alphabet. The Hagal rune was the expression of inner strength overcoming adversity. The interpretation of the Hagal rune was the development of the inner man inorder for him to conquer the universe.

FYRFOS (SWASTIKA).

The ancient symbol of eternity. The swastika also symbolised the Gibor Rune which denoted Gib = Give and OR = Descendant, used as a traditional blessing for the prosperity and survival of the Germanic race: broadly interpreted as "Man being one with God and one with eternity".

TYROS (CIRCLE). This was a multiple symbol holding within the circle the twin SS Runes and the inverted arrow symbolising Tyr = the God of War and the Sword and OL = the Spirit. The interpretation of this symbol was as an exhortation to "Be fearless, true and brave" and that "Death cannot kill".

SS-TOTENKOPFRING
(Award Document)

Der Reichsführer-SS   Feld-Kommandostelle, den 20.August 1943

SS-Untersturmführer Hans P e r k o
SS-Nr. 261 324, Stammabteilung Donau, Bezirk II

Ich verleihe Ihnen den Totenkopfring der SS

Er soll sein:

Ein Zeichen unserer Treue zum Führer, unseres unwandelbaren Gehorsams gegen unsere Vorgesetzten und unserer unerschütterlichen Zusammengehörigkeit und Kameradschaft.

Der Totenkopf ist die Mahnung, jederzeit bereit zu sein, das Leben unseres Ichs einzusetzen für das Leben der Gesamtheit.

Die Runen dem Totenkopf gegenüber sind Heilszeichen unserer Vergangenheit, mit der wir durch die Weltanschauung des Nationalsozialismus erneut verbunden sind.

Die beiden Sig-Runen versinnbilden den Namen unserer Schutzstaffel. Hakenkreuz und Hagall-Rune sollen uns den nicht zu erschütternden Glauben an den Sieg unserer Weltanschauung vor Augen halten.

Umkränzt ist der Ring von Eichenlaub, den Blättern des alten deutschen Baumes.

Dieser Ring ist käuflich nicht erwerbbar und darf nie in fremde Hände kommen.

Mit Ihrem Ausscheiden aus der SS oder aus dem Leben geht dieser Ring zurück an den Reichsführer-SS.

Abbildungen und Nachahmungen sind strafbar, und Sie haben dieselben zu verhüten.

Tragen Sie den Ring in Ehren!

SS-Totenkopfring Award Document of SS-Untersturmfuhrer Hans Perko, awarded on the 20th of August, 1943 and signed by Heinrich Himmler.

The Reichsführer-SS
Field Headquarters, 20th August 1943

SS-Untersturmfuhrer Hans Perko
SS-Nr. 261 324, Stammabteilung Donau, Bezirk II

I bestow upon you the Deathshead Ring of the SS

It shall be:

A symbol of our loyalty to the Fuhrer, our undivided attention to our leaders, and our unwavering unity and comradeship.

The Deathshead is a warning that we must hold ourselves ready at all times and be prepared to sacrifice ourselves for the good of the Nation.

The runes opposite the Deathshead are symbols of our past, through which we are bound to the world concept of National Socialism.

The two Sieg runes remind us of the name of our Schutzstaffel. The Hakenkreuz and Hagall runes shall ensure we never fail and keep before our eyes our abiding faith in the victory of our vision of the world.

The ring is encircled with oakleaves, the leaves of the ancient German trees.

This ring cannot be purchased and must never be allowed to fall into the hands of strangers.

In the event of your departure from the SS or upon your death, this ring must be returned to the Reichsführer-SS

Reproductions and copying of the ring are a punishable offence. You are to always safeguard your ring.

Wear your Ring with Honour!

H.Himmler

SS HONOUR RING

Date: 20 April 1937
REUM WILLY - SS Obersturmführer (11 Sept 1938)
SS-Haüptsturmführer (9 Nov 1940)
Born: 4 Jan 1908
SS-Totenkopfstandarte 4 "Ostmark"
Party number 39248
SS number 124557
Dagger
SA sports badge - bronze
DRL sports badge - bronze

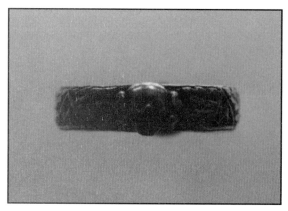

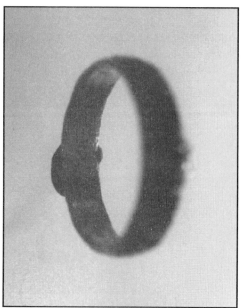

SS-Totenkopfring of SS-Haüptsturmführer Willy Reum who received the Award on the 20th of April, 1937 at which time he held the rank of SS-Untersturmführer.

This is an English translation of the original order from Reichsführer-SS Heinrich Himmler issued on the 10th of April, 1934 instituting the SS-Totenkopfring. The award criteria contained in this original order was relatively straightforward, but was later qualified and extended by subsequent amendment orders.

THE REICHSFÜHRER-SS   **Munich, 10.4.1934**

SS-ORDER

I.

The Deathshead Ring should be presented to:

IMMEDIATELY:

1.) All SS members up to Identity Card number 3,000,
2.) All SS Leaders from SS-Sturmfuhrer upwards, who joined the SS before 30th of January, 1933 and have served for at least two years;

FOR THE FUTURE:

3.) All SS Leaders who joined after the 30th of January, 1933 and serve as SS Leaders for 3 years;

EXCEPTIONS:

4.) SS Leaders who were unable to join before the 30th of January, 1933 because they served in the Police or the National Army will be eligible after two years service in the SS.

II.

Every SS Leader, who has presented with this Ring must wear it at all times, on his left ring finger. I forbid the SS-Totenkopfring to be shown or be made known to any newspaper. The presentation of the Ring is an otward sign of inner worth, won through struggle and duty, and of tried and tested communion with the Fuhrer and his ideology. The Ring is not a medal or Order and may not be used by the bearer for personal propaganda.

The Reichsführer-SS

Berlin, 13 September 1936

The Reichsführer-SS
Staff Chancery Office
Section P 6 Tgb. No. 1480/36

Distributor Va

Regulations

with regard to the bestowal of the Totenkopfring of the SS

A. Bestowal

1. Conditions

The Totenkopfring will be bestowed to:

1.) Every SS Member up to the SS No. 5,000.
2.) Every SS Leader from the rank of Untersturmführer upwards who entered an SS detachment before the 30.1.33
3.) Every SS Leader who entered the SS after 30.1.33 and has three years service.
4.) Every SS Leader, who was not able to enter the SS before the 30.1.33 due to membership of the German Forces or Police and has completed 2 years service in the SS.
5.) Every SS Leader who, before 30.1.33 did active duty in different organisations of the Party (SA, HJ, NSKK, PO,) and without interruption of duties entered the SS and has completed 2 years service in the SS.
   In this case his superior administrative department have to certify the date of joining the SS.
6.) Exceptional individual cases have to be presented to the Personnel Office for the decision of the Reichsführer-SS.
7.) All who carry a Golden Party Badge no matter what rank.

II. Special statements

1.) The bestowing of the Totenkopfring depends on past disciplinary action as follows:

a) degraded	3 years	b) time limited expulsion	2 years
c) arrest	1 year	d) stern reprimand	$\frac{1}{2}$ year
e) formal reprimand	$\frac{1}{4}$ year		

In the case of Z.V. position the SS Leader will receive the SS Ring after expiration of a year after he has shown good conduct and if he complies with the conditions A 1-6.

2.) Reasons for disqualification from the bestowing of the Totenkopfrings are:

a) SS Members who do not comply with the conditions A 1-6.
b) SS Members who face a disciplinary charge against them at a Party or SS Court.
c) SS Members who have leave of absence from the Reichsführer-SS for disciplinary reasons.

B. Revision of Applications

1.) The lists of applications for granting of the Totenkopfrings have to be forwarded by the Principal Office in the official way to the Personnel Department Reichsführer-SS.
2.) The applications have to contain:
a) Name and christian names of the ring applicant.
b) Rank
c) SS number
d) Position
e) Measurement of the left ring finger
3.) The lists of applications should be accompanied by a verification from the provisions officer that all checks have been made in accordance with the issued regulations.
4.) The applications may be continuously submitted to the Personnel Office.

C. Returning of the SS Ring

1.) All SS Leaders who resign from the SS, even those who resigned honourably, have to return, with no exception, the ring and Investiture Citation to the Personnel Office.
2.) SS Members (look at instruction - the Chief of the SS - main offices V 17 E 2, Tgb. No. 4550. Re.) have to return the ring without the Investiture Citation for storage at the main Personnel Office.
3.) SS Leaders who have been reprimanded have to return the ring with Investiture Citation to the Personnel Office as per stipulated in the exclusions
4.) SS Leaders, who have been reduced in rank to Unterführer or SS man though remaining in the SS, have to return the SS ring with

Investiture Citation, without delay to the Personnel Office.

5.) SS Leaders, who are in possession of SS rings, but are given leave of absence from the Reichsführer-SS pending legal action, have to present the ring and papers to the Personnel Office until the legal proceedings are completed.

6.) In case of punishment of a holder of the ring by arrest or rebuke, the ring will stay the property of the Führers.

7.) According to which we point to the DBO C le, to this the Reichsführer SS has defined the withdrawal of the Totenkopfrings as punishment.

8.) Naturally it follows that Unterführen (SS No. 1-5,000 who are wearers of Totenkopfrings, have to return the ring regarding C 1-7.

9.) If a ring has been wrongly sized or ground and made unsightly through years of wear and tear, the ring alone will have to be returned to the Personnel Office and at the same time an application as in "D" number 7.

D. Re-bestowing

The Totenkopfring being restored:

1.) At the re-confirmation of an SS Leader who left the organisation honourably.

2.) At the re-confirmation of an SS Member at an official office.

3.) At the end of a disciplinary procedure and lifting of the consequent leave.

4.) After three years of the inforced reduction of rank.

5.) Two years after the date of expulsion the expiration of an imposed time of disqualification from the SS.

6.) After the loss of the SS ring through no fault of the holder. In this case a short report of the facts by the SS Member in question.

7.) By official applications for re-instatement or exchange of the Totenkopfring .

Besides this is to add:

a) the engraved date of the last issued ring.

b) if the ring candidate is still in possession of the Investiture Citation.

E. Other regulations

1.) Every SS Member, who had been bestowed with the Totenkopfring is obliged to wear it at all times on the ring finger of his left hand.

2.) The bestowing of the SS ring is the outward sign of an achievement reached through effort and allegiance of a special value achieved by years of faithfulness to the Führer and his philosophy.
The ring is no decoration, and should not be used for personal propaganda. Therefore it is forbidden to announce the bestowal of the Totenkopfring in a newspaper.

3.) It is referred to special regulations in the Investiture Citation.

4.) The rings of deceased SS Leaders are kept as a permanent memory to them at the Personnel Office. The dependents of deceased SS Leaders are duty bound to return them to the Personnel office of the Reichsführer-SS. The citation remains property of the next of kin.

5.) From now on the Investitures Citation will be presented in a frame. Orders of frame do not exist. SS Members who have already received the Totenkopfring and would like to own a frame can order them through Schreinermeister Braun, George, Makt Grafing (Oberbayern) Marktplatz 14, for the price of Reichsmark 1.45.

6.) All previous regulations will now be considered obsolete.

F. d. R.   **The Reichsführer SS**

signed   **gez. H. Himmler**

SS Brigadeführer

Berlin 30 September, 1937

The Reichsführer-SS
SS Staff Chancery Offices
Department P 6 Tgb. No. 432/37

Distributor Va

Ref: Bestowal of the SS-Totenkopfring

Point A 1-7 of the conditions for the bestowal of the Totenkopfrings of the SS from 13.9.36 - Tgb. No. 14890/36 is an additional order that:

every SS Member, who is the bearer of the Golden Party Badge will receive the Totenkopfring.

Applications for granting the ring to SS Members who come under the above conditions have to be sent by 1.12.37 to the SS Staff Chancery Office, with regard to paragraph 'B' of the bestowal conditions dated 13.9.36.

Approval for wearing the Golden Party Badge has to be confirmed through the Principal Office and by enclosure of the proof.

The Reichsführer-SS

F.d.R.
for the SS-Leader

signed: H. Himmler

signed:

SS-Gruppenführer

Berlin, 1 August, 1939

The Reichsführer-SS
The Chief of the Personnel Head Office
Abt. I B 2 - v.k./T.

Contributor V

Covering letter to the orders
about bestowal of the Totenkopfring SS
from 13.9.36 - Tgb. No. 1480/36

A. Bestowal

I. Conditions

The Totenkopfring will be bestowed to:

1) Every SS Member up to the SS nr. 10,000
2) Every SS Leader - from the rank of Unterführer upwards, who entered the SS before the 30.1.33.
3) Every SS Leader, who entered the SS after 30.1.33 and has been <u>3 years a leader.</u>
4) Every SS Leader, who because of his membership to the Reichswehr (Austrian Bundeswehr) or police (Austrian Bundespolizei) could not enter the SS before the 30.1.33, if he has

had <u>two years service in the SS.</u>

5) Every SS Leader who did active service in different organisations of the Party (SA, NSKK,PL? HJ.) and without interruption of those duties came over to the SS, if he has had <u>two years SS service.</u>

6) SS Members in cases of special consideration which the Reichsführer-SS decides.

7) Every SS Member, who carries a badge of honour, the Golden Party Badge.

8) Every SS man, who is the owner of the Coburg Insignia. By Unterführern and men the certificate of the ownership of the Coburg insignia is to be added to the application.

9) Every member of the Police, who is SS Leader or SS Unterführer and entered as a member of the Police before 30.1.33 and is a member of the party.

The SS Totenkopfring will be further bestowed:

10a) Every SS Leader, who was resident in Austria during the struggle for its annexation and belonged to the illegal SS, if he has been an <u>SS Leader for two years.</u>

10b) Every SS Leader who was resident in Sudetenland if he, after the return of the Sudetenland to the Reich, entered the SS by, at the latest, 31.12.38 and has served as an <u>SS Leader for two years.</u>

10c) Every SS Leader who was a resident of the Memel District if he entered the SS as soon as the Memel District became part of the Reich and not later than 1.6.39 and has been an <u>SS Leader for two years.</u>

The conditions C 1-8 of the bestowal order from 13.9.36 in connection with the return of the Totenkopfrings is again specially referred to.

The Reichsführer SS

F.d.R.

gez. H. Himmler

gez. Signature
SS-Gruppenführer   **F.d.R.d.A.**

Berlin, 6 December 1939

The Reichsführer SS
Tgb. Nr. 37/67/39
SS P.H. Tgb. No. 226/3

SS - Order

In the citation dealing with the bestowal of the SS Totenkopfring it is laid down that on the death of the holder the ring should be returned to me.

The rings of the deceased SS members are kept for ever as a permanent memory to them by the Reichsführer SS.

To have the rings back from our comrades killed in action I order:

1) The commanders of the Waffen-SS should ensure that the rings of members killed in action should be taken from them before burial and handed over to the Commanders so that they can be sent to the SS Personnel Office.
2) The same applies for Totenkopfrings from SS members who died as a result of war wounds in home hospitals or of SS members killed in action with an army unit. There the local officers would, by a visit to relatives and through tactful explanations, explain why the ring should be returned to the Reichsführer-SS and make the request that the relatives hand back the ring in accordance with the investiture citation and then be sent to the SS Personnel Head Office.

The Reichsführer - SS

signed: H. Himmler

17.10.1944

The Reichsführer SS
The Head of SS Principal Personnel Office
1 3 - v. K./H1 -

<u>Ref:</u> Bestowal of the Ring

The Reichsführer SS has in consideration of the war efforts of all available forces, decided to discontinue the production and bestowal of the Totenkopfring. Applications for the bestowal are to cease from this date.

The applications already presented to the Principal Personnel Office and not dealt with, will take first place after resuming the bestowals. At the same time we refer to the obligation of returning the Totenkopfring from those killed in action deceased and those who cease to be SS Members.

The Head of SS Principal Personnel Office

signed: v. Horff

SS Obergruppenführer und
General of the Waffen-SS

DOCUMENT GROUP OF GEORG MULLER

This important group of SS personnel documents relates to Georg Muller, an officer in the Allgemeine-SS, and spans a period of almost 20 years from him joining the Nazi Party in October, 1926 until his award of the War Service Cross on Hitler's birthday April 20th, 1945. Muller had an extremely varied association with various branches of the NSDAP including membership in the SA, Allgemeine-SS, and culminating in his joining the German Army during World War II where he received a number of medals and awards for bravery.

Georg Muller joined the Nazi Party very early in its history and consequently had a very low Party Number (Nr. 46581). He was a very early recipient of the Gold Party Badge, being awarded the honour as early as 1933. It is extremely rare for such a significant group of documents and photographs to survive intact and in their entirety for more than half a century.

Obverse and reverse views of the SS-Fuhrer Ausweis (SS Officer's ID Card) issued to Georg Muller in 1936. The ID card is printed on white card stock with a grey eagle and swastika watermark: the watermark was an additional security measure to deter forgers. The ID card contains basic information regarding the holder i.e. ID card number, NSDAP membership number, name, rank and organisation and his signature. The card bears a photograph of Muller taken in Allgemeine-SS uniform wearing the black service cap which bears early SS insignia. An embossed validation stamp has been applied over the bottom lefthand corner of the card encompassing Muller's photograph. Note that on the reverse of the card the red rectangular validation stamp has been removed. This was done after Muller ceased to be an active member of the Allgemeine-SS after joining the Wehrmacht in WWII. The card bears an ink pad facsimile signature of Heinrich Himmler and the ink signature of the endorsing officer.

A closeup photograph of Georg Muller taken from his NSDAP Party book showing him bareheaded and wearing civilian clothing.

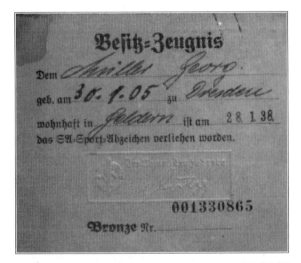

Obverse and reverse views of the certificate for the award of the SA Sport's Badge in Bronze awarded to Muller on the 28th of January, 1938. The obverse side bears the recipients name, date and place of birth and the number of the bronze award. A fascimile of the award is embossed into the card. The reverse of the card bears a photograph of Muller wearing the black Allgemeine-SS uniform.

A closeup photograph of Muller dressed in the black Allgemeine dress uniform and service cap.

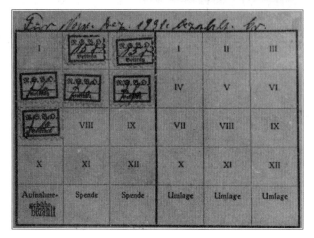

Obverse and reverse sides of Muller's NSDAP membership card. This card issued in December, 1931 relates to a particular cell of the Party in Munich. The reverse of the card has several stamps affixed to it: these were proof of payments of Party dues and span the period February to July, 1932.

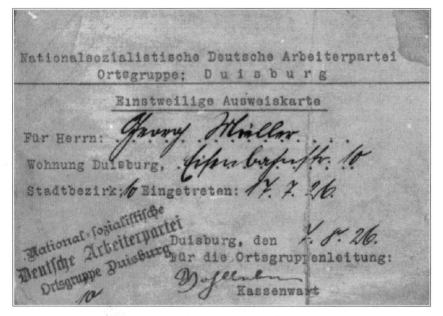

Muller's NSDAP membership card for his own particular cell of the organisation "Ortsgruppe; Duisburg".

Muller's NSDAP Traditions Award Certificate (Gauabzeichens). This Ausweis for NSDAP Gau Essen indicates that Muller was an area organisation leader for the NSDAP.

Muller's Besitzurkunde (Award document) for the NSDAP Gold Party Badge Nr. 46581. The document issued to Muller on the 12th of September 1933 states that George Muller is entitled to wear the Gold Honour Badge of the NSDAP and that he can wear the badge at all times providing he maintains his party membership.

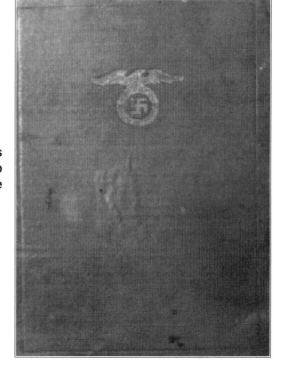

The front cover of Muller's NSDAP Party membership book issued to him at the time he joined the party.

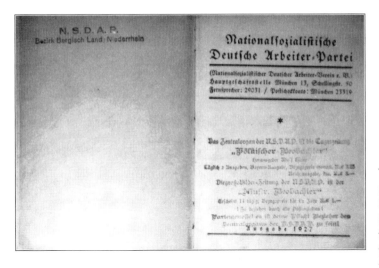

This group of three photographs of Muller's NSDAP Party book starts with the title page which is followed by a foreword written by Adolf Hitler outlining the duties and responsibilities of all members of the Nazi Party and instructing the individual Party member in the correct manner of deportment and how to present himself to other members of the Party and to other persons. The instructions from Hitler go on to impress upon every Party member that they should conduct themselves correctly in public in order to make the most favourable impression possible on others.

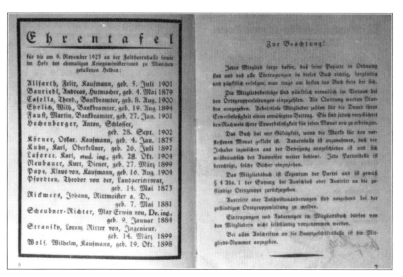

Pages 6 and 7 of Muller's NSDAP book showing on the left the Roll of Honour of the "16 Fallen Martyrs" who sacrificed their lives at the Feldherrenhalle in Munich on November 9th, 1923 whilst taking part in the abortive Munich Putsch. On the righthand page 7 is a directive instructing all NSDAP members to keep their papers in order and to be punctual in making their monthly Party contributions. It goes on to state that should a member become unemployed a lesser amount of contribution can be paid, however he must report and show evidence of his unemployed status on a monthly basis to local Party officials. The local NSDAP leadership has the authority to withdraw membership at any time. Changes in membership and Party status is to be reported to the Party officials at local level. Any enquiry regarding these points should be accompanied by the individual's Party membership number.

Pages 8 and 9 of Muller's NSDAP Party book contain the following personal information: his name, profession, address, date of birth, date of joining the Party, validation authority, member's photograph and his signature.

Pages 10 and 11 contain details of actions which will invalidate the individual's Party membership: for example unpaid Party dues, unauthorised entries in the Party membership book, etc. It states that the only person(s) authorised to make entries or alterations in the Party membership book are the Gauletier and area Group Leader.

Pages 12 through 15 are a provision for entries to be made when the holder of the membership book relocates or transfers to another area.

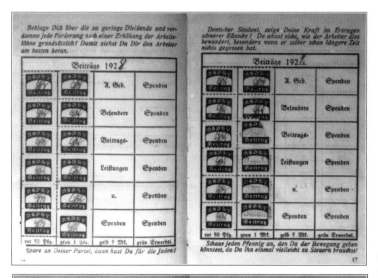

Pages 16 through 21. These six pages contain spaces where stamps were affixed monthly to show proof of payment of Party dues. Additional stamp entries could also be made for donations and special payments to charity etc., however judging from the entries Muller has only paid his Party dues and contributed no additional payments to any of the optional charities.

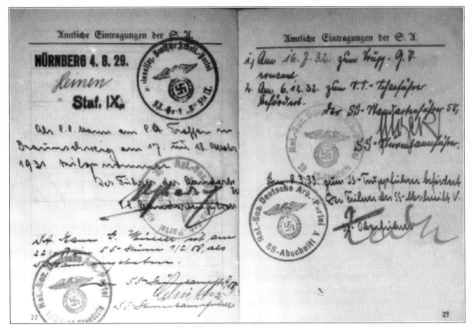

Pages 22 and 23 were reserved for official entries detailing temporary duty assignments, Party meetings, rallies and other special events. Between 1929 and 1933 Georg Muller attended five Party events.

This form is a summary of officer personnel information relating to Georg Muller. It records: the name of the individual, his entrance date into the SS, date of attaining rank, educational qualifications, and NSDAP Party membership details. Further information blocks are provided to record any Awards such as the SA Sport's Badge, Reichs Sport's Badge, the Totenkopfring and Jullechter.

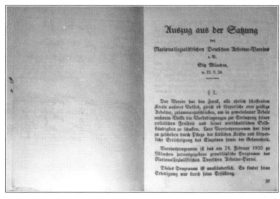

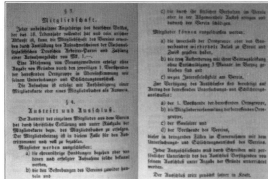

Pages 25 through 31 give a detailed breakdown and explanation of the constitution of the NSDAP: paragraph 2 is an introductory preamble to the Party giving the reasons for its formation and also the date of its institution; paragraph 3 deals with membership; paragraph 4 deals with entering and leaving the Party; paragraph 5 covers the Annual General Meeting; paragraph 6 to 14 deal with the organisation and structure of the Party.

Pages 33 through 38 cover various aspects of the Nazi Party platform. Its principles and organisations. On the page facing number 38 there is a list of NSDAP related publications written by Nazi noteables including works such as Adolf Hitler's MEIN KAMPF, works by the Party ideologue Alfred Rosenburg and Hitler's chief of propaganda Josef Goebbels who has no less than four titles listed. There are also several publications relating to the Jews and Zionism.

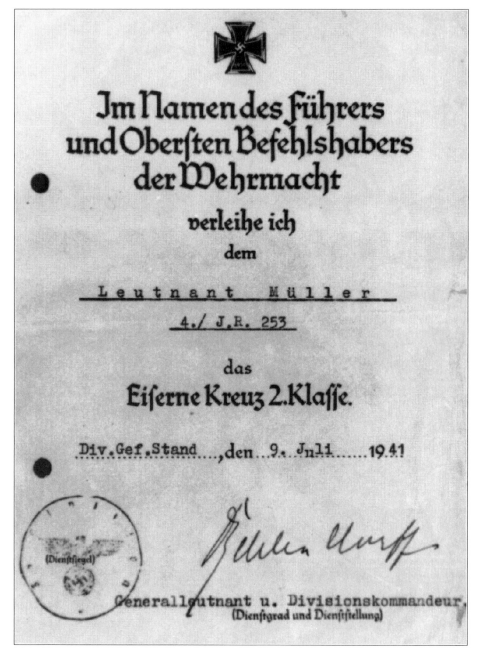

Award document for the Iron Cross 2nd Class presented to Muller on the 9th of July, 1941 whilst he was serving in the 4th Company of the 253rd Infantry Regiment. Muller saw considerable action between 1941 and 1945 receiving a total of six different awards. He served in the Army and not the Waffen-SS having been discharged from the Allgemeine-SS prior to the outbreak of hostilities. At the time of being awarded the Iron Cross Muller held the rank of Leutnant.

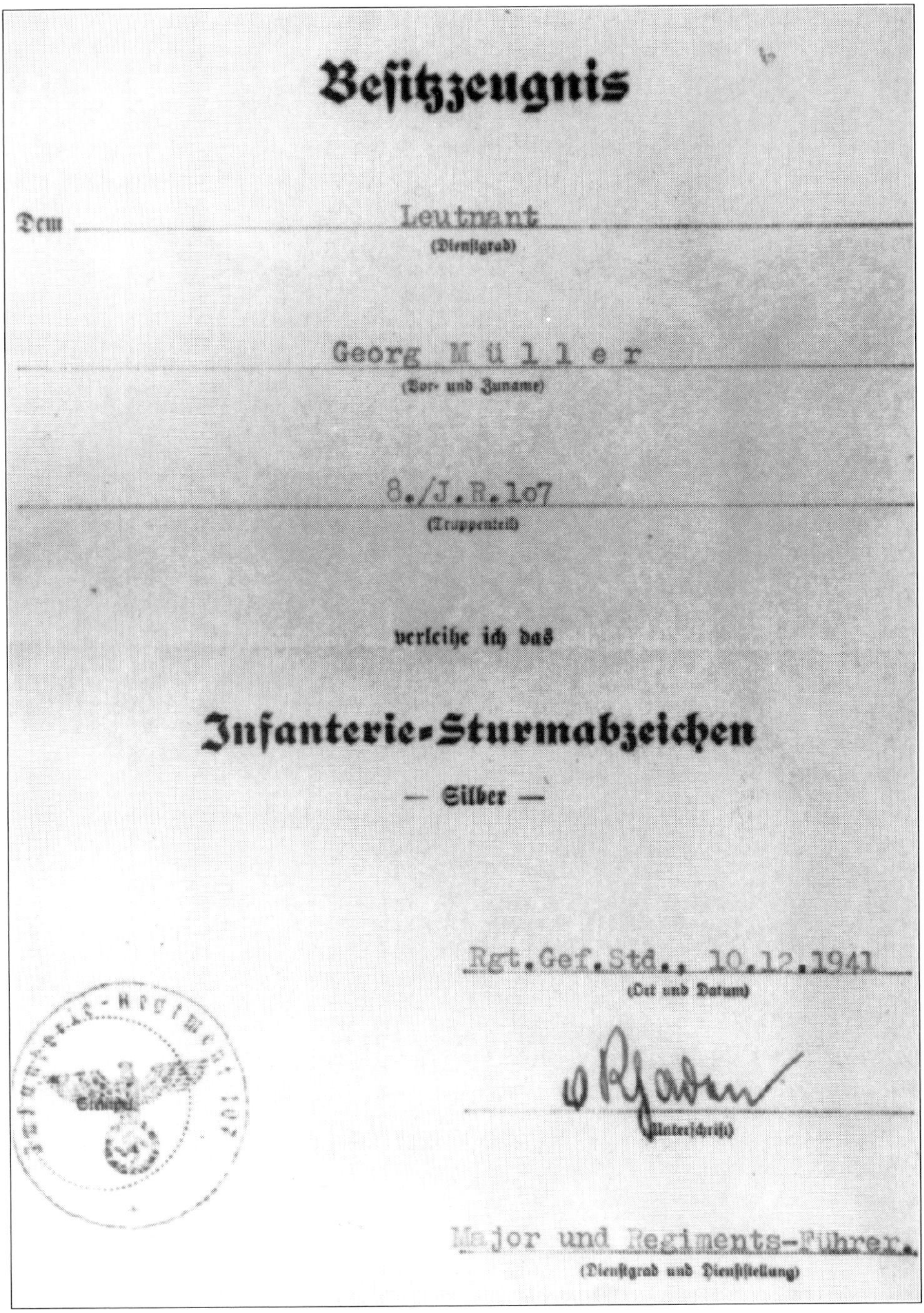

Besitzeugnis

Dem _____ Leutnant _____
(Dienstgrad)

Georg M ü l l e r
(Vor- und Zuname)

8./J.R.107
(Truppenteil)

verleihe ich das

Infanterie-Sturmabzeichen

— Silber —

Rgt.Gef.Std., 10.12.1941
(Ort und Datum)

(Unterschrift)

Major und Regiments-Führer.
(Dienstgrad und Dienststellung)

Preliminary Award document for the Infantry Assault Badge in Silver awarded to Muller on the 10th of December, 1941. At the time of the award Muller was serving with the 8th Company of the 107th Infantry Regiment.

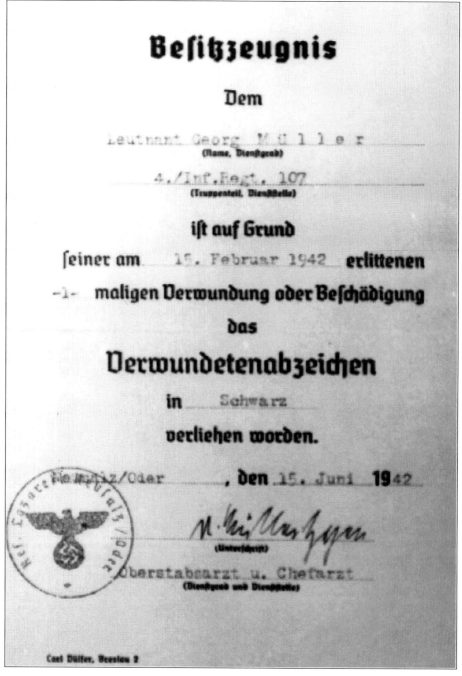

Besitzeugnis

Dem

Leutnant Georg M ü l l e r
(Name, Dienstgrad)

4./Inf.Regt. 107
(Truppenteil, Dienststelle)

ist auf Grund

seiner am   15. Februar 1942   erlittenen

-1- **maligen Verwundung oder Beschädigung**

das

Verwundetenabzeichen

in   Schwarz

verliehen worden.

Ho.Nitz/Oder   , **den** 15. Juni **19**42

(Unterschrift)

Oberstabsarzt u. Chefarzt
(Dienstgrad und Dienststelle)

Carl Dülfer, Breslau 2

Award document for the Wound Badge in Black. The document is dated
the 15th of June, 1942.

Jm Namen des führers und Obersten Befehlshabers der Wehrmacht

verleihe ich

dem

Leutnant Georg M ü l l e r
8./J.R.1o7

das

Eiserne Kreuz 1. Klasse

Div.Gef.Stand ......,den......13. 6. ....19.42

(Dienstsiegel)

Generalmajor und Kommandeur
der 34. Jnf.Div.
(Dienstgrad und Dienststellung)

On the 13th of June, 1942 Muller was awarded the Iron Cross 1st Class:
illustrated here is the Award document for that medal.

IM NAMEN DES FÜHRERS
UND
OBERSTEN BEFEHLSHABERS
DER WEHRMACHT
IST DEM

Leutnant

Georg M ü l l e r

AM 5.9.1942

DIE MEDAILLE
WINTERSCHLACHT IM OSTEN
1941/42
(OSTMEDAILLE)
VERLIEHEN WORDEN.

FÜR DIE RICHTIGKEIT:

Gren.-Erf.- Btl. 107

Major u. Btl.-Kommandeur

Award document for the Eastern Front Medal earned by Muller for participating in the Winter War of 1941/42 dated on the 5th of September, 1942.

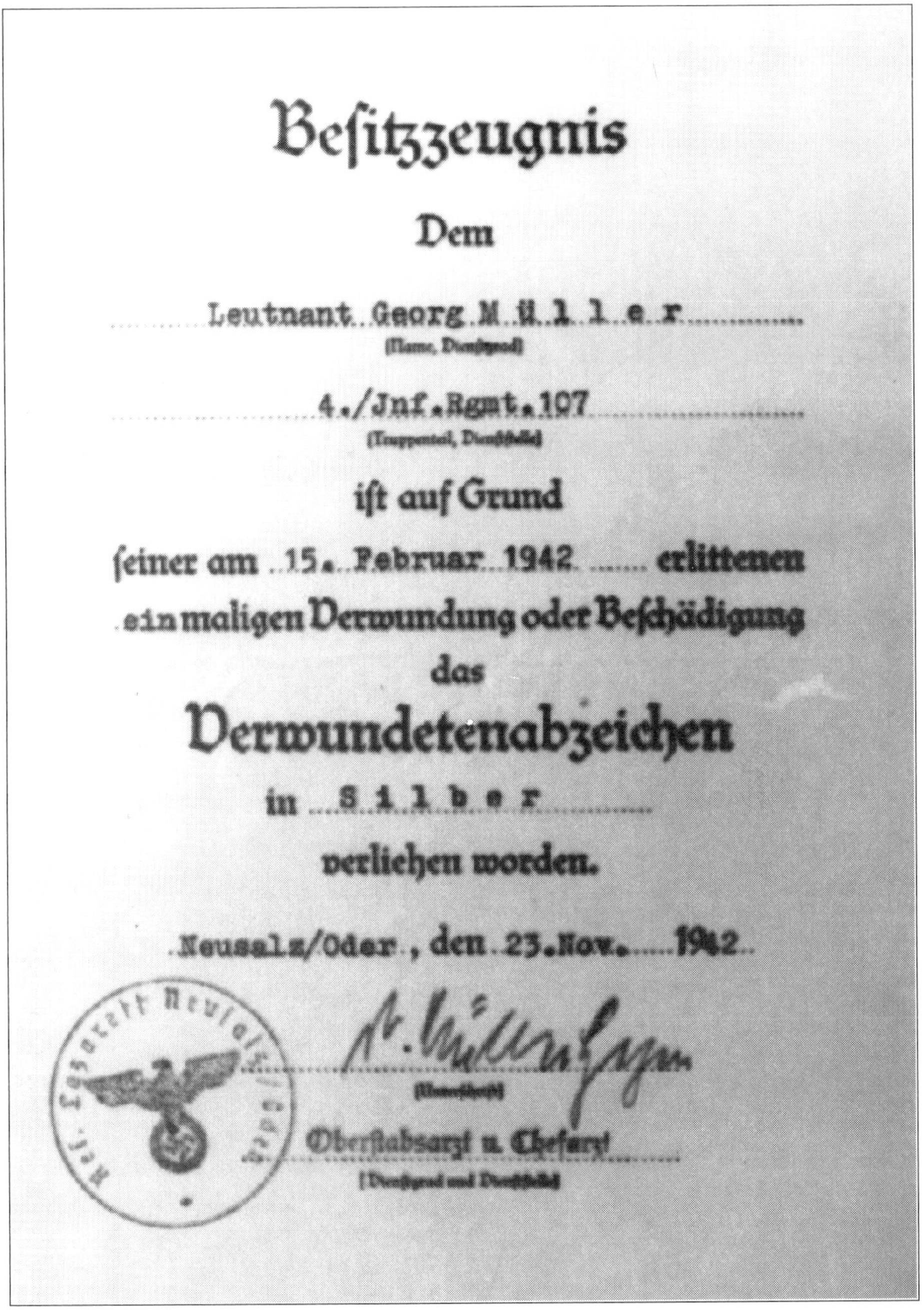

Beſitzzeugnis

Dem

Leutnant Georg M ü l l e r
(Name, Dienſtgrad)

4./Jnf.Rgmt.107
(Truppenteil, Dienſtſtelle)

iſt auf Grund

ſeiner am 15. Februar 1942 erlittenen

ein maligen Verwundung oder Beſchädigung

das

Verwundetenabzeichen

in S i l b e r

verliehen worden.

Neuſalz/Oder , den 23.Nov. 1942.

(Unterſchrift)

Oberſtabsarzt u. Chefarzt
(Dienſtgrad und Dienſtſtelle)

Award document for the Wound Badge in Silver awarded to Muller on the 23rd of November, 1942.

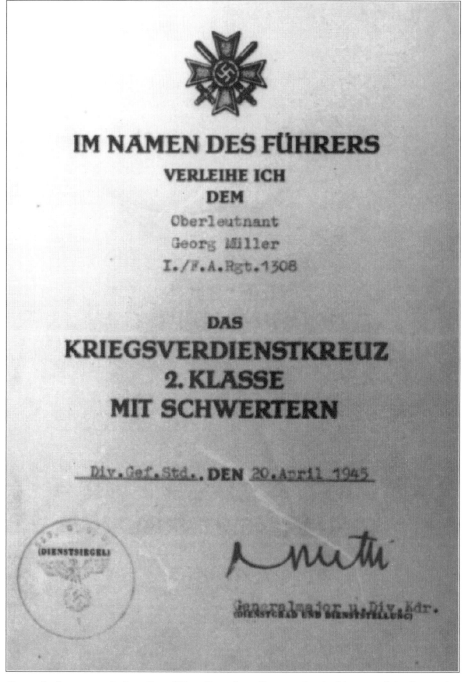

Award document for the War Service Cross 2nd Class with Swords, awarded to Muller on Hitler's birthday on the 20th of April, 1945 less than 3 weeks before the end of the war in Europe. Note that by the time of this award Muller had been promoted to Oberleutnant.

(Marriage Application)

The questionnaire form for the SS Engagement and Marriage Application was designed to determine that the main racial qualities of the prospective spouse were compatible with those of the SS-Mann. No SS-Mann was permitted to marry a prospective bride until such times as she had been examined by an SS Medical Tribunal. The RUSHA (Race and Settlement Department) was the approving authority.

The main criteria applied when judging the suitability of marriage applicants of SS men were: first racial purity, and second physical compatibility between the two partners which would likely result in a fertile marriage.

The engagement and marriage laws of the SS were one of the oldest and most fundamental laws of the SS and were first issued in December, 1931. The following rules applied to applicants:

1. No SS-Mann may marry without the express consent of the Reichsführer-SS

2. The decision to approve any proposed marriage was governed solely by racial and physical considerations.

3. The competent department for examining each case individually and rendering a decision on each application rested with the racial department (later the RUSHA)

4. Non-compliance with the SS marriage laws would render the individual liable for disciplinary action and dismissal from the SS.

This marriage questionnaire pertains to Georg Muller's prospective spouse. Entries relate to personal information concerning: her mother, father, grandmothers, grandfathers, numbers of children born to each of her relatives, their dates and locations of birth and dates of any marriages and deaths etc.

B l a t t 1

Fragebogen zur Erlangung der Heiratsgenehmigung.

Nr.1 N a m e (leserlich schreiben): ..*Josef Zittgret*.............

in SS seit:...........Dienstgrad:...................Truppe:.....

Mitgliedsnummer in Partei:.................. in SS :..............

geb. am:*11.7.1908*...zu:*Simmerstein*..........Kreis:*Uxxx*.....

Land:*Priatn*.....jetziges Alter:*17 jahr*.Glaubensbekenntnis:*rkl*.

Jetziger Wohnsitz:*Marktheim.....*Wohnung:*Hohenweg.22*

Beruf und Berufsstellung:.........*Nostier*...................

Liegt Berufswechsel vor?.....................................

Ausserberufliche Fertigkeiten und Berechtigungsscheine, z.B.

Führerschein, Sportabzeichen:................................

....

Sportauszeichnungen:...

Ehrenamtl.Tätigkeit:...

Dienst im alten Heer: Truppe:..........von:.........bis:.........

     Reichsheer: " :..........von:.........bis:.........

     Schutzpolizei: " :..........von:.........bis:.........

Letzter Dienstgrad:..

Frontkämpfer von:...........bis:...........verwundet:.......

Orden und Ehrenzeichen einschl. Rettungsmedaille:...........

....

Nr. 2 Name d. Vaters:*Jan von Zittgret*.......Vorname:,.......

geb.a,*17.11.1873*....zu:*Simmerstein*..........Kreis:*Kxxx*.....

Jetziger Wohnsitz:...*Marktheim*..............Kreis:...........

Land:.............Glaubensbek.:*rkl*.....jetziges Alter lbd:.....

Beruf:...*Nostier*............Erreichtes Alter falls gest.:*72 jr*.

Bemerkungen ob Kriegsteilnehmer, Verwundung, Auszeichnung usw.

....

Todesursache:...*Herzverschlimmerung*..........................

Nr. 3 Geburtsname d.Mutter:...*Krupp*.........Vorname:*Josefine*..

geb.am:*4.6.1885*.zu:...*Jefferi*..............Kreis:...*Kxxx*.....

Verheiratet am:*15.11...*..zu:*Simmerstein*....Kreis:...*Kxx*.....

Erreichtes Alter falls lebd.:*54*...falls gest.:......Bekenntnis:*rkl*.

Bemerkungen:...

Todesursache:...

Kinder zu Nr. 2 u. 3: Zahl:*4*.........männlich:*3*...weiblich:*1*...

Nr. 4 Grossvater väterl.;Name:.............Vorname:...............
geb.am:.........zu:.................Kreis:...........
Land:.............Glaubensbek.:.....jetziges Alter lebd.:.....
Beruf:................Erreichtes Alter falls gest.:....
Bemerkungen:...
Todesursache:..

Nr. 5 Grossmutter väterl.; Geburtsname:.................
geb.a.:.........zu:...............Kreis:...........
Verheiratet am:.........zu:.............Kreis:...........
Erreichtes Alter falls lebd.:.........falls gest:....Bek.:....
Bemerkungen:...
Todesursache:..

Kinder zu Nr. 4 u. 5: Zahl:......, männlich:.....weiblich:....

Nr. 6 Grossvater mütterl.:...............Vorname:.........
geb.am:.........zu:...............Kreis:...........
Land:...........Glaubensbek.:.....jetziges Alter falls lebd.:....
Beruf:................Erreichtes Alter falls gest.:....
Bemerkungen:...
Todesursache:..

Nr. 7 Grossmutter mütterl.Geburtsname:.................
geb.am:.........zu:...............Kreis:...........
Verheiratet am:.........zu:.............Kreis:...........
Erreichtes Alter falls lebd.:.........falls gest.:....Bek.:....
Bemerkungen:...
Todesursache:..

Kinder zu Nr. 6 u. 7: Zahl:......männlich:.....weiblich:....

(Weitere Angaben von Vorfahren sind erwünscht und in ähnlicher
Weise auf einem besonderen Bogen beizufügen:)

Ort:....................Datum:..........
....   Gesehen:...........
     Unterschrift d. Ausfüllers   SS-Führer:...........

155

B l a t t I

Fragebogen zur Erlangung der Heiratsgenehmigung.

Nr.1 N a m e (leserlich schreiben): ....

in SS seit:.............Dienstgrad:.......................Truppe:......

Mitgliedsnummer in Partei:...............in SS :............

geb. am:.............zu:....................Kreis:.............

Land:.............jetziges Alter:.....Glaubensbekenntnis:.....

Jetziger Wohnsitz:.................Wohnung:.............

Beruf und Berufsstellung:.........................

Liegt Berufswechsel vor?.........................

Ausserberufliche Fertigkeiten und Berechtigungsscheine, z.B.

Führerschein, Sportabzeichen:.........................

....

Sportauszeichnungen:.........................

Ehrenamtl.Tätigkeit:.........................

Dienst im alten Heer: Truppe:...........von:.........bis:.........

Reichsheer: " :...........von:.........bis:.........

Schutzpolizei: " :...........von:.........bis:.........

Letzter Dienstgrad:.........................

Frontkämpfer von:...........bis:...........verwundet:.........

Orden und Ehrenzeichen einschl. Rettungsmedaille:.........

....

Nr. 2 Name d. Vaters:...............Vorname:.........

geb.a,:.............zu:.................Kreis:.............

Jetziger Wohnsitz:.................Kreis:.............

Land:.............Glaubensbek.:.......jetziges Alter lbd:.....

Beruf:...............Erreichtes Alter falls gest.:.....

Bemerkungen ob Kriegsteilnehmer, Verwundung, Auszeichnung usw.

....

Todesursache:.........................

Nr. 3 Geburtsname d.Mutter:...............Vorname:.........

geb.am:.............zu:.................Kreis:.............

Verheiratet am:.............zu:.................Kreis:.............

Erreichtes Alter falls lebd.:.......falls gest.:.....Bekenntnis:.....

Bemerkungen:.........................

Todesursache:.........................

Kinder zu Nr. 2 u. 3: Zahl:.......männlich:.....weiblich:.....

Nr. 4 Grossvater väterl.;Name: ....Vorname: ....
geb.am: ....zu: ....Kreis: ....
Land: ....Glaubensbek.: ....jetziges Alter lebd.: ....
Beruf: ....Erreichtes Alter falls gest.: ....
Bemerkungen: ....
Todesursache: ....

Nr. 5 Grossmutter väterl.; Geburtsname: ....
geb.a,: ....zu: ....Kreis: ....
Verheiratet am: ....zu: ....Kreis: ....
Erreichtes Alter falls lebd.: ....falls gest.: ....Bek.: ....
Bemerkungen: ....
Todesursache: ....

Kinder zu Nr. 4 u. 5: Zahl: ...., männlich: ....weiblich: ....

Nr. 6 Grossvater mütterl.: ....Vorname: ....
geb.am: ....zu: ....Kreis: ....
Land: ....Glaubensbek.: ....jetziges Alter falls lebd.: ....
Beruf: ....Erreichtes Alter falls gest.: ....
Bemerkungen: ....
Todesursache: ....

Nr. 7.Grossmutter mütterl.Geburtsname: ....
geb.am: ....zu: ....Kreis: ....
Verheiratet am: ....zu: ....Kreis: ....
Erreichtes Alter falls lebd.: ....falls gest.: ....Bek.: ....
Bemerkungen: ....
Todesursache: ....

Kinder zu Nr. 6 u. 7: Zahl: ....männlich: ......weiblich: ....

(Weitere Angaben von Vorfahren sind erwünscht und in ähnlicher
Weise auf einem besonderen Bogen beizufügen:)

Ort: ....Datum: ....
.............Gesehen: ....
Unterschrift d. Ausfüllers   SS-Führer: ....

HORST MARCKS

The following group of documents pertain to SS Panzer Grenadier Horst Marcks assigned to the 6th Company, 2nd Battalion, 1st Regiment of the 1st SS Panzer Division "Liebstandarte Adolf Hitler" (LSSAH). The group includes the Soldbuch, Fuhrerschein and several Prisoner of War documents relating to Marcks dating from 1946-1950. Marcks was captured by the Americans, and was interned as Flossenburg-Weiden. He was in captivity for over a year and following the end of the war he was employed by the US Army to clear minefields. Sadly he was killed by a mine during the course of the minefield clearing operations. Two of the documents in this group relate to Marcks' death: one item giving the date of his death and the location where he was buried; the second item is a letter written on YMCA notepaper from one of Horst Marcks' comrades who wrote to his next-of-kin giving details of the tragedy and informing her that Marcks had been given a proper burial by his fellow soldiers.

A photo montage of the various documents relating to SS Panzer Grenadier Horst Marcks.

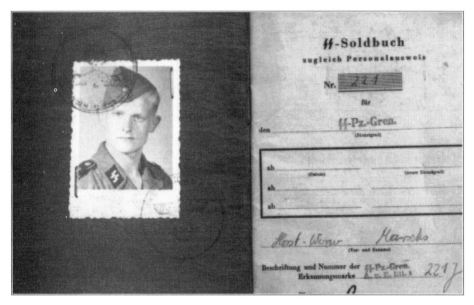

Inside front cover and page 1 of Horst Marcks' SS Soldbuch. The cover has a photograph of Marcks wearing an SS sidecap. The photograph is held in place by two staples top right and bottom left, and has validation stamps on the top left and bottom right. Page one of the Soldbuch gives its number, the holder's rank, full name, unit, blood group, gas mask size and his service number.

Pages 4 and 5 of the Marcks Soldbuch give details of the training he received at the SS Panzer Grenadier Ausbildungs and Ersatz (Training) Battalion at Berlin-Lichterfelde. Page 5 of the Soldbuch records the name and address of the holder's next-of-kin.

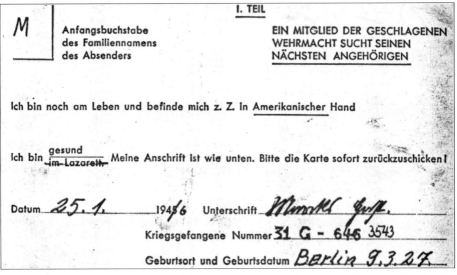

Letzte bekannte Anschrift des nächsten Angehorigen IN BLOCKSCHRIFT I	*Fr. Irmgard Ludwig Berlin-Falkensee Krommerstr. 18*	Gebühren- frei

IV. TEIL Falls Addressapt unauffindbar	in der Amerikanischen Zone, Weitergabe an....	HAUPTVERMITTLUNGSSTELLE FRANKFURT a/M
	in der Britischen Zone, Weitergabe an....	HAUPTVERMITTLUNGSSTELLE HAMBURG

V. TEIL Nur für den Dienst- gebrauch durch die Hauptermittlungsstelle zwecks Weiterbeförderung	*Insbruk...ff... P.W.E. 422. Flossenburg-Weiden A.P.O. 109*

Front side of a Prisoner of War postcard sent by Marcks to his family. These cards were filled out by captured enemy prisoners to notify their families of their health, and also their location for any return mail. The card indicates that Marcks was held at Prisoner of War Enclosure 422 in Flossenberg. The front side of the POW card records the recipient's address and the address of the POW camp.

M	Anfangsbuchstabe des Familiennamens des Absenders	I. TEIL EIN MITGLIED DER GESCHLAGENEN WEHRMACHT SUCHT SEINEN NÄCHSTEN ANGEHÖRIGEN

Ich bin noch am Leben und befinde mich z. Z. In Amerikanischer Hand

Ich bin ~~gesund~~ ~~im Lazarett~~. Meine Anschrift ist wie unten. Bitte die Karte sofort zurückzuschicken!

Datum *25.1.* 194~~5~~6 Unterschrift *Marcks Wff.*

Kriegsgefangene Nummer *31 G - 646 3543*

Geburtsort und Geburtsdatum *Berlin 9.3.27*

The reverse of the POW card informs the receiver that the sender is in American hands and that they are either in good health or in a Field Hospital. Marcks has indicated on his card that he is in good health by striking out the "hospital" option. The bottom section of the card records the date, signature, POW number and date of birth of the sender. These cards had no provision for any personal messages from the sender; the captors were merely required under the terms of the Geneva Convention to inform families of POWs of their whereabouts and health.

An information card from the Deutsche Dienststelle (German Service Records Office) dated 20th July, 1950 and addressed to a Mrs. Irmgard Prietzel who had enquired about Marcks. The reverse side of the form records the date of his death and the location of his burial. (The individual requesting this information would appear to be the same lady who had earlier received the POW notification card from Horst Marcks in 1946 though her surname has changed probably due to marriage.

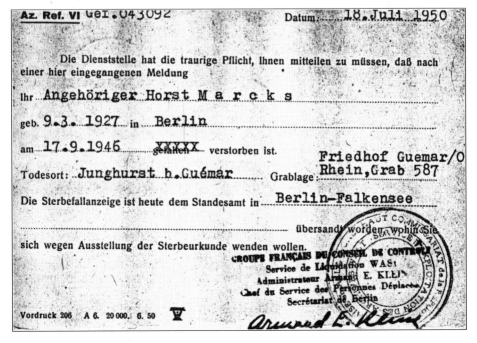

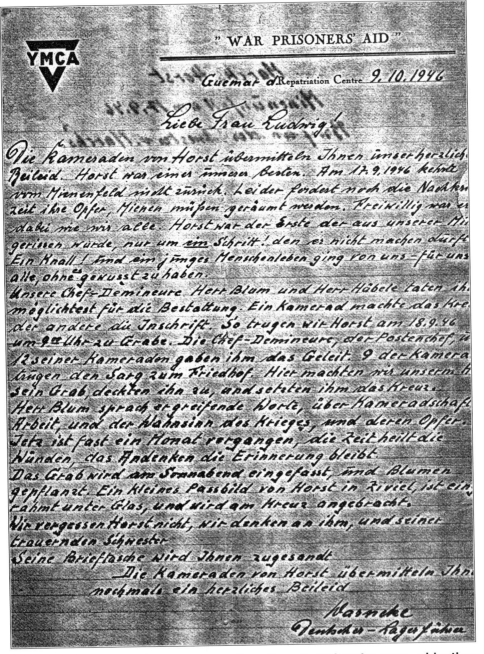

A letter written on YMCA notepaper to a Frau Ludwig who was evidently a relative of Horst Marcks. The letter outlines the circumstances of Marcks's death whilst clearing a minefield and goes on to tell her how well loved he was by the other men and that he was given a soldier's burial by his comrades. The letter is signed by the SS Lagerfuhrer at the Prisoner of War Enclosure in Flossenburg. The letter was written on the 9th of October, 1946 less than a month after Horst Marcks had been killed by a mine.

ALFRED SCHRADER

The following group of original documents relate to former SS-Obersturmführer Alfred Schrader. Schrader served in both the Allgemeine SS and Waffen-SS during the course of his ten year SS career. As a member of the Waffen-SS during World War II Alfred Schrader served in Waffen SS Divisions, "Das Reich", "Skanderberg" and "Prinz Eugen".

The various documents contained in this grouping constitute a record of Schrader's SS career covering the period December 1934 through to September 1944.

SS-Oberscharführer Alfred Schrader.

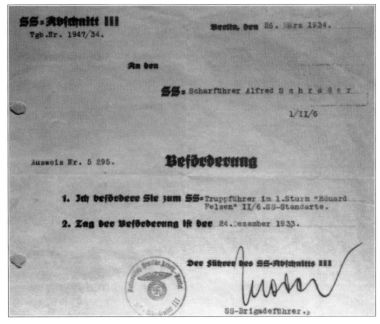

Promotion document from the SS Abschnitt III (personnel) for Schrader. Promoted to rank of SS-Trüppenfuhrer with the 2nd Batt., 6th SS-Standarte (Regiment-Allgemeine SS). Promotion effective 24th December, 1933.

Undated message directing Schrader to report for temporary duty with the Air Defence Dept. (Luftschutz) in Berlin. Serves as a temporary I.D. and allows him to ride buses and trams free while serving. Signed by a police captain.

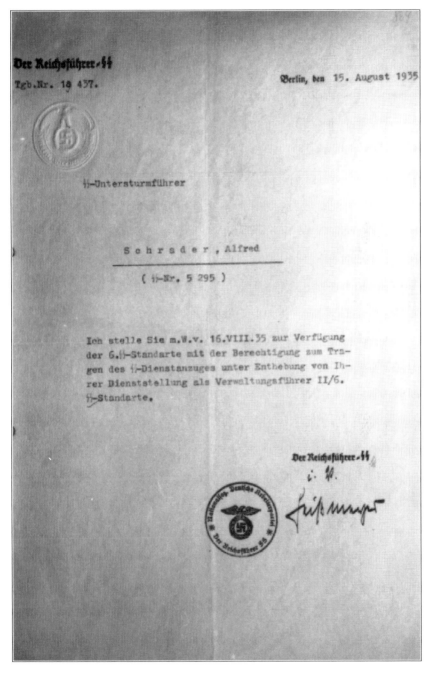

Der Reichsführer-SS

Tgb.Nr. 18 437.

Berlin, den 15. August 1935

SS-Untersturmführer

S c h r a d e r , Alfred

(SS-Nr. 5 295)

Ich stelle Sie m.W.v. 16.VIII.35 zur Verfügung
der 6.SS-Standarte mit der Berechtigung zum Tragen des SS-Dienstanzuges unter Enthebung von Ihrer Dienststellung als Verwaltungsführer II/6.
SS-Standarte.

Der Reichsführer-SS
i. A.

Order dated 15th August, 1935, directing Schrader to serve in uniform for the 6th SS-Standarte as administrative supervisor. Signed by one of Himmler's adjutants in the SS Head Office.

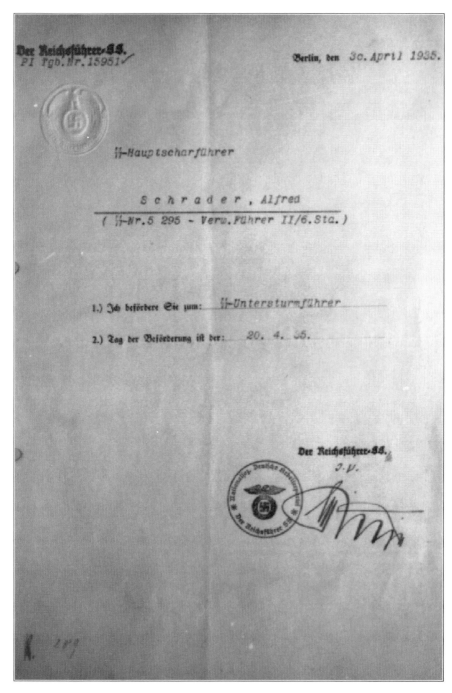

Promotion document dated 30 April, 1935 promoting Schrader to SS-Untersturmfuhrer with effective date of 20 April, 1935. Signed by one of Himmler's adjutants in SS Head Office.

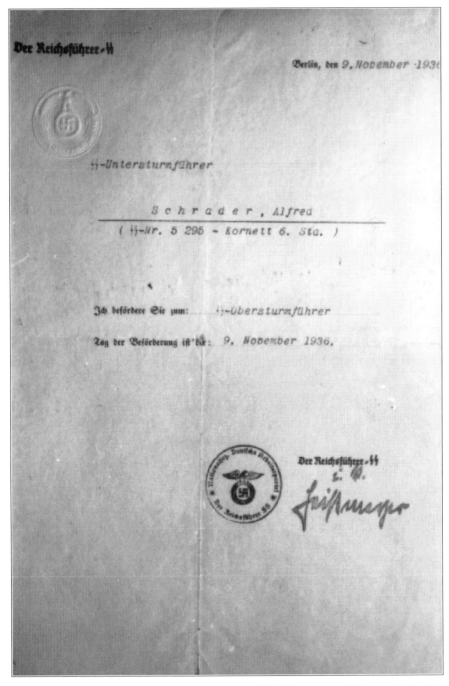

Schrader's promotion document to SS-Obersturmführer dated 9 November, 1936, effective same date. Signed by one of Himmler's Adjutants. Schrader still with 6th SS-Standarte.

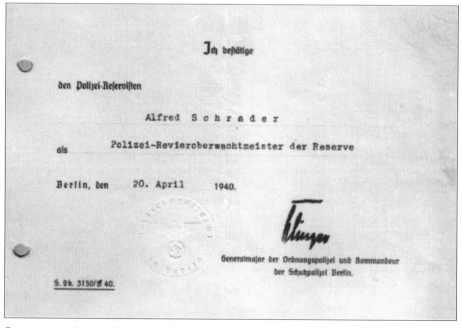

Training Certificate from the head of the Berlin Paramiltary Police, dated 15 September 1938, showing that Schrader completed a course on Police training.

Statement from Commander of the Berlin Paramilitary Police, date 20 April, 1940, that Schrader holds the rank of a Police Warrant Officer of the Reserve.

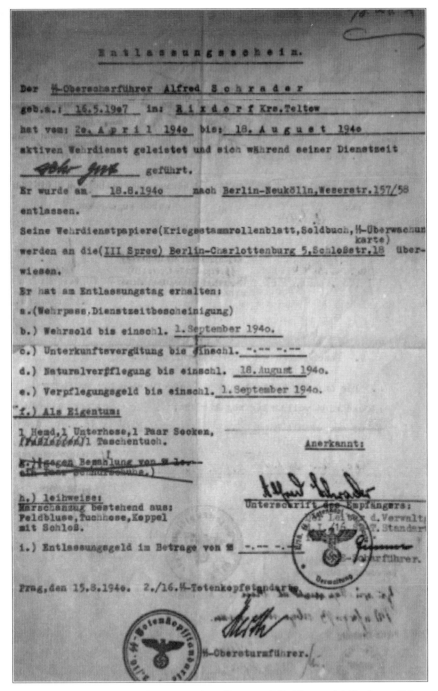

Entlassungsschein.

Der ⚡-Oberscharführer Alfred S c h r a d e r

geb.a.: 16.5.1907 in: R i x d o r f Krs.Teltow

hat vom: 20. A p r i l 1940 bis: 18. A u g u s t 1940

aktiven Wehrdienst geleistet und sich während seiner Dienstzeit

_____ geführt.

Er wurde am 18.8.1940 nach Berlin-Neukölln,Weserstr.157/58

entlassen.

Seine Wehrdienstpapiere(Kriegsstammrollenblatt,Soldbuch,⚡-Überwachungs
                                                        karte)
werden an die(III Spree) Berlin-Charlottenburg 5,Schloßstr.18 über-

wiesen.

Er hat am Entlassungstag erhalten:

a.(Wehrpass,Dienstzeitbescheinigung)

b.) Wehrsold bis einschl. 1.September 1940.

c.) Unterkunftsvergütung bis einschl. -.-- -.--

d.) Naturalverpflegung bis einschl. 18.August 1940.

e.) Verpflegungsgeld bis einschl. 1.September 1940.

f.) Als Eigentum:

1 Hemd,1 Unterhose,1 Paar Socken,
1 Taschentuch.

Anerkannt:

leihweise:
Marschanzug bestehend aus:
Feldbluse,Tuchhose,Koppel
mit Schloß.

Unterschrift des Empfängers:

i.) Entlassungsgeld im Betrage von ℳ -.-- -.--

Prag,den 15.8.1940. 2./16.⚡-Totenkopfstandarte

⚡-Obersturmführer.

Discharge Certificate/Record (similar to DD Form 214) describing
Schrader's four months of active duty service as an Oberscharführer
with the 2nd Company, 16th SS-Totenkopf Regiment (20 April - 18
August 1940) in Prague, Czechoslovakia.

Reverse side of Schrader's Discharge Certificate which bears numerous validation stamps applied by different SS departments involved in the processing of Schrader's Discharge from active duty. The final entry is dated 21 August 1940.

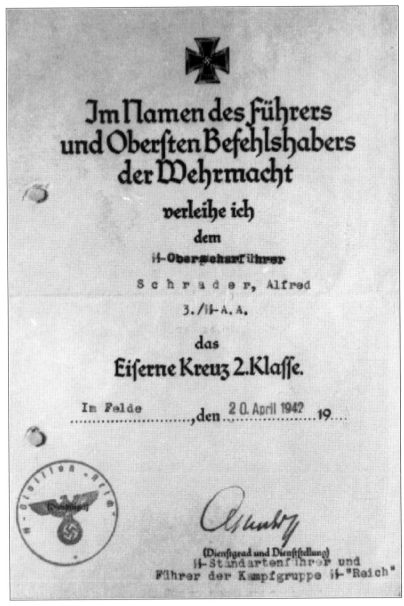

Iron Cross 2nd Class award document for SS-Oberscharführer Schrader, dated 20 April, 1942, while assigned to 3rd Company, - Aufklarungs Abteilung (Recon Batt) 2, 2nd SS-Panzer Gren. Division "Das Reich" (which was serving on the Russian Front at the time). Signed by SS-Standartenführer Werner Ostendorf, who commanded the Division Kampfhgruppe "Das Reich" in the spring of 1942 in Russia. Ostendorf, won the Knights Cross and Oakleaves, died May 4, 1945, from wounds while serving as Commander of "Das Reich" in Austria.

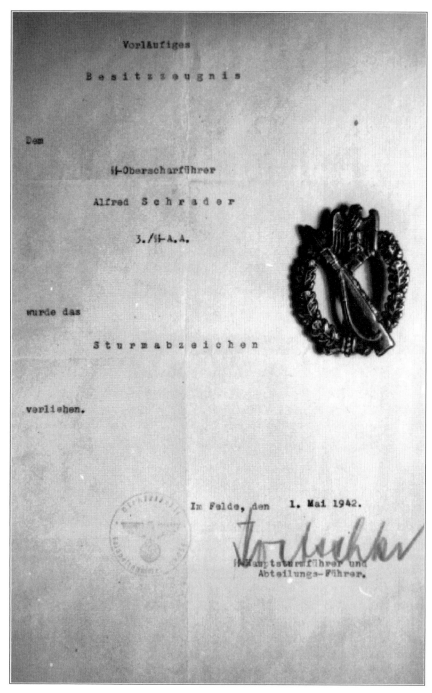

Preliminary award certificate for the Infantry Assault Badge awarded to Schrader, while still with "Das Reich", dated 1 May, 1942, signed by his battalion commander.

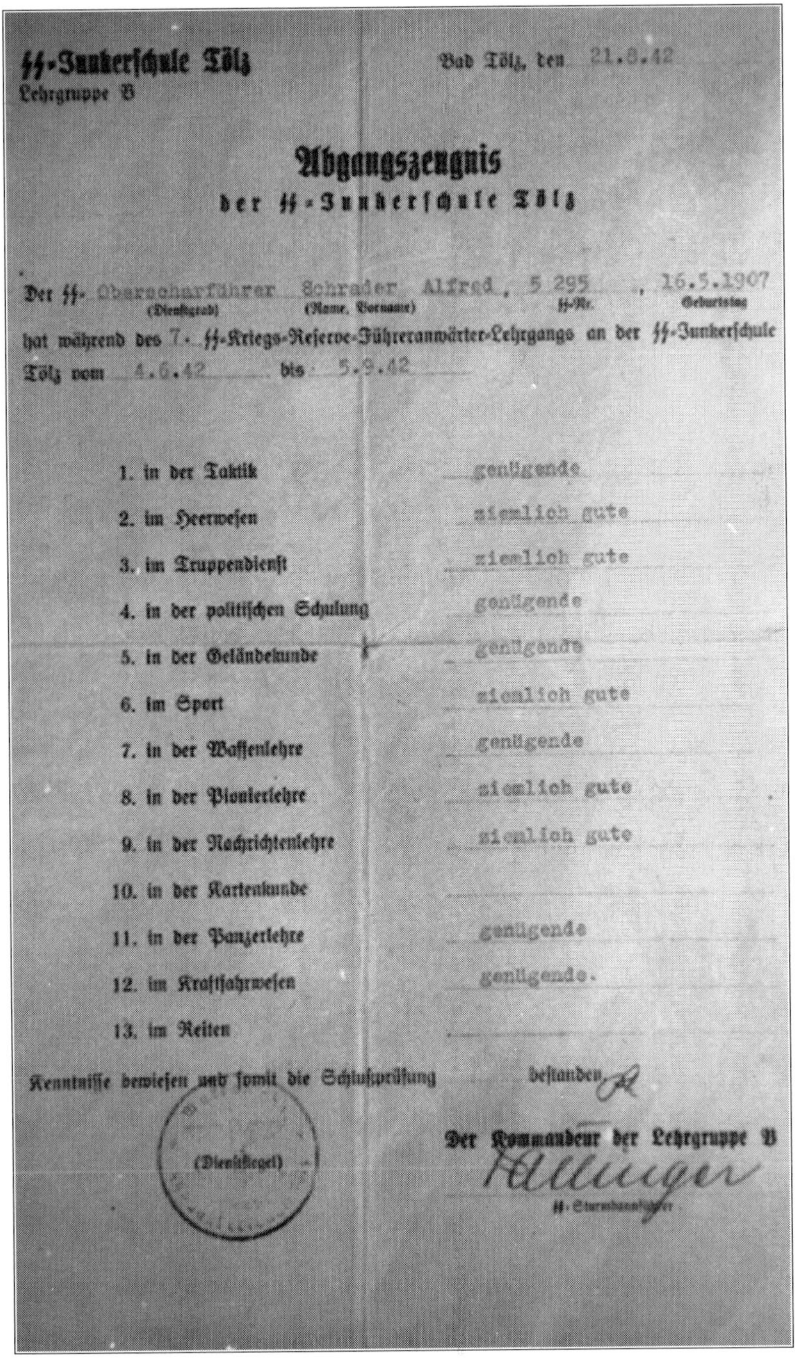

SS-Junkerschule Tölz
Lehrgruppe B

Bad Tölz, ten 21.8.42

Abgangszeugnis
der SS-Junkerschule Tölz

Der SS- Oberscharführer Schrader Alfred, 5 295 , 16.5.1907
    (Dienstgrad)   (Name, Vorname)   SS-Nr.   Geburtstag

hat während des 7.- SS-Kriegs-Reserve-Führeranwärter-Lehrgangs an der SS-Junkerschule
Tölz vom 4.6.42 bis 5.9.42

1. in der Taktik	genügende
2. im Heerwesen	ziemlich gute
3. im Truppendienst	ziemlich gute
4. in der politischen Schulung	genügende
5. in der Geländekunde	genügende
6. im Sport	ziemlich gute
7. in der Waffenlehre	genügende
8. in der Pionierlehre	ziemlich gute
9. in der Nachrichtenlehre	ziemlich gute
10. in der Kartenkunde	
11. in der Panzerlehre	genügende
12. im Kraftfahrwesen	genügende.
13. im Reiten	

Kenntnisse bewiesen und somit die Schlußprüfung   bestanden

(Dienstsiegel)

Der Kommandeur der Lehrgruppe B

SS-Sturmbannführer

Completion certificate for OCS (SS-Junkerschule at Bad Tolez)
for Schrader who attended from 4 June - 5 September 1942.
Gives grades for various subjects evaluated during the course
(either "Sufficient" or "Very Good").

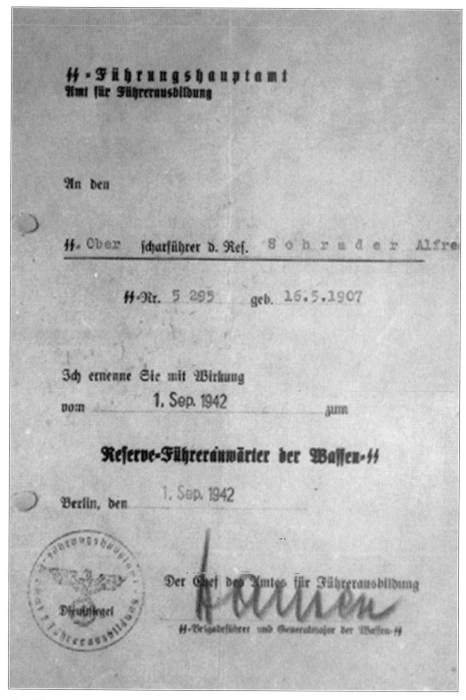

Certificate from SS-Head Office appointing Schrader as an Officer Candidate of the Waffen SS Reserve, dated 1 September 1942.

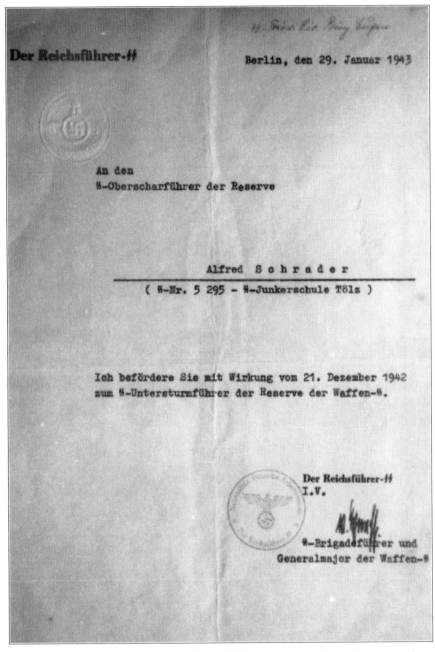

Promotion document effective 21 December, 1942, promoting Schrader to SS-Obersturmführer LT. of the Waffen-SS Reserve, from the Head Office (signed by one of Himmler's Adjutants). At the time of this promotion, Schrader was apparently assigned to the 7th SS-Volunteer Mountain Division "Prinz Eugen".

Award document dated 19 May, 1943, for the Croatian Bravery Medal of Poglavnik 4th Class, given to SS-Untersturmfuhrer Schrader, while serving in Croatia with "Prinz Eugen" Division. (This is an EXTREMELY rare document)

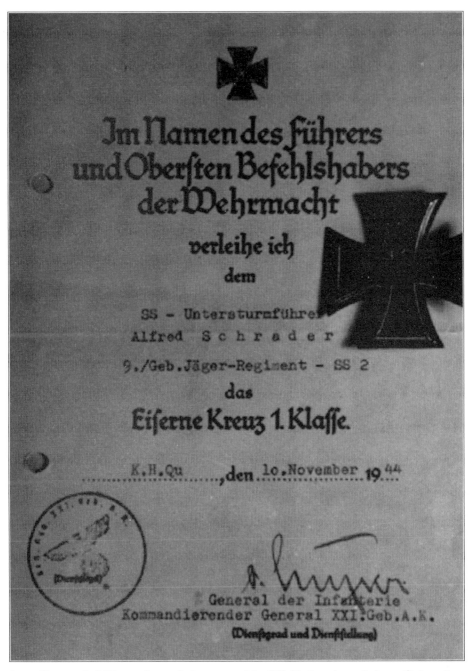

Iron Cross 1st Class Award document to SS-Untersturmfuhrer Schrader, dated 10 November, 1944, while assigned to the 21st SS-Volunteer Mountain Division "Skanderberg" (Albanian Nr. 1), serving in Yugoslavia fighting Tito's partisans. Signed by the Commander of the 21st mountain Corps. (Von Meyer)

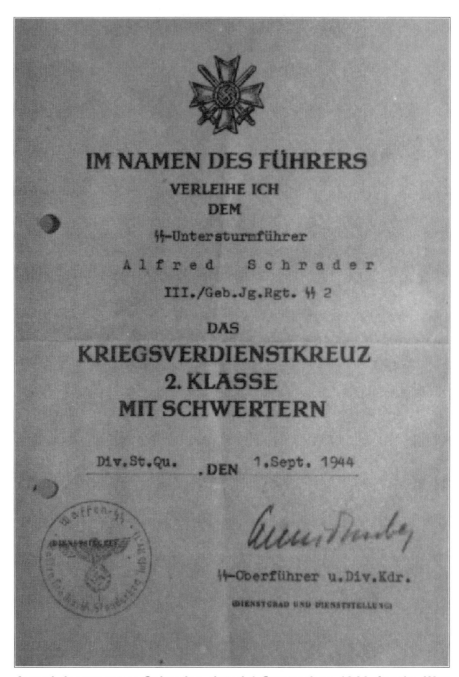

Award document to Schrader, dated 1 September, 1944, for the War Service Cross, 2nd Class, with Swords. Signed by the Commander of "Skanderberg", SS-Oberführer August Schmidhuber, who had commanded a Regiment in "Prinz Eugen" previously.

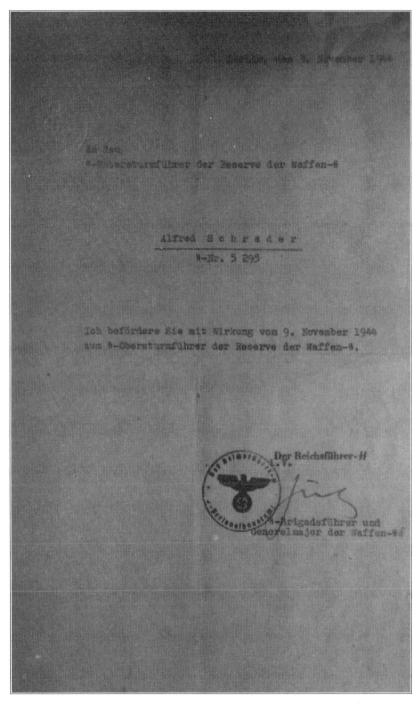

Promotion orders dated 9 November, 1944, promoting Schrader to SS-Oberstürmführer of the Reserve. Signed by one of Himmler's adjutants.

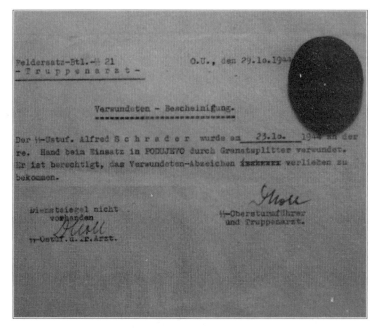

Preliminary award Certificate to Schrader for the Black Wound Badge, for wounds received 23 October, 1944, in action in Padujevo, Yugoslavia.

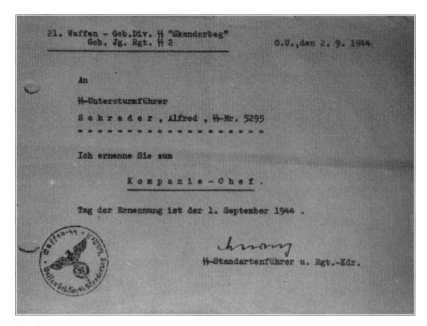

Order appointing Schrader as Company Commander of 9th Company, 2nd Mountain Regiment, 21st SS Mountain Division "Skanderberg", dated 1 September, 1944. Signed by Regimental Commander.

GUNTHER KROLL

Front cover of SS-Sturmann Gunther Kroll's Wehrstammbuch (Master Military File). Note that the file has an inked Waffen-SS stamp in the top lefthand corner and includes Kroll's personal details.

Page 3 of Kroll's Wehrstammbuch bear a Munich validation stamp for his service in the RAD and is dated the 1st of April, 1939.

IV. Aktiver Wehrdienst

Einstellungsuntersuchung

Tag, Monat, Jahr	Truppenteil u. Standort	Ärztliches Urteil
I 6.4.38	11. T. A. Ob.	11. tauglich
II	Dachau	

Einstellung

Einstellungstag am	Eingestellt (Ausgehoben — Freiwilliger*) bei
6. 4. 38	9./11-1- T. A. Oberbayern (Truppenteil)
(Tag, Monat, Jahr)	Dachau (Standort)

Dienstzeit rechnet ab:	Vereidigt am:
1. April 1938	9. November 38
(Allgemeiner Einstellungstag)	(Tag, Monat, Jahr)

Tag der ersten Belehrung über Geheimhaltung militärischer Dinge und Spionageabwehr:

(Tag, Monat, Jahr)	(Name, Dienstgrad, Dienststellung)

Nicht eingestellt auf Grund der Einstellungsuntersuchung

In Marsch gesetzt nach:	am:	überwiesen an:
I		
II (Behalte)	(Tag, Monat, Jahr)	(Wehrmeldeamt)

Bemerkungen:

*) Nichtzutreffendes durchstreichen.

The entries on page 6 of Kroll's Wehrstammbuch relate to his military service and periods of active duty. Indicated on this page are details of Kroll's service with SS-Totenkopf Verbande, SS-Standarte Oberbayern at the Dachau Concentration Camp. The dates for Kroll's service at Dachau are from 6/4/38 - 9/1/38.

Page 21 of Kroll's Wehrstammbuch indicates that he served with the SS-Gebirgsjager Regiment Nr.6 in Lappland and that he was killed in action on the Lappland Front on the 16th of April, 1943. The Waffen-SS ink stamp for E-Stelle VII is the final stamp applied to the Wehrstammbuch by the Waffen-SS Personnel Office to indicate that Kroll's death has been officially recorded and that the book is no longer valid.

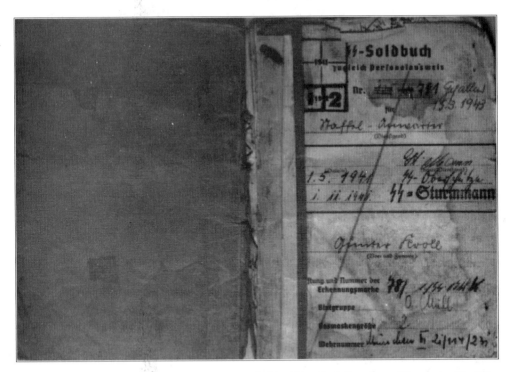

The inside cover and first page of Kroll's Soldbuch, although Kroll's photograph is missing and the overall condition of the book is quite poor it is still possible to glean a considerable amount of information from what remains. Entries in the book show that Kroll had received three promotions rising from SS-Mann to SS-Sturmann. At the foot of the page are details of Kroll's bloodgroup, gasmask size and Wehr number. The inked block at the top left of the page is for quarterly administration checks and for recording updated details. Kroll's Soldbuch has been invalidated by having a red line drawn diagonally across the whole page with the entry "Gefallen 15.3.1943" (Killed in Action the 15th of March, 1943).

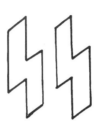

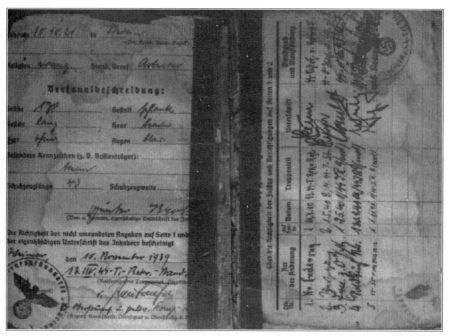

Page 2 lists Kroll's personal data such as: physique, date of birth, religion, civilian profession and his payroll signature. Page 3 documents the various units to which Kroll had been assigned during his period of active service with the SS validation stamp at the end of all their entries.

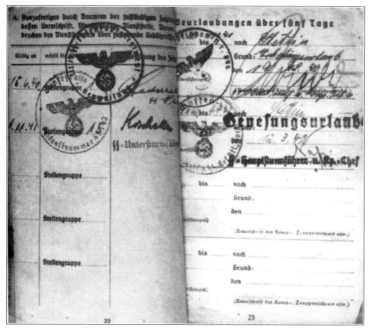

Pages 22 and 23 of Kroll's Soldbuch contain entries for periods of leave lasting more than 5 days: indicating that he took four extended leaves from his units between 15.6.40 and 4.4.42. Each of the four separate leaves have had a validation stamp and officer's signature applied when the leave was granted and also when Kroll returned from leave.

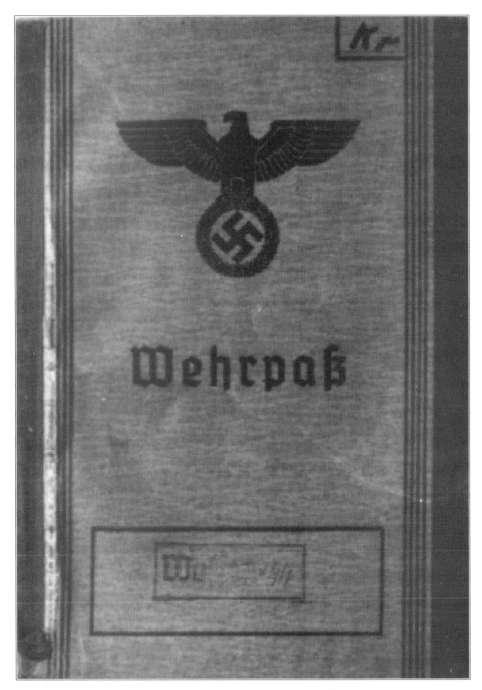

Front cover of Gunther Kroll's Wehrpass which is the regular green cloth Wehrmacht type with a Waffen-SS ink block stamped into the bottom unit identification panel. In the top righthand corner are the initials "Kr" which were an abbreviated form of Kroll's surname used for administration and filing purposes by the unit's clerk.

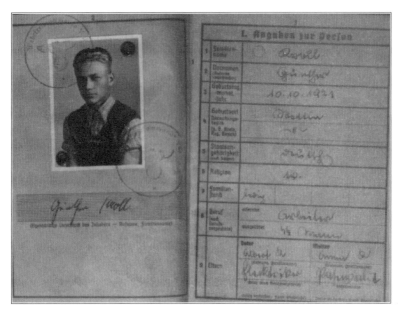

Page 2 of this Wehrpass has a pre-war photograph of the young Kroll wearing casual civilian clothes. The photograph is rivited onto page 2 and has SS validation stamps applied to top and bottom corners. There is a specimen of Kroll's signature beneath his photograph. Page 3 records Kroll's personal details such as: name, date of birth, religion, etc.

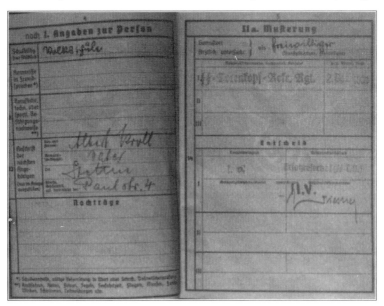

Page 4 records details of the school Kroll attended and his next-of-kin who lived in Stettin; whilst page 5 indicates Kroll's status as a Freiwillinger (Volunteer), and that he entered service with the SS-Totenkopf Regiment on the 2nd of December, 1939. The bottom entry on this page shows that at one time he was placed in the SS-Ersatzreserve (SS Replacement Reserve Battalion).

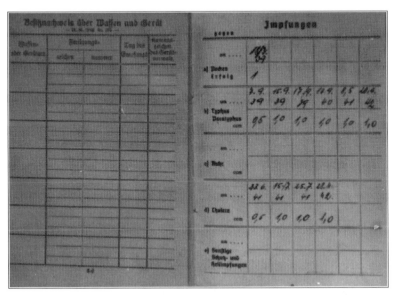

Page 8 has no entries whilst page 8a documents the weapons which were issued to Kroll by his unit when he arrived to serve on the Eastern Front on 8.4.42. The serial numbers of the four items issued to Kroll have also been recorded.

Page 8d is a continuation page from page 8a for recording the issue of weapons on which there are no entries. Page 9 is for IMPFUNGEN (Immunisations) indicating that Kroll had received innoculations for: Smallpox, Typhus and Paratyphus and Cholera. The boxes within each of the sections record the day and month of each innoculation with the year beneath. The box underneath the date indicates the dosage in CC (cubic centimetres) of each innoculation administered.

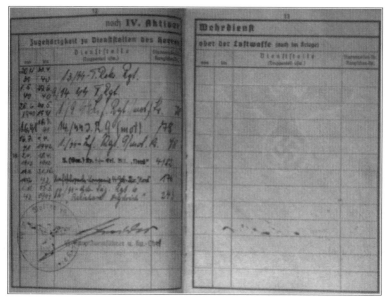

Pages 12 and 13 of Kroll's Wehrpass were for recording details of the individual's unit assignments and show that between 20.1.39 and his death on 15.3.43 Kroll had served with no less that 8 different SS regiments ending with his final unit 12th SS-Gebirgs Jager Division Regiment Nr. 6 "Reinard Heydrich" in which Kroll was killed in action while fighting in Lappland.

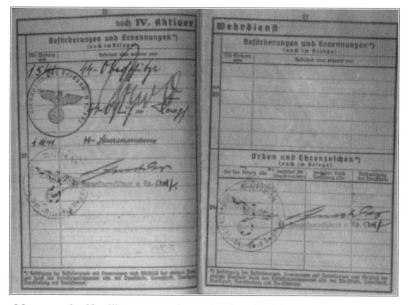

Page 22 records Kroll's promotions both of which took place in 1941, ending with the rank of SS-Sturmann. Each of the promotion entries has a unit validation stamp and the commanding officer's signature. Page 23 records that at the time of his death Kroll had received no awards indicated by the word "Keine" (None) which appears beneath the unit's validation stamp and above his unit Commanders signature.

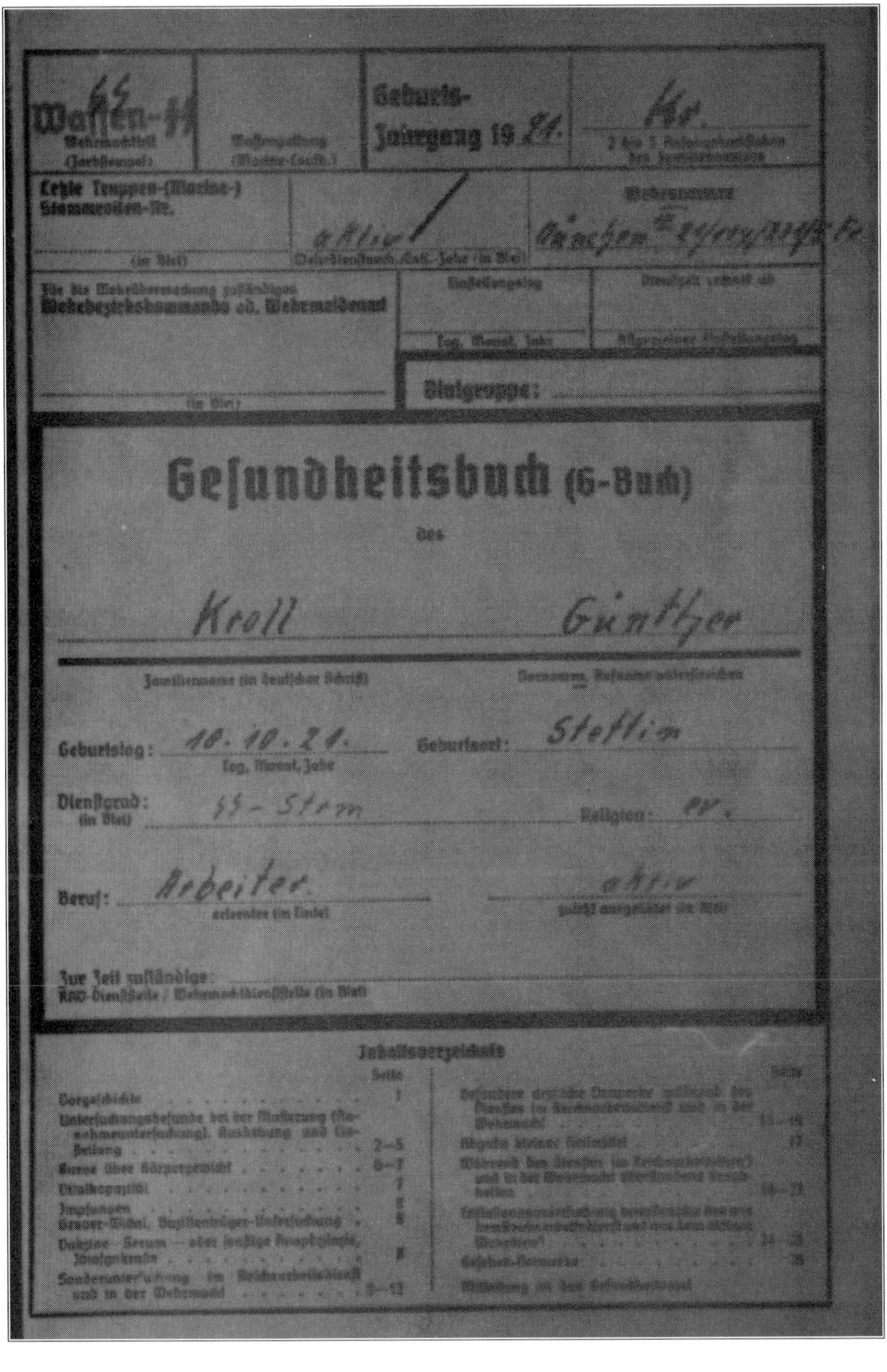
Waffen-SS
Wehrmachtteil (Truppenteil)
Waffengattung (Marine-Laufb.)
Geburts-Jahrgang 19 21.
Kr.
2 bis 5 Anfangsbuchstaben des Familiennamens
Letzte Truppen-(Marine-) Stammrollen-Nr.
(in Blei)
aktiv /
Wehrdienstverh. (Ggf. Jahre (in Blei))
Wehrnummer
München ...
Für die Wehrüberwachung zuständiges Wehrbezirkskommando od. Wehrmeldeamt
(in Blei)
Einstellungstag
Tag, Monat, Jahr
Dienstzeit rechnet ab
Allgemeiner Einstellungstag
Blutgruppe:

Gesundheitsbuch (G-Buch)

des

Kroll Günther

Familienname (in deutscher Schrift)
Vornamen, Rufnamen unterstreichen

Geburtstag: 10.10.21.
Tag, Monat, Jahr
Geburtsort: Stettin

Dienstgrad: SS-Strm
(in Blei)
Religion: ev.

Beruf: Arbeiter
erlernter (in Tinte)
aktiv
zuletzt ausgeübter (in Blei)

Zur Zeit zuständige
RAD-Dienststelle / Wehrmachtdienststelle (in Blei)

Inhaltsverzeichnis

PAK 3.7 anti-tank gun, Gunther Kroll was qualified to operate this weapon.

A questionnaire sent to Kroll's father almost one year after his sons death requesting information about Gunther Kroll's civilian occupation, date of enlistment etc.

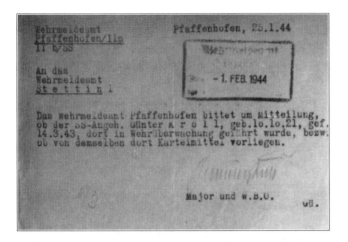

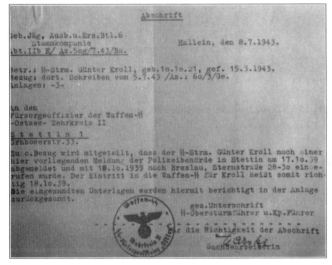

These three letters graphically illustrate that long after a soldiers death his service documentation continued to accumulate. The letters circulated between the Enlistment Registration Office and SS Records Offices from July 1943 to February 1944, almost a year after Kroll's death in Northern Russia.

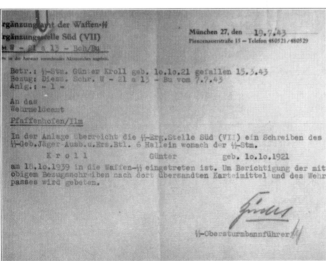

Kroll's Vermendungskarte.

Gunther Kroll's punishment record whilst serving with SS Regiment "Reinard Heydrich". The record indicates that Kroll was sentenced to five days close arrest on 1-11-1942. His sentence was served in his unit from 2-11-1942 to 7-11-1942 and he was released at 19.00 hours on that date. Kroll would appear to have fallen foul of his Company Commander very soon after joining his new unit. The record has been closed on 10th April 1943 with the Company Commanders signature and unit stamp. The record shows that Kroll was killed in action on 15-3-1943.

Kriegstammrole sheet used to update Kroll's records following his transfer from one SS unit to another, also any other details which had changed since the original records were entered.

Kriegstammrole update sheet indicating that Kroll was transferred from 4th SS Battalion "Nord" to 6th SS Gebirgsjager Regiment Reinhard Heydrich. Also recorded is Kroll's attendance at the SS Drivers School in Berlin-Lichterfelde.

Kriegstammrolle update sheet recording Kroll's death on 15-3-1943 on the Lappland Front whilst serving with 6th SS Geburgsjager Regiment "Reinard Heydrich".

Ergänzungsamt der Waffen-SS   München 27, den 7.7.43
Ergänzungsstelle Süd (VII)   Pienzenauerstraße 15
Abt.II/T - 21 a 13 - Mu

Betr.: Karteimittel gefallener SS-Angehöriger
Bezug: Ohne
Anlg.: W.St.Buch, G.Buch, V.Karte, 2 Krista, Strafbuchauszug,
       Wehrpaß, Soldbuch

An das
Wehrmeldeamt

Pfaffenhofen/Ilm

In der Anlage überreicht die SS-Ergänzungsstelle Süd (VII)
die Karteimittel und den Wehrpaß für den SS-Stm.

     K r o l l   Günter   geb. 1o.1o.21

der am 15.3.43 an der Lapplandfront
gefallen ist.

Beerdigt: Karelien, Friedhof May-Weg.
Einschreiben gilt als Empfangsbestätigung.

            Der Leiter der Ergänzungsstelle Süd (VII)
                     der Waffen-SS

     i.V.

                     SS-Sturmbannführer
                     SS-Hauptsturmführer

Deceased transmittal form, recording the details of Kroll's death and showing that his document such as Soldbuch Wehrpass etc. were sent to the records office of his SS district.

HEINZ KASSEL

The following Soldbuch, Wehrpass and associated documents relate to SS Pioneer Heinz Kassel who served with the Stabs Kompanie (Headquarters Company) of SS Pioneer Battalion 17th SS Panzer Grenadier Division "Gotz Von Berlichingen". Kassel joined the SS as a volunteer on the 21st of January, 1944 and was killed a year later on the 22nd of January, 1945 during the Norwind Offensive in Alsace Lorraine.

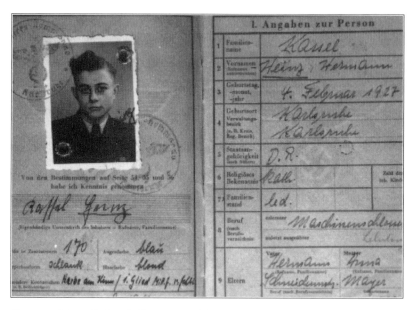

Pages 2 and 3 of Kassel's Wehrpass with his photograph rivited to the top of page 2 and endorsed with two SS rubber stamps. His personal details including his name, address, next-of-kin, height, colour of eyes, hair and blood group are also recorded.

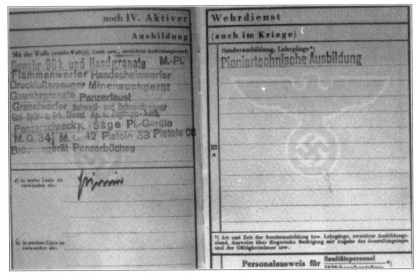

Pages 20 and 21 of Kassel's Wehrpass indicate that he was trained as a combat engineer and that he was qualified to operate the following weapons: K-98, MP-40, MG-34, MG-42, P-38, P-08, flamethrower, flashlight, mine detector, rifle grenades, Panzerfaust, mortar, Panzerschreck, anti-tank rifle, chain-saw, welding equipment (gas and arc), engineer construction tools, expolsives and bridging equipment.

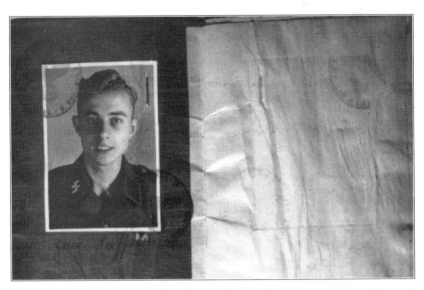

Inside cover of Kassel's Soldbuch. The uniformed picture of Kassel has been stapled onto the page rather than being rivited, and has been stamped on the upper right and lower left corners with the battalion stamp. Kassel's signature appears below his photograph.

Page 1 of Kassel's Soldbuch bears his personal details over which an invalidation line has been applied diagonally from bottom left to top right in red with the words "Gefallen am 22.1.45" written along the red line indicating that Kassel was killed on that date and that his Soldbuch was no longer valid. The lefthand page of the Soldbuch has a portrait picture of Adolf Hitler which Kassel had obviously glued into the book himself.

Pages 20 and 21 of the Kassel Soldbuch were used to record details of his death and the location where he was buried, 3 kilometres south of Zweibrucken in Althornbach Community Cemetery. The final entries in Heinz Kassel's Soldbuch were completed in Dresden on the 8th of February, 1945 and bear the official Waffen-SS Stamp and signature of an SS Untersturmführer.

Service Record Sheet relating to Heinz Kassel which was completed following his death. This form of record sheet consists of 41 entries and contains personnel information about the soldier. Entries include name, date of birth, religion, next-of-kin, Service Grade, where he was trained, roster number and unit, information recording death or missing in action status, training, Awards and promotions.

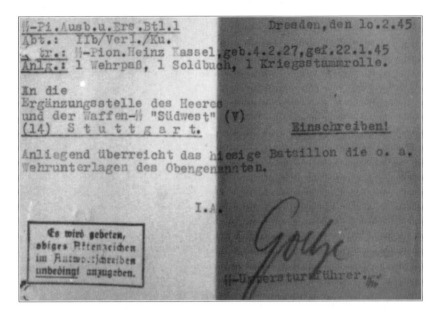

Transmittal slips from Kassel's Home Replacement battalion to the SS Recruiting District Southwest notifying them of his death and the transfer of his Wehrpass, Soldbuch and Service Record Sheet. The place and date of the final piece of processing of Kassel's documents after his death was in Stuttgart on the 17th of April, 1945, almost 4 months after his death.

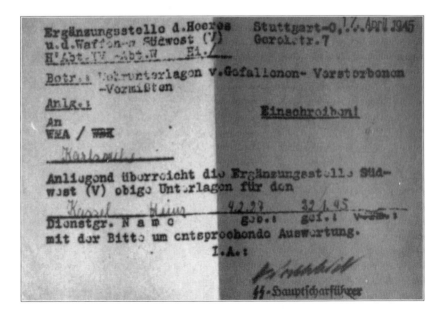

JOHANN MUNK

The following set of documents all relate to SS Sturmann Johann Munk, a Dutch volunteer who served with the 1st Battalion SS Regiment "Westland" of the 5th SS Panzer Division "Wiking". Johann Munk who is still alive and residing in England today had a varied and interesting career in the Waffen SS rising through the ranks to eventually attend the SS Officer's School at Bad Tolz. Munk retained a wide variety of material relating to his service career in the Waffen-SS and also kept notes on events and actions in which he was involved. He recorded incidents on note paper bearing the Westland emblem in the top left hand corner. His notes covering the period of the war on the Russian Front give an interesting insight not only into the disposition of his unit but also the terrain features and locations of suspected or known enemy positions. Munk also documented his views on the prevailing political situation and how he perceived Germany's position and war aims. He graphically describes the rural areas of the Soviet Union as crude and primitive, often without any form of plumbing or electricity. Amongst his notes, photographs and Award documents which he has scrupiously preserved, there is also an extremely interesting chart which details the members of his cadet class at Bad Tolz showing their ranks and originating units.

Johann Munk.

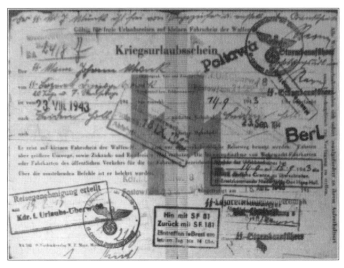

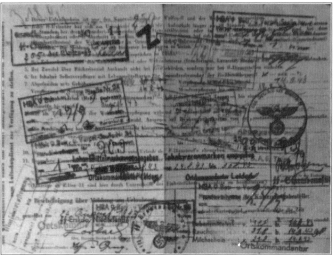

Obverse and reverse sides of a Kreigsurlaubsschein (wartime leave pass). This extremely flimsy form is printed on tissue paper and has red SS runes stamped in the centre along with a wide variety of validation stamps from numerous military, police and civilian authorities. This form was required when a soldier went on leave from the Front, and without it a soldier could be immediately detained by military authorities until his disposition could be verified. In the closing months of the war a soldier not having a valid Kreigsurlaubsschein could quite easily be subject to arrest and summary execution as a deserter. This type of leave pass also afforded the bearer permission to cross Reich frontiers whilst travelling from the Front to his home destination. This gave the Kreigsurlaubsschein the status of a military passport.

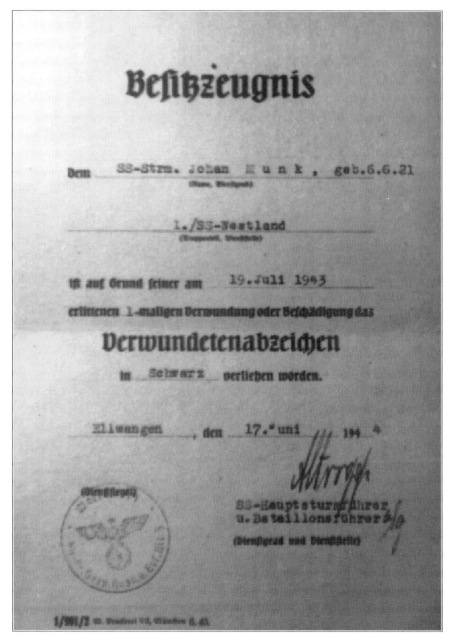

Award document for the Black Wound Badge awarded to Munk on the 19th of July, 1943. The Award of the Wound Badge has a signature of approval from his battalion commander.

Obverse and reverse sides of an SS Lazarett (Field Hospital) discharge slip giving details of Munk's admission date, wounds which were treated and subsequent discharge on the 14th of August, 1943. Munk had received a bullet wound in his right shoulder on the 19th of July, 1943. The form authorises a change in his duty status from active to invalid, and grants him 3 weeks convalescence leave. The document is signed by the Chief Medical Officer, and SS Sturmbannführer, and was countersigned by an SS Hauptsturmführer who was the physician treating Munk.

Award document to SS Sturmmann Johann Munk for the Wound Badge in Silver dated the 15th of July, 1944. The document states that Munk received three wounds on three separate occasions 19/7/43; 8/10/43 and 2/11/1943. As a result of the severity of these wounds Munk was unable to make a full recovery. This disablement prevented Munk from returning to combat duty status at that time.

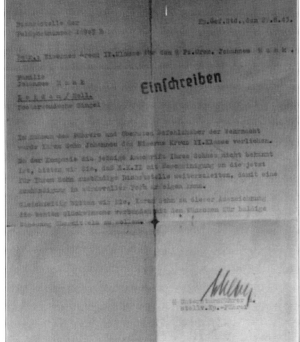

A letter dated 22nd of August, 1943 from Munk's Company Commander informing Munk's family that their son has been awarded the Iron Cross 2nd Class. The letter is written in German and is addressed to the family of Johannes Munk in Leiden, Holland.

II. Mit Wirkung vom 1.8.1944 werden unter gleichzeitiger Kommandierung
zu dem in der Zeit vom 1.8. bis 12.10.1944 stattfindenden 10. Führer-
bewerber-Lehrgang für germanische ﬀ-Führerbewerber an der ﬀ- und
Waffen-Junkerschule Tölz, versetzt:

  1.) zur ﬀ-Führerschule des VT-Dienstes:

    a) vom ﬀ-Begleitkommando des Führers:
       ﬀ-Oscha. Malta   Paul   geb. 26.11.20

    b) vom ﬀ-Pz.Gren.Ausb.u.Ers.Btl. 5:
       ﬀ-Ustf.   Braams   Gerard-Willem " 4. 8.18
       ﬀ-Sturm. Munk   Johann   " 6. 6.21

    c) vom ﬀ-Pz.Gren.Ausb.u.Ers.Btl. 11:
       ﬀ-Uscha. Knudsen   Emil   " 28.11.20

    d) vom ﬀ-Art.Ausb.u.Ers.Rgt. 5:
       ﬀ-Sturm. Riemeijer   Johannes   " 20. 5.16

    e) von der ﬀ-Pz.Jg.Ausb.u.Ers.Abt. 1(mot.Z.):
       ﬀ-Uscha. de Haan   Hendrik   " 10. 7.17

    f) von der Ausb.u.Ers.Abt.d.ﬀ-Verw.Dienstes:
       ﬀ-Uscha. Eggendaal   Jakobis   " 18. 9.13
       ﬀ-Uscha. van Farteijk Carmelius   " 15. 8.22
       ﬀ-Uscha. Verbrüggen   Hendrik   " 3.10.18

    g) vom ﬀ-Hauptamt - Ers.Kdo. "Norwegen" -
       ﬀ-Uscha. Graijner   " 5.10.15

    h) vom Landsturm "Nederland":
       ﬀ-Sturm. Vuist   Dirk   " 9. 3.22

    i) vom ﬀ-Pz.Gren.Ausb.u.Ers.Btl. 9:
       ﬀ-Uscha. Heiserl   Rudolf   " 22. 4.22

  2.) zur ﬀ-Kraftf.Ausb.u.Ers.Rgt.:

    a) vom ﬀ-Pz.Gren.Ausb.u.Ers.Btl. 5:
       ﬀ-Ustf.   Buitenhuis   Floor   " 1. 5.25

    b) vom ﬀ-Hauptamt - Ers.Kdo."Norwegen" -
       ﬀ-Ustf.   Gulbrannsen Asbjørn   " 5. 7.19

    c) vom ﬀ-Pz.Gren.Ers.Btl. 18:
       ﬀ-Oscha. Krause   Adolf   " 19. 8.18

    d) vom ﬀ-Pz.Gren.Ausb.u.Ers.Btl. 8:
       ﬀ-Ustf.   Huber   Sonnjörg   " 6. 7.20

    e) vom ﬀ-I.G.Ausb.u.Ers.Btl. 1:
       ﬀ-Sturm. Menthe   Jörn   " 20. 6.23

A copy of orders directing SS Sturmann Munk to report for duty at the
Junkerschule in Bad Tolz on the 12th of January, 1944. Munk was selected
to attend the Officer's Candidate School after demonstrating his leadership
qualities in various actions on the Eastern Front.

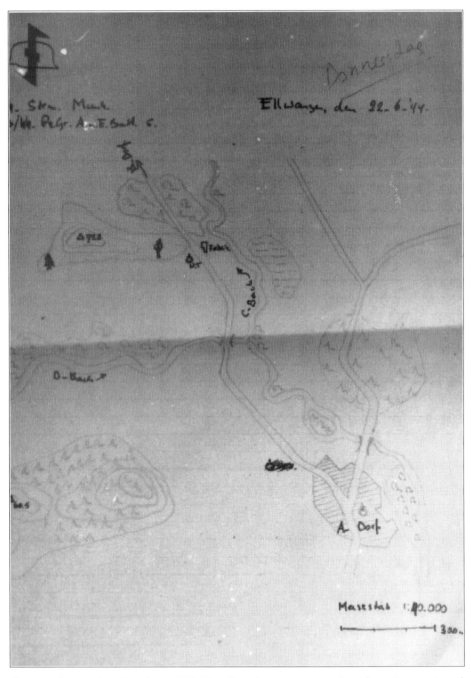

A map drawn by Munk on SS Westland notepaper showing the route of his escape carrying a wounded comrade following heavy fighting on the Eastern Front.

A photograph of Munk with his unit.

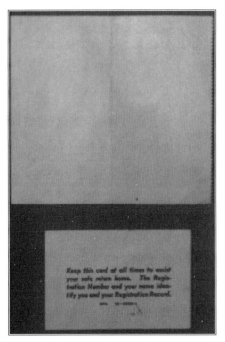
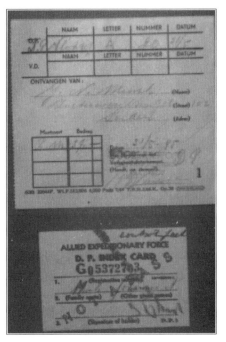

Munk's displaced person index card issued to him by the Allied expeditionary forces in May 1945.

SS-UNTERSCHARFÜHRER WALTER POELZL

The following group of original documents relate to former SS-Unterscharführer Walter Poelzl who served with Waffen-SS Panzer Division "Leibstandarte SS-Adolf Hitler". The documents contained in this grouping cover the period from November, 1938 through to June, 1953.

Walter Poelzl was born on the 4th of November, 1920 in Vienna, Austria. He grew up in the town of Graz where he attended school and studied to become an electrician. On his 18th birthday in November, 1938 he became eligible for National Service and entered the RAD (Reich Labour Service): serving with RAD detachment 7/280 in Marktredwitz, Bavaria. His records show that whilst serving with the RAD in Bavaria he received two weeks camp arrest for being 25 minutes late for bed check on the 10th of June, 1939. On the 30th of September, 1939 Poelzl completed his service in the Labour Corps and was honourably discharged from the RAD with the rank of Vormann (Senior Private).

Shortly after leaving the RAD in 1939 Walter Poelzl volunteered to serve in the Waffen-SS. Upon completion of his training Poelzl was assigned to the prestigious Waffen-SS unit "Leibstandarte SS-Adolf Hitler" (LSSAH). Although Poelzl's original Soldbuch and Wehrpass are absent from this grouping it is still possible to trace his career in the Waffen-SS quite well based upon the available surviving documents.

The Poelzl documents indicate that he married Eva Josefa Kopp on the 26th of October, 1940, one week after the birth of a child! It was not until the 11th of July, 1941 that Poelzl was officially registered as the father of the child although the marriage had been declared racially acceptable by the SS Race and Settlements Office (RUSHA) on October 18th, 1940.

Walter Poelzl served with LSSAH throughout World War II, and it can be assumed that he took an active part in: the 1940 French, Belgium and Dutch Campaigns; the 1941 Balkan Campaign; Russian Front 1941-44; Normandy and West Front 1944-45, and the final campaigns of LSSAH in Austria-Hungary in 1945. It is evident from his numerous surviving Award documents that Poelzl was involved in a considerable amount of action during his career in LSSAH.

On the 27th of March, 1942 Poelzl was promoted to the rank of SS-Sturmann (Corporal) followed shortly thereafter by a further promotion to SS-Rottenführer (Senior Corporal). On January 30th, 1943 Poelzl was promoted to SS-Unterscharführer (Sergeant) on the recommendation of the LSSAH commander SS-Obergruppenführer Sepp Dietrich. Following this promotion Poelzl's records show that he served with the headquarters company of the 1st SS-Panzer Regiment of the LSSAH. Although it is difficult to ascertain his specific duties in this position there is a document dated the 6th of August, 1944 indicating that Poelzl had received training as a Rechnungführer (Senior Clerk). The final record entry for Poelzl with the 1st SS Panzer Regiment of LSSAH is on Hitler's birthday, the 20th of April, 1945: at this time the regiment was commanded by Joachim Peiper.

Walter Poelzl was captured by the US Army at the end of the war in Austria, and entered a US POW Camp on the 11th of May, 1945: he was interned in Camp Maurice L. Tyler close to Wegscheid bei Linz, where he remained until his ultimate discharge over one year later on the 24th of May, 1946.

US Army records show that during Poelzl's one year in captivity he carried out work in the Camp as an electrician, driver, cleaner and carpenter. Under the rules in operation Poelzl was entitled to payment from the US Army for carrying out these various jobs which at the time of his release Poelzl did not receive. Between 1951 and 1953, Walter Poelzl tried without success on several occasions to petition the headquarters of the US Forces in the European Theatre for the payment he believed he was due for work carried out in the POW Camp in 1945-46.

The records of Walter Poelzl indicate that as of June, 1953 he was living in his home town of Koflach in Austria. In total the Poelzl documents span a period of 15 years (1938-1953) and record his various fortunes successively in the RAD, Waffen-SS and as a Prisoner of War.

Photograph taken in 1940 showing SS-Mann Walter Poelzl alongside his father.

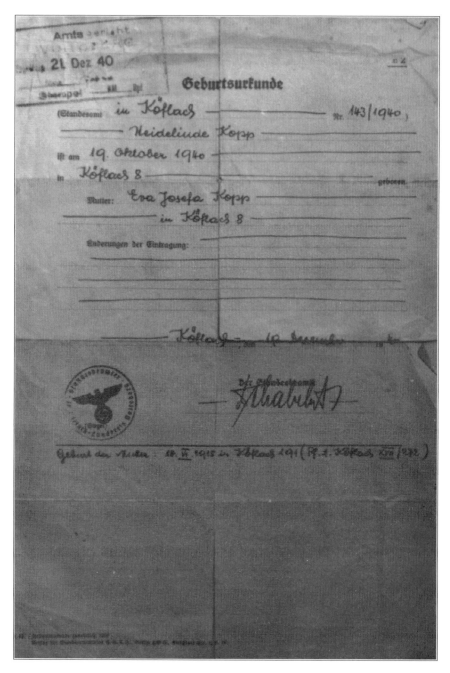

Birth certificate for Heidelinde Kopp, daughter of Eva Josefa Kopp. The child was born one week before Poelzl and Eva Kopp were officially married.

Marriage certificate for SS-Mann Walter Poelzl and Eva Josefa Kopp, married on the 26th of October, 1940 in Koflach, Austria.

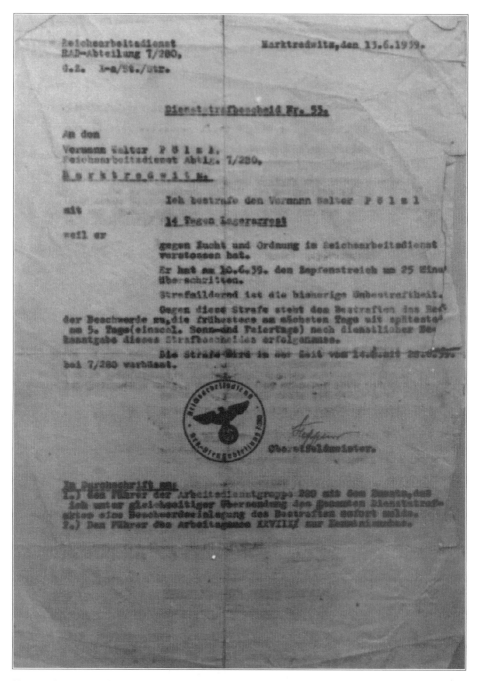

Record on non-judicial punishment duly administered to Walter Poelzl on the 13th of June, 1939 whilst he was serving with the RAD Abteilung 7/280 in Marktredwitz, Bavaria. He was found guilty of being 25 minutes late for bed check and was sentenced to 14 days camp arrest.

RAD travel permit issued to Poelzl authorising him to travel from Marktredwitz to his hometown of Koflach in Austria between the 17th and 19th of October, 1939. The pass bears his RAD unit validation stamps.

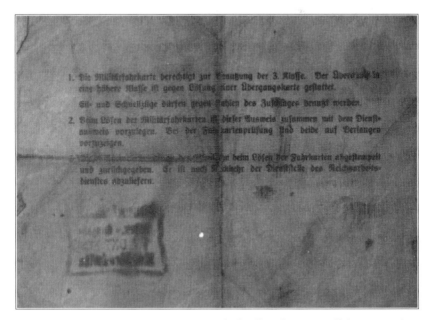

Reverse of Poelzl's travel permit indicating conditions under which it was issued and stipulating that the permit was only valued for 3rd class travel.

The revised birth certificate of Poelzl's Heidelinde dated the 11th of July, 1941 identifying Poelzl as the father.

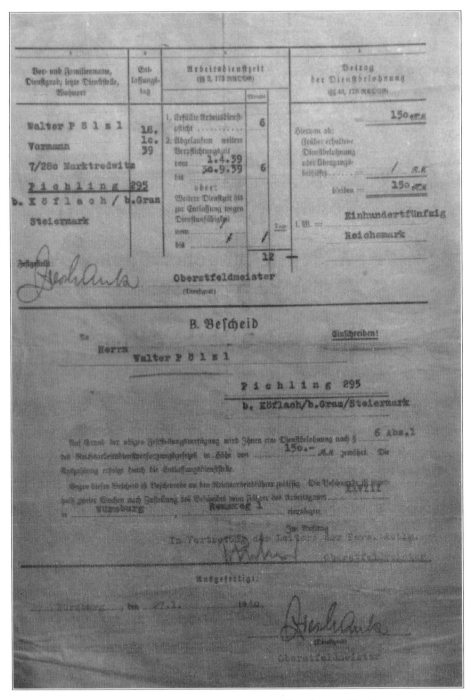

Poelzl's pay record from his RAD service indicating a discharge payment of 150 RM paid upon the successful completion of six month's RAD service dated on the 30th of September, 1939.

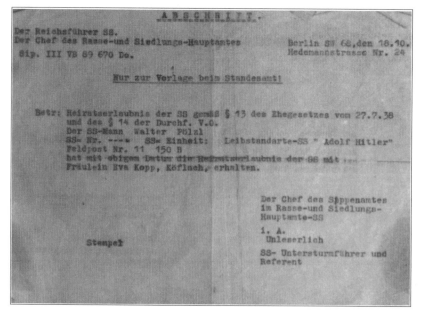

Waffen-SS pay statement which accompanied Poelzl's promotion to SS-Sturmann. The statement indicates that his pay is being deposited in a bank account in his hometown of Koflach.

A statement which indicated that Poelzl had received permission from the SS Race and Settlements Office (RUSHA) to marry Eva Kopp. The statement further shows that Poelzl was assigned to "Leibstandarte SS-Adolf Hitler".

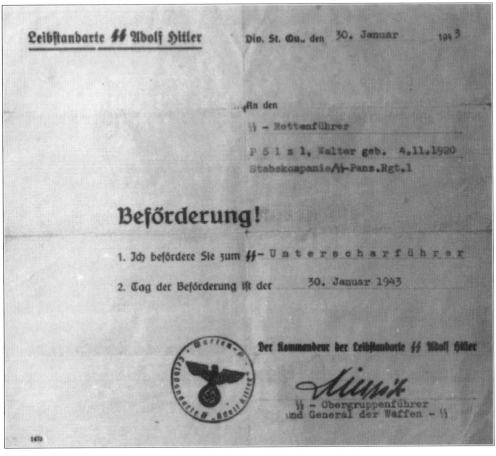

Leibſtandarte 𝕾𝕾 Adolf Hitler   Dio. St. Qu., den   30. Januar   194 3

An den

𝕾 - Rottenführer

P 5 l z l, Walter geb. 4.11.1920
Stabskompanie/𝕾-Panz.Rgt.1

Beförderung!

1. Ich befördere Sie zum 𝕾𝕾 - U n t e r s c h a r f ü h r e r

2. Tag der Beförderung ift der   30. Januar 1943

Der Kommandeur der Leibſtandarte 𝕾𝕾 Adolf Hitler

𝕾 - Obergruppenführer
und General der Waffen - 𝕾

Promotion document dated the 30th of January, 1943 promoting Poelzl from SS-Sturmann to the rank of SS-Rottenführer. The document is on official Leibstandarte paper and is signed by SS-Obergruppenführer Sepp Dietrich.

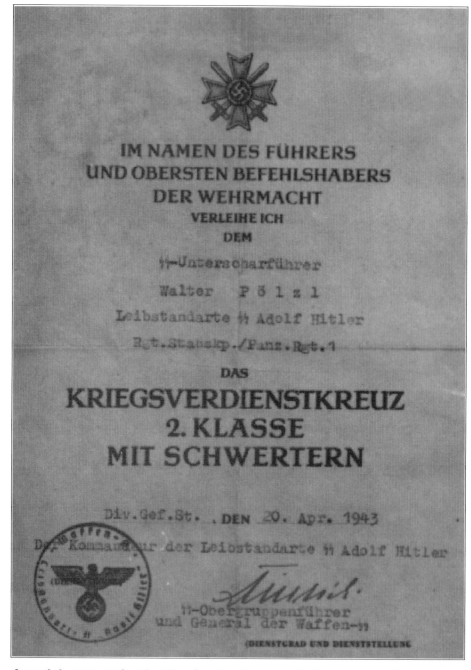

Award document for the War Service Cross with Swords 2nd Class dated the 20th of April, 1943 awarded to SS-Unterscharführer Walter Poelzl. The document bears the official LSSAH stamp and the ink signature of SS-Obergruppenführer Sepp Dietrich.

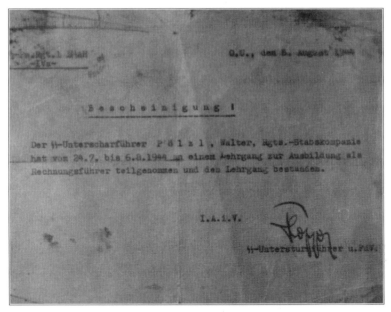

A certificate issued to Poelzl upon the completion of a course for training as a clerk/bookeeper. The two week course was held between the 27th of July and the 6th of August at the regimental headquarters of the 1st SS-Panzer Regiment, then stationed in Normandy.

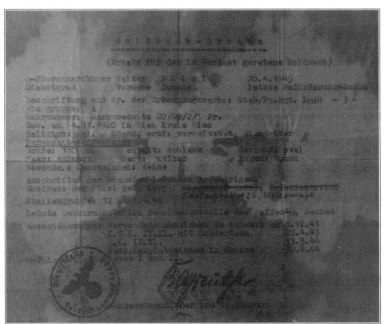

Soldbuch replacement document for Walter Poelzl which temporarily replaced his original Soldbuch lost in April, 1945. The document gives a brief summary of the details which would have appeared in his original Soldbuch including: his personal details, military career and decorations, etc.

RAD identification booklet issue to Walter Poelzl on the 21st of November, 1938 - the date he joined the Labour Service. Unfortunately Poelzl's photograph has been removed.

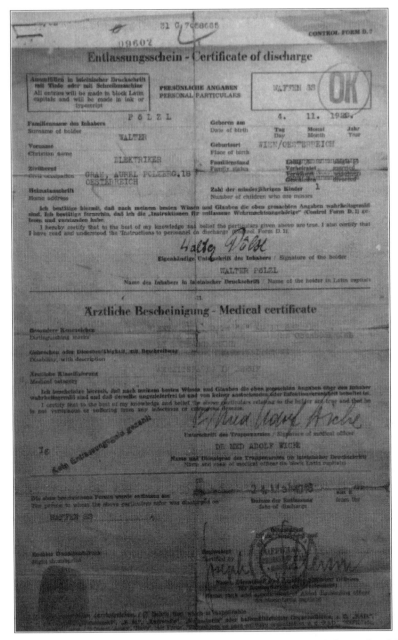

US Prisoner of War discharge certificate issued to Poelzl on the 24th of May, 1946 upon his release from captivity. The document gives personal details of Poelzl and incorporates a medical certificate certifying his medical condition at the time of his release. The document indicates that Poelzl had been a member of the Waffen-SS and includes an inked impression of his right thumb print along with the official camp validation stamp.

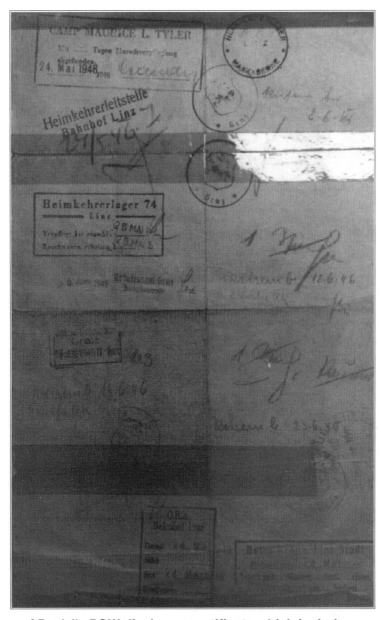

Reverse of Poelzl's POW discharge certificate which includes numerous ink stamps beginning with his release from Camp Maurice L.Tyler on the 24th of May, 1946. Other stamps on the reverse show Poelzl passing through the railway station at Linz in Austria the day after his release and several other stamps which carry over into June, 1946. Released SS Prisoners of War were required to carry their POW release document and have it validated when using public transport or any other public services.

An affidavit signed by Poelzl in Graz, Austria and dated the 30th of April, 1951 which stated that whilst he was a Prisoner of War he carried out work for the US Army.

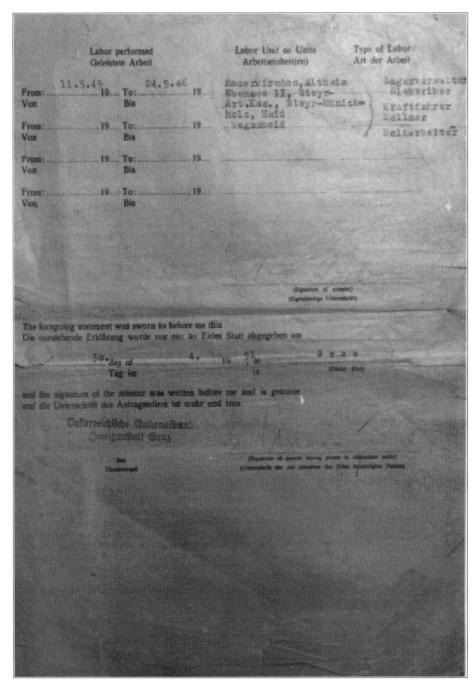

Reverse of the Poelzl affidavit stating the date, unit and type of work carried out for US Forces whilst he was in captivity between the 11th of May, 1945 and the 24th of May, 1946.

A certificate of credit from headquarters US Forces European Theatre to
Poelzl dated the 30th of April, 1951. This was the official US form for
paying POWs who had carried out work for US Forces. At the foot of the
document is the stamp which rejected Poelzl's claim and states he was
not a former US-Held Prisoner of War.

HEADQUARTERS
UNITED STATES FORCES IN AUSTRIA
COMPTROLLER SECTION
APO 174   U.S. ARMY

11 June 1953

Mr. Walter Poelzl,
Gradenberg 129,
Post Koeflach, Stmk
Austria

Dear Sir:

Reference is made to your claim for payment as former U.S.
held prisoner of war.

This headquarters received reply from the Enemy Prisoner of
War Information Bureau, Camp Holabird, Maryland, and was informed
that you are not listed, nor were you ever reported to or by that
bureau as a prisoner of war and that your status while in custody
of the U.S. Forces is not known.

Therefore, favorable consideration cannot be given your claim
for payment.

Very truly yours,

3 Incls:
1-Cert.of Discharge
2-Rejected CCC
3-Affidavit

L.B. MEASHEY
Major   FC

A letter to Poelzl dated the 11th of June, 1953 from headquarters US Army Forces in Austria informing Poelzl that he had never been on record as a Prisoner of War with the US Army! The letter concluded by denying his claim for payment for work carried out during his alleged captivity.

SS-UNTERSCHARFÜHRER FRIEDRICH KOFFLER

This interesting SS document set includes the three main SS documents required for analysing the service career of any SS member. Friedrich Koffler who ultimately held the rank of SS-Unterscharfuhrer obviously had a varied and eventful career: first serving with the SS-Totenkopf Verbande at Dachau and later with the Waffen-SS from 1938 until his death in Russia on the 15th of September, 1942.

The document set comprises Koffler's SS-Soldbuch (Paybook/ID book); SS-Wehrpass (Service Book) and SS-Wehrstammbuch (Master Military Record). The first two documents would have been in the possession of Koffler whilst the Wehrstammbuch was held and maintained with the regimental replacement battalion in Germany. Generally the Wehrstammbuch does not appear along with the individual's Soldbuch and Wehrpass except in instances where an SS soldier had died: at which time the three documents would have been brought together in the individual's regimental office records. This procedure was to insure that the final closing out details were entered not only in the Wehrstammbuch, but also in the Soldbuch and Wehrpass.

In addition to the three aforementioned documents Koffler's effects also contained 10 other miscellaneous documents and papers pertaining to various aspects of his service. These supplementary items give a fascinating insight into the movement of Koffler's documents both before and after his death, and reveal the amount of documentation which related to any personnel in the SS and also show that the paperwork continued to accumulate long after the SS man's death.

Koffler's induction notice. This form is from the RAD and is directing him to report for service at Dachau on 20.7.38.

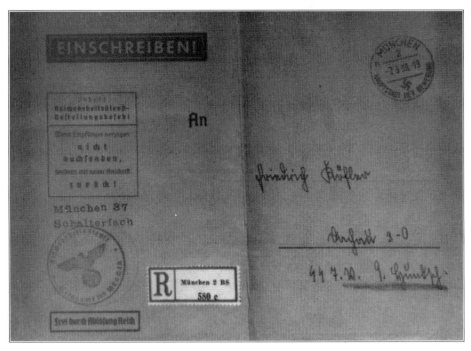

A registered envelope from the Reichsarbeitsdienst (RAD) in Munich postmarked 7.3.39 addressed to Friedrich Koffler at his home address in Munich.

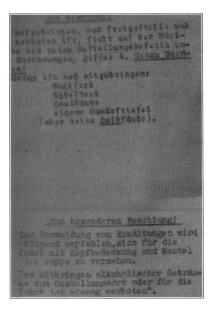

A letter from the RAD to Koffler informing him of the type of clothing to bring to the registration centre and also informing him that it was strictly forbidden to drink alcoholic beverages whilst at or travelling to the RAD registration office.

The RAD order contained in Koffler's registered envelope directing him to report to the Munich Registration Office of the RAD on the 1st of April, 1939 not later than 18:00 hours.

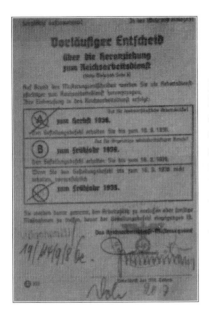

A questionnaire form from the SS Records Office asking Koffler's father to verify his son's entry date into the SS and other information. This form was sent to Koffler's father on the 29th of March, 1944 almost two years after Koffler's death! The document was to clarify details for the SS Personnel Office to enable documentation to be completed on the deceased Friedrich Koffler.

Notification from the RAD informing Koffler that he could expect to be called up for service in the Spring of 1939, and that he would receive notification before the 10th of March, 1939. The document is stamped by the Munich Induction Office of the RAD and countersigned by a RAD Leader.

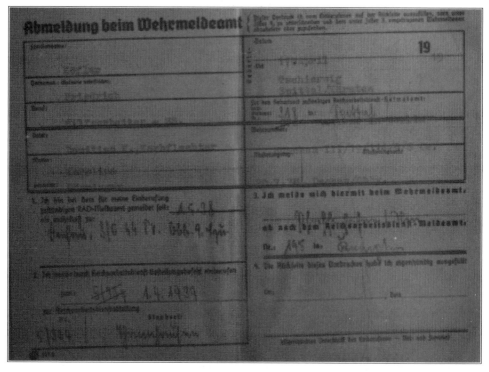

A RAD Service Exemption Certificate issued to Koffler on the 1st of April, 1939 indicating that he was not required to report for service with the RAD as he was already serving with the SS as of 20.7.38 at Dachau, Oberbayern.

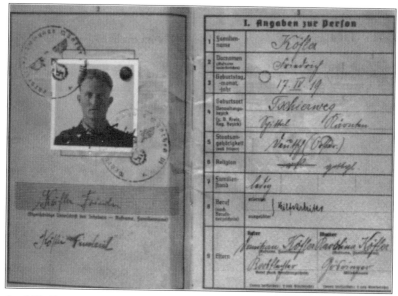

Page 2 of Koffler's Wehrpass bearing a photograph of Koffler in Allgemeine-SS uniform. The photograph is affixed in the regulation rivited manner and overstamped on the top left and bottom right corners. The foot of the page carries two specimens of Koffler's signature. Page 3 carries entries stating Koffler's name, date of birth, hometown, religion, civilian profession and next-of-kin.

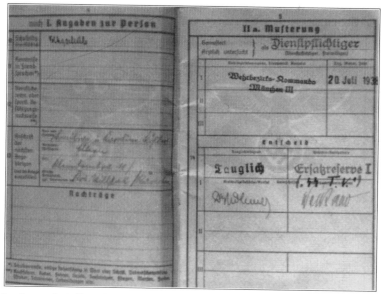

Page 4 gives details of Koffler's education and shows he graduated from High School. Page 5 carries details of Koffler's induction into the SS on the 20th of July, 1938 into the Ersatz Reserve of the SS-"TV" (Totenkopf Verbande). The top section of page 5 indicates that Koffler was a "Dienstpflichtiger" (Conscript).

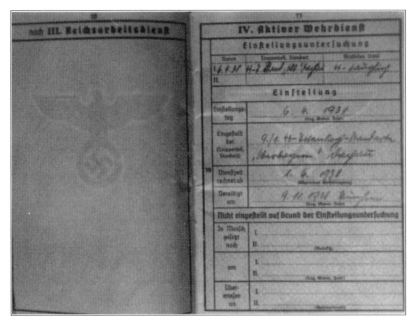

Page 10 of the Wehrpass was reserved for RAD entries, however Koffler had been exempted from service in the RAD: consequently no entries appear (note the Nazi eagle Watermark on this page). Page 11 shows Koffler being assigned to SS-Totenkopf Verbande at Oberbayern (Dachau). He joined his unit there on 6.4.38 where he served as a Concentration Camp Guard.

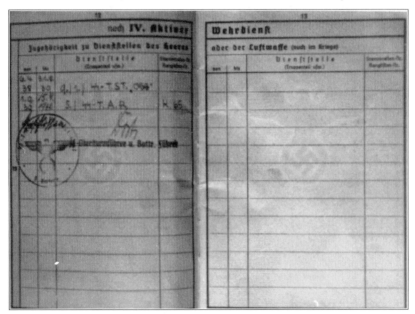

Page 12 carries chronological entries of the units in which Koffler served: 6.4.38 to 31.8.39 with SS-Totenkopf Verbande, Dachau; 1.9.39 to 15.9.42 service with 5th Battery Totenkopf Artillery Regiment 3rd SS-Grenadier Division "Totenkopf".

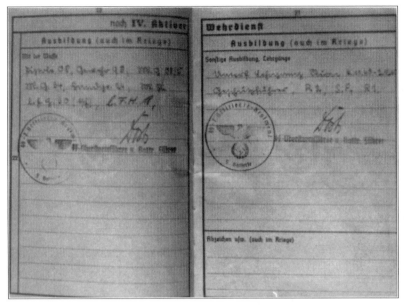

Pages 20 and 21 indicate weapons training received by Koffler showing that he qualified with the following weapons: Pistol P-08; Rifle K-98; Machine Guns Mg-08-15 and MG-34; Handgrenade M-24; and Machine Pistol (MP-40), Other entries indicate that Koffler was assigned as the section gun loader with his Battery.

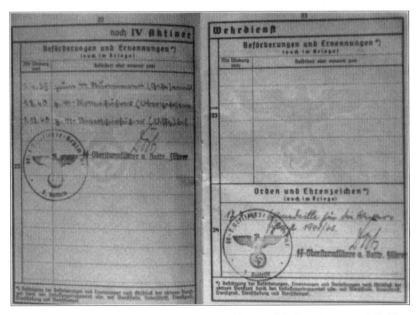

Page 22 lists Koffler's promotions: 1.4.39 to SS-Sturmann; 1.2.40 to SS-Rottenführer; 1.12.40 to SS-Unterscharführer. Page 23 indicates that Koffler received only one award, the Ostmedille (The Eastern Front Medal 1941/42). The award page has been closed out by Koffler's Battery commander after Koffler was killed in action on the 15th of September, 1942 near Godilowa in the Demyansk Pocket in Russia.

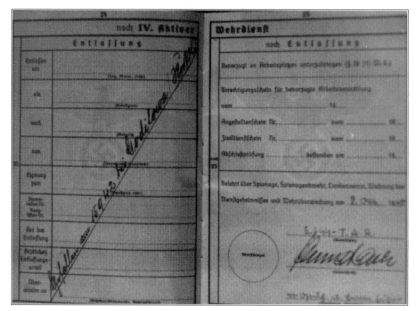

Page 24 bears a red diagonal line attesting to Koffler's death on 15.9.42 and thereby invalidating the Wehrpass. The entry along the line reads "Gefallen aus 15.9.42 bei Godilowa Russland." (Killed in action on 15.9.42 near Godilowa, Russia.) Page 25 carries the signature of the commander of 5th Battery SS-Totenkopf Artillery Regiment.

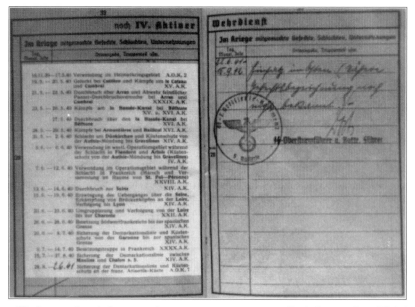

Page 32 is a glued in supplementary page compiled from the Divisional operational log and chronologically records the date and location of combat engagements in which Koffler participated. There are 17 combat entries in all, dating from 16.11.39 to 2.6.41 mainly relating to Koffler's service in the French Campaign of 1940. Page 33 carries an inked entry recording Koffler's final combat assignment ending with the date of his death on 15.9.42

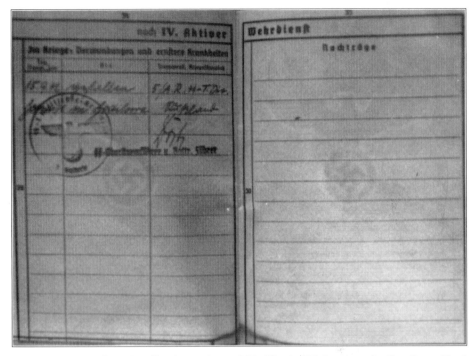

Page 34 contains the final entries of Koffler's Wehrpass indicating: that he was killed in action, the date and location, and the unit he was serving with at the time of his death.

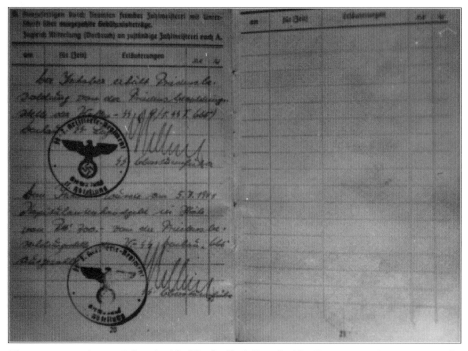

Two paymaster entries in Koffler's Soldbuch. Both payments were made at Dachau.

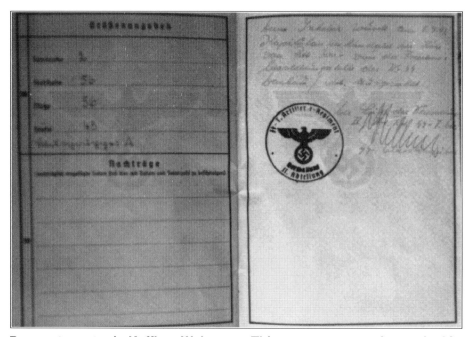

Paymaster entry in Kofflers Wehrpass. This same entry can be tracked in his Soldbuch and Wehrstammbuch.

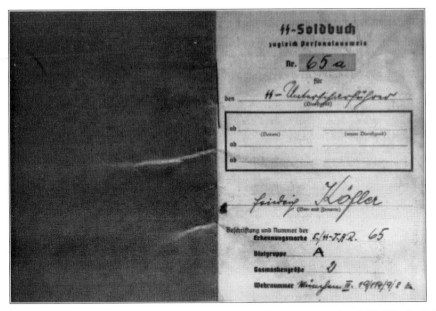

Inside cover (holder's photograph removed) and page 1 of Koffler's SS-Soldbuch.

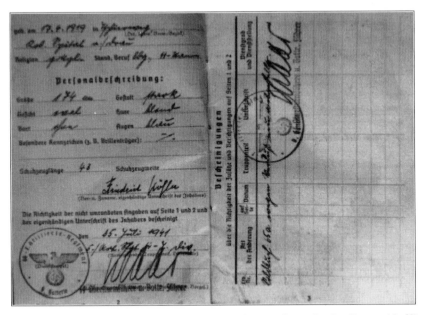

Pages 2 and 3 record personnel information including: Koffler's physique, date of birth, religion, civilian occupation and payroll signature. The validation stamp indicates Koffler was assigned to the 5th Battery SS-Totenkopf Artillery Regiment. Page 3 bears the unit stamp and commanding officer's signature overstamped on the entry closing out Koffler's Soldbuch after he was killed in action.

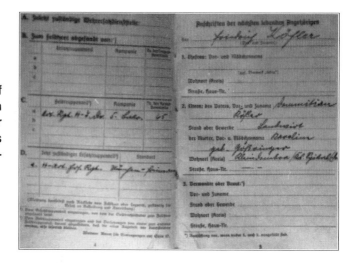

Pages 4 and 5 of Koffler's Soldbuch contain entries for personal entries regarding his next-of-kin, etc.

Pages 6 and 7 give details of the different articles of clothing issued to Koffler.

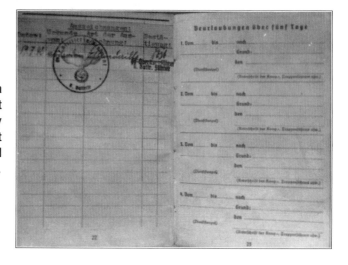

Page 22 is a continuation sheet filled out on 17.7.42 by Koffler's unit confirming the Award of the East Front Medal.

KOFFLER'S WEHRSTAMMBUCH
(Master Military File)

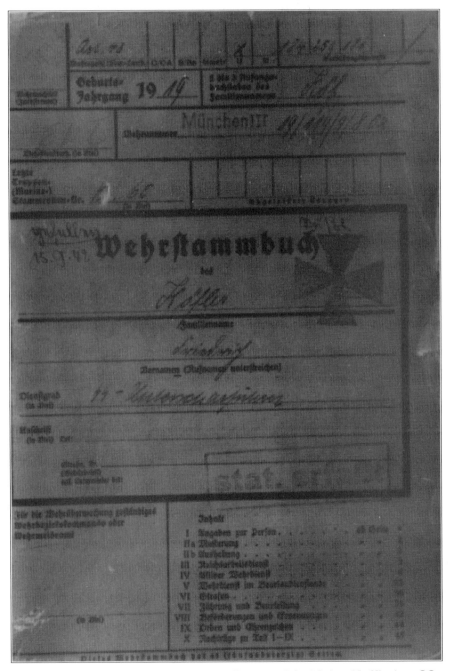

Front cover of SS-Unterscharführer Friedrich Koffler's SS-Wehrstammbuch, (master military file).

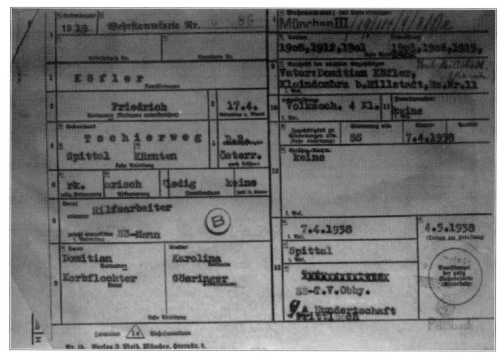

Wehrstammbuch insert card showing Koffler's: name, date and place of birth, civilian occupation, mother and father's names, home address and his SS induction date into SS-Totenkopf Verbande, Oberbayern (Dachau).

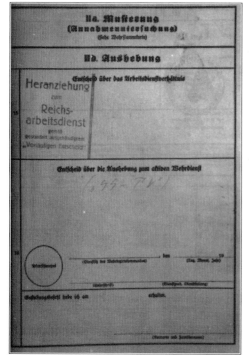

Page 2 of the Wehrstammbuch is for RAD Service entries: with a RAD ink stamp applied indicating Koffler was exempt from RAD Service due to serving in the SS-TV.

Separate glued in entry sheet documenting Koffler's Active Service Record dating from 16.11.39 through to his death on 15.9.42: recording the various actions he was involved in mainly in the French Campaign of 1940.

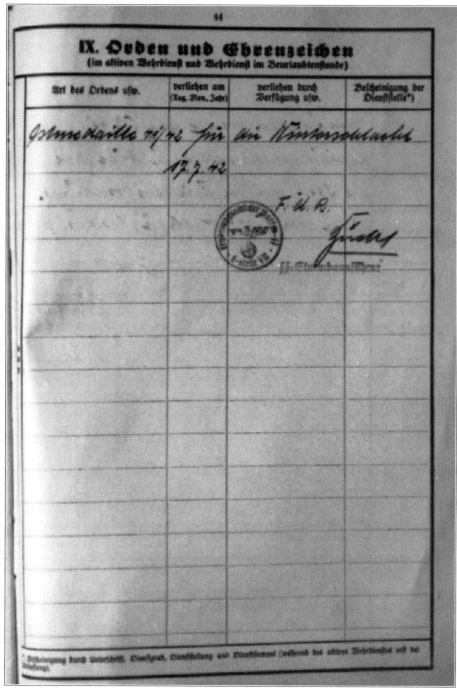

Page 44 of Koffler's Wehrstammbuch indicating the award of The Winter War Medal (Medaille Winterschlacht im Osten) on 17.7.42.

Inside page to Koffler's Wehrstammbuch recording personal details.

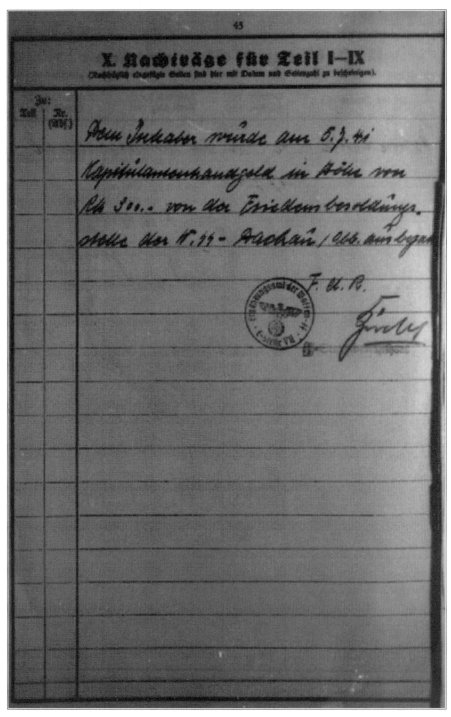

Entry in Koffler's Wehrstammbuch, section I-IX. The holder received 300 RM on 5.7.41 at Dachau, Obb.

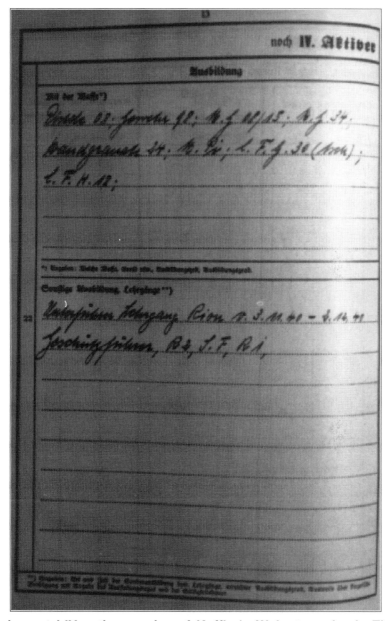

Entry in part I-IV active service of Koffler's Wehrstammbuch. The top section lists the weapons Koffler was qualified on.

P-08	Handgrenade M-24
K-98	L. F. H. 30 *
MG 08/15	L. F. H. 12 *
MG 34	* L. F. H. = Light Field Howitzer

The bottom section records attendance at an NCO training course Koffler attended in Rion from 3.11.40 to 2.12.40.

Entry recording Koffler's units of assignment in chronological order: SS-Totenkopf Standarte Oberbayern and 5th Battery Totenkopf Artillery Regiment.

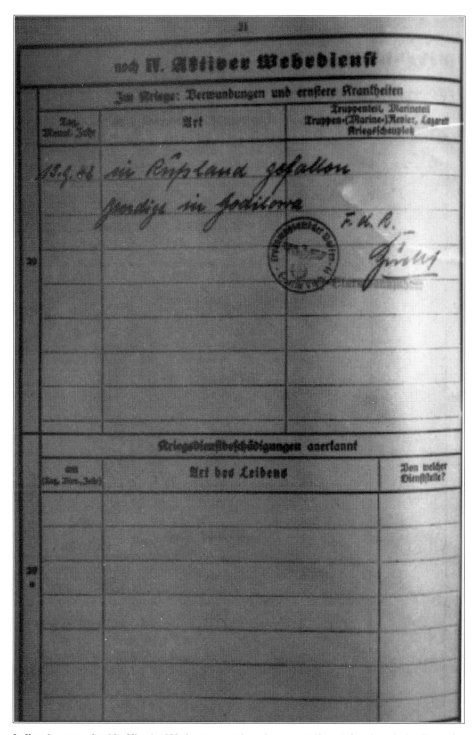

A final entry in Koffler's Wehrstammbuch recording his death in Russia on 15.9.42.

A Verwendungskarte (Utilisation Card) relating to Koffler. This form was filled in the Werstammbuch and served as a record of information about: the individual's name, date of birth, hometown, civilian occupation, professional skills, military service etc.

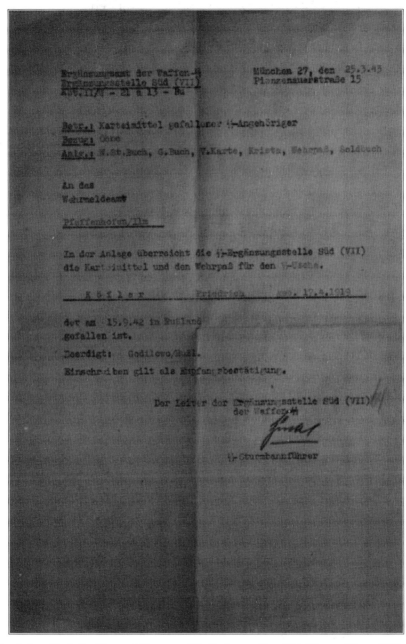

A Karteimettel (Letter of Transmittal) from the SS Recruiting Office in Munich to the SS Central Records Office. This document accompanied Koffler's Wehrstammbuch, Soldbuch, Wehrpass and Medical Records ("G" Book) to the Central SS Records Office and also carried details of his death on 15.9.1942 in Russia and the location "Godilowo" where he was buried.

Kriegstammrole (War Muster Roll) 65. This document was used by SS Field units to update SS personnel details requiring entry into an individual's Wehrstammbuch and was sent by Koffler's FIeld unit to his Home Replacement Battalion in Germany. The entries indicate that in 1942 Koffler was serving with the SS-"Totenkopf" Division in Russia and that on 1.10.1942 his records were transferred to SS-Artillery Ersatz Regiment in Munich-Freimann following his death. Other entries at the foot of the document contain updated information on Koffler having qualified with additional weapons such as pistol, hand grenade and machine pistol, etc.

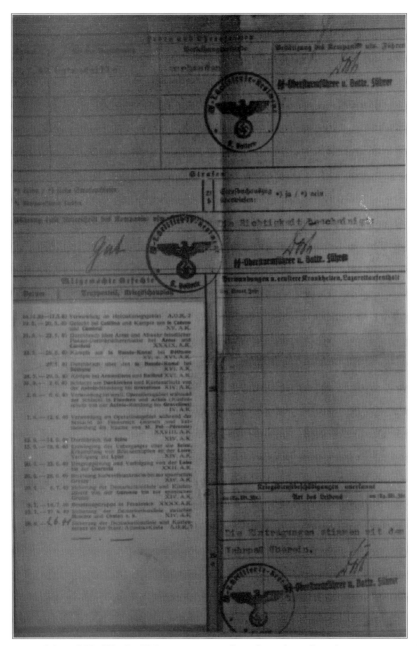

Reverse side of Koffler's Kriegstammrole: showing that he was awarded the East Front Medal on 7.7.42 and indicating his conduct was "Gut" (Good). Attached in the appropriate box is a typed list of the actions which Koffler was involved in between 16/11/39 and 2/6/41. This added document mainly relates to his service during the French Campaign of 1940 which included actions at Cambrai, Dunkirk and later service on the Atlantic Coast of France.

CARL-HEINZ FRUHAUF

Carl-Heinz Fruhauf was born in Hamburg on the 14th of February, 1914, and attended a private boys school from 1 April, 1920-31 March, 1924. Following grammer school he entered a technical university and studied to become a mechanical engineer between 1st April, 1930 and 31st March, 1934. During this period Fruhauf also joined the NSDAP and SS and attended courses in policework given by the Hamburg Police.

After completing his degree program, Fruhauf entered the SS-Verfugungstruppe. During the period 1 April, 1934 to March, 1935, he was assigned duties as an instructor at the SS Sports School at Sternberg/Mecklenberg. On 9 Nov., 1937 Fruhauf was promoted to SS-Oberscharführer. From the Period Nov. 1937 thru June 1938 he held various duty assignments such as primary marksmanship instructor and platoon leader in both the 1st and 3rd, companies of SS Regiment "Germania".

At the outbreak of the war Fruhauf was assigned as platoon leader in the regiments armoured reconnaissance squadron. he took part in the Polish Campaign and was awarded the Iron Cross 2nd. class on 17 Sept., 1939. After demonstrating outstanding leadership qualities, he was selected to attend the officers training course at Braunschweig in February 1940. He successfully completed this course in May, 1940 and was then selected to attend the army cavalry school for armoured reconnaissance training in Krampnitz. He completed training in July 1940 and on 1 Aug, 1940 he was promoted to SS-Untersturmführer. Returning to SS Regiment Germania, Fruhauf was assigned to duty as the battalion adjutant 2nd. battalion. On 1 March, 1941 he was assigned as an ordnance officer to the divisional staff of the newly formed SS division "Wiking". The SS "Wiking" Division was formed in December 1940 and became fully operational on April 1st, 1941, under the command of Felix Steiner.

At the beginning of Operation Barbarossa (Invasion of Russia) Fruhauf was assigned as an ordnance officer on the regimental staff SS infantry regiment Germania, in August, 1941 he was awarded the Iron Cross 1st Class. From Sept., 1941 to May, 1942 he was transferred and assigned as company commander of the 15th Kradschutzen (motorcycle reconnaissance) company. In May he was again transferred and reassigned to the SS-Versorgungs (supply and service) regiment as regimental adjutant. While serving in this position, Fruhauf was informed that his brother was killed in action, he was now the only surviving son in his family.

During the spring offensive of 1942, Fruhauf was wounded during the drive towards the Caucasus oilfields on 18 Sept., 1942 and spent two months recovering in a hospital after receiving a bullet wound in the neck.

Following convalescence leave, he was assigned as commander to an SS armoured reconnaissance company training centre at Ellwangen. He served in this position from Nov., 1942 thru Sept., 1943.

Due to attrition after severe setbacks at Stalingrad and Kursk, Fruhauf, now a SS-Hauptsturmführer was reassigned to combat duty in early 1944. From Jan. thru March 1944 he served as battalion commander of the 23rd pioneer battalion SS Panzergrenadier Regiment "Nederland". On 13th March he was reassigned as battalion commander of SS Panzergrenadier Regiment "De Ruyter". Both of these units were engaged in action in the Kurland sector.

During March 1944 Fruhauf's battalion was engaged in heavy fighting at Narwa. It was during this battle that he received the Knight's Cross. While fighting in the Narwa bridgehead, the 5th companies position was overrun by assault after a heavy artillery preparation. Because the battalion reserve had been committed the situation was desperate. Fruhauf immediately assessed the situation and gathered every non essential soldier. He then led a counter-attack and successfully threw back the enemies local gain after intense hand to hand fighting. The success of the counter-attack retained key terrain and restored the former forward line of troops. The award of the Knight's Cross was announced on 4th June, 1944.

On 27th July, 1944 Fruhauf was severely wounded by a tank hi-explosive shell. He received shrapnel wounds to the right hand and knee, upper thigh, lower left leg, left side of the temple and to the chest as well as a damaged lung. He spent 4 months recovering in the field hospital in Zappot East-Prussia. On 9th November he was promoted to SS-Sturmbannführer and assigned to the 1st SS armoured reconnaissance detachment (training) at Senne-Lager near Paderborn, After the U.S. forces crossed the Rhein at Remagen in March 1945, Fruhauf fought with his unit until the closing of the Ruhr pocket and subsequent end of hostilities.

Carl Heinz Fruhauf served 11 years on active duty and rose to the rank of SS- Sturmbannführer coming up through the ranks. He fought almost entirely on the Eastern Front and won the Knight's Cross. Fruhauf died from a stroke in Hamburg in 1976.

"Das Reich" Hamburg-Langenhorn Barracks.

Fruhauf is pictured here wearing the black SS dress uniform.

Exhausted and black faced Fruhauf takes a rest during a lull in the fighting on the Eastern Front.

Fruhauf in Russia July, 1941.

Fruhauf pictured on the Eastern Front following the award of the Iron Cross 1st Class in August, 1941

Fruhauf with two fellow officers following him being awarded the Knight's Cross of the Iron Cross.

A potrait photograph of Carl Heinz Fruhauf taken in 1943.

Felix Steiner Commanding General of SS Division "Wiking" who recommended Fruhauf for the award of the Iron Cross 1st Class and later the Knight's Cross of the Iron Cross.

Nationalsozialistische Deutsche Arbeiterpartei

Gau Hamburg — Kreis 2

Ortsgruppe Weiher
205

Bankkonto: Hamburger Sparcasse von 1827, Konto Nr. 5/599
NSDAP, Gau Hamburg, Ortsgruppe Weiher
Sprechstunden: Dienstag und Freitag, 20 bis 22 Uhr
und sonst jederzeit nach Vereinbarung

Abteilung: Ortsgruppenleiter
(Bitte im Antwortschreiben angeben)

Ihr Brief:

Hamburg 30, den   9. Juni 1944.
Geschäftsstelle: Eidelstedter Weg 11
Fernsprecher: 55 70 38

                    Herrn
Wilhelm F r ü h a u f   und Frau,
H a m b u r g 19 .
=====================
Otterbeckallee 1

Im Rundfunk höre ich heute morgen, dass Ihr Sohn der SS - Haupt-
sturmführer Karl-Heinz F r ü h a u f   vom Führer mit dem
Ritterkreuz des Eisernen Kreuzes ausgezeichnet wurde.
Ich spreche Ihnen als Eltern zu dieser hohen Auszeichnung Ihres
Sohnes die allerherzlichsten Glückwünsche der Ortsgruppe
Weiher aus.
Mit Ihnen freue ich mich und bin stolz auf den ersten Ritter-
kreuzträger der Ortsgruppe Weiher.
Mögen Sie auch fernerhin recht viel Freude an Ihrem Sohn er-
leben.

                    Heil Hitler !

                    (Kern)
              Ortsgruppenleiter V.i.A.

Letter from Ortsgruppenleiter Kern of Orstgruppe Weiher. The letter is addressed to Wilhelm Fruhauf and is congratulating their son, SS-Hauptstürmfuhrer Carl-Heinz Fruhauf on his receiving the Knight's Cross.

Fernspruch - Fernschreiben - Funkspruch - Blinkspruch

Nachr.-Stelle		Nr.	Befördert				
			an	Tag	Zeit	durch	Rolle
Nachr.Kp. 54		63					
Vermerke:							

Angenommen oder aufgenommen				
von	Tag	Zeit	durch	
	11.6.	1110	H.	

Abgang	An:	Absendende Stelle
Tag:	Brig. "Nederland"	
Zeit:		
Dringlichkeits-Vermerk		Fernsprech-Anschluß:

++++ SSSS 4881   10/6/44   1645 //

/// AN DIE SS-FRW:/+ PZ GREN/+BRIGADE/+ N E D E R L A N D

UEB/+ GEN/+ KDO/+ ROEM 3//+ SS PZ/+ KORPS

// ICH BITTE DEM SS HSTUF KARL HEINZ FRUEHAUF ZUR VERLEIHUNG

DES RITTERKREUZES MEINE

HERZLICHSTEN GLUECKWUENSCHE

ZU UEBERMITTELN /+//

DER CHEF DES SS FUEHRUNGSHAUPTAMTES H /+   JUETTNER /+//++

F.d.R.d.A.

SS - Untersturmführer
und Btl. - Adjutant

Fernspruch Fernschreiben Funkspruch Blinkspruch	Nr.	Von	An	Tag	Zeit	Annehmender Offz. (Uffz.)	
						Name	Dienstgrad

C/0872

Field teletype message announcing the award of the Knight's Cross to Fruhauf. The message was released by Hans Juttner, Chief of the Waffen-SS central office.

SS-Frw.Pz.Gren.Brig."Nederland"   Brig.Gef.Std.,d.8.6.1944
      IIa

              Brigade Tagesbefehl !

      Der Führer und Oberste Befehlshaber der Wehrmacht

                    hat den

      SS-Hauptsturmführer F r ü h a u f ,
      Führer II./SS-Frw.Pz.Gren.Rgt. "De Ruyter"

                    und den

      SS-Obersturmführer S c h o l z ,
      Chef 7./SS-Frw.Pz.Gren.Rgt. "De Ruyter"

                  am 6.6.1944

                    mit dem

      Ritterkreuz des Eisernen Kreuzes

                  ausgezeichnet.

      Die Brigade beglückwünscht die Ausgezeichneten und ihre
      tapferen Männer zu dieser hohen Auszeichnung.

Brigade order of the day. Announcement of the Knight's Cross to SS-Hauptstürmführer Fruhauf and SS-Obersturmführer Scholz.

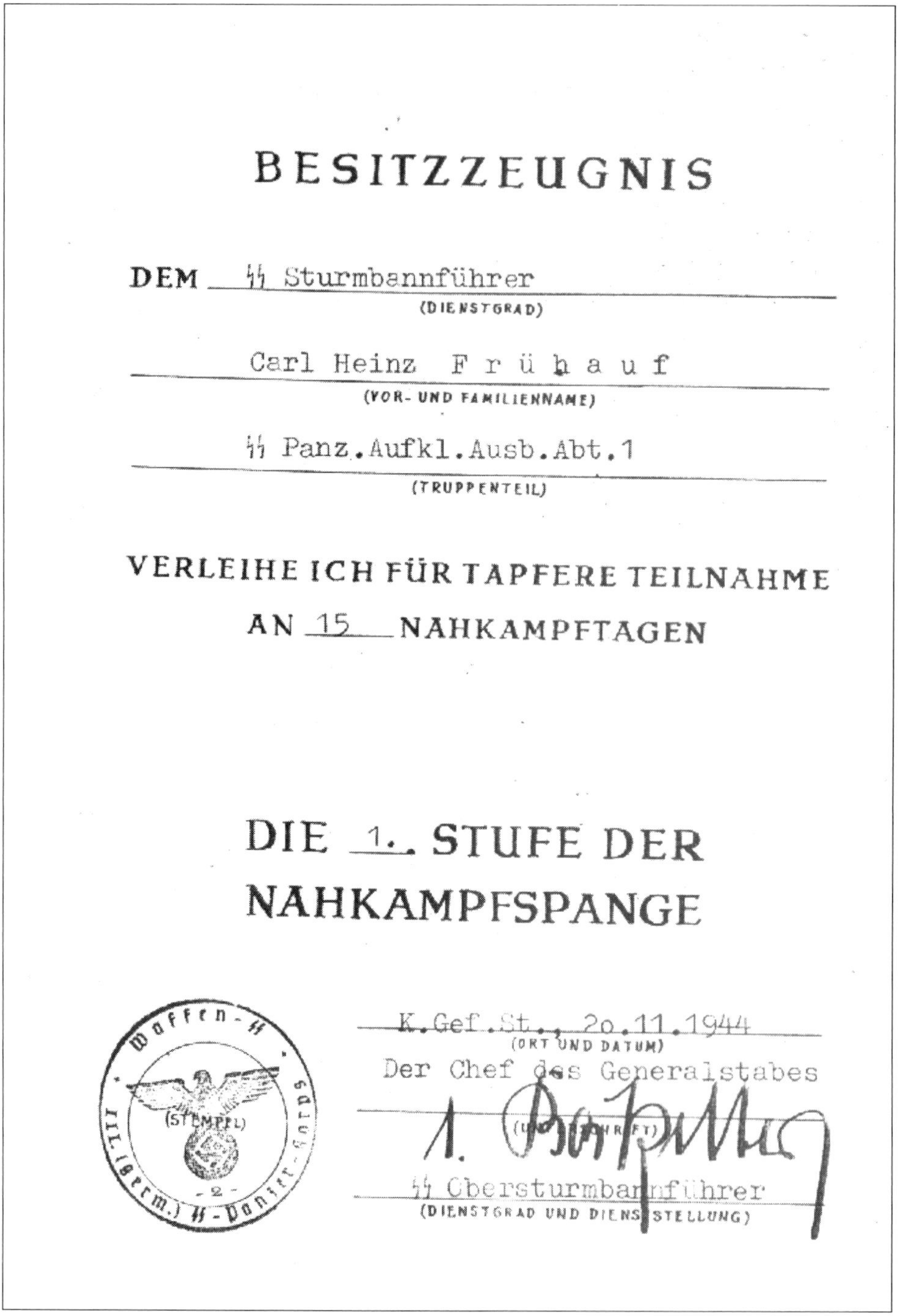

BESITZZEUGNIS

DEM ϟϟ Sturmbannführer
(DIENSTGRAD)

Carl Heinz F r ü h a u f
(VOR- UND FAMILIENNAME)

ϟϟ Panz.Aufkl.Ausb.Abt.1
(TRUPPENTEIL)

VERLEIHE ICH FÜR TAPFERE TEILNAHME
AN 15 NAHKAMPFTAGEN

DIE 1. STUFE DER
NAHKAMPFSPANGE

K.Gef.St., 20.11.1944
(ORT UND DATUM)

Der Chef des Generalstabes

(UNTERSCHRIFT)

ϟϟ Obersturmbannführer
(DIENSTGRAD UND DIENSTSTELLUNG)

Award document for the close combat clasp in bronze, awarded to Fruhauf on 20.11.44.

IM NAMEN DES FÜHRERS
UND
OBERSTEN BEFEHLSHABERS
DER WEHRMACHT
IST DEM

ᛋᛋ-Sturmbannführer

F r ü h a u f , Karl-Heinz

AM 15.September 1942

DIE MEDAILLE
WINTERSCHLACHT IM OSTEN
1941/42
(OSTMEDAILLE)

VERLIEHEN WORDEN.

FÜR DIE RICHTIGKEIT:

Award document for the East Front medal.

GEMEINDEVERWALTUNG DER HANSESTADT HAMBURG

DER LEITER DER VERWALTUNG
DES KREISES 9

Hamburg-Bergedorf, den 7.Juli 1944
Rathaus

An den
Ritterkreuzträger SS Hauptsturmführer Karl-Heinz Frühauf,
Hamburg 19
Ottersbeckallee 1

Mein lieber alter Arbeitskamerad Frühauf!

Mit großer Freude nahmen Ihre alten Arbeitskameraden der Vermessung
wie auch ich Kenntnis von der Ihnen durch den Führer verliehenen
hohen Auszeichnung. Wir alle gratulieren Ihnen von ganzem Herzen
und sind stolz auf Sie. Da ich inzwischen nach Bergedorf übergesie-
delt bin, trotzdem die Verbindung mit meinem mir seit vielen Jahren
lieb gewonnenen Vermessungsamt aufrechterhalte, wäre es mir eine
ganz besondere Freude, Sie gelegentlich eines Besuches im Berge-
dorfer Rathaus begrüssen zu können. Manch alter Ihnen bekannter
Arbeitskamerad wird dann meine Freude teilen.
Bis auf ein baldiges Wiedersehn wünsche ich Ihnen weiterhin Solda-
tenglück und begrüsse Sie mit

Heil Hitler !

Ihr

Baudirektor

Anschrift: Hamburg-Bergedorf 1, Wentorfer Straße 38. Fernsprecher: 21 38 72-77.

A letter to Fruhauf from a former RAD comrade congratulating him on
the award of the Knight's Cross.

Your ref.   My ref.   Date

Subject   Carl Heinz Fruehauf   - Personal and Military Record

Born 14/2/14, Haburg, Father:Masterbuilder, school:HH secondary school Hamburg, learned trade: Mechanical Engineer

14 yrs.:Band der Geusen(Youth League) and NS School league

18 yrs.:(1932) NSDAP and SS

1933: voluntary 8-week training with "Schwarzer Reichswehr"(Black Reichs Defence) and 2 x 4 weeks with Hamburg Police.

1934: sub-leader choice training with AW chief, Sports school Moelln, 1/4/34 to 31/3/35 sub-leader at SS Sports school Sternberg.

From 1/4⁻/35 as SS Scharfuehrer in the VT, 3rd Rgt. Germania as group leader and substitute platoon leader, from 1936 1st Rgt. Germania as Kp.Troopleader +Shooting instructor. 9/11/37 promoted to Oberscharfuehrer(group leader)

June 38 transfered to newly formated Tank Reconnaissance platoon Germania as Reconnaissance patrol leader and substitute platoon leader.(stand-in)

As such in 1939 took part in Poland campaign, awarded with EK 2

Feb.-April 1940 took part in first crash course SS Leader-School Braunschweig, followed by Army Cavalry School Krampnitz,May-July'40,Tank Reconnaissance training. 1/8/40 promoted to SS Untersturmfuehrer, posted back to Rgt. Germania, employed as O.O. (Ordinance Officer) and adjutant at II. Germania.

With formation Div. Wiking transfered to AA5 (aufklarungs Abt.) and commissioned as lower grade (aide) with the formation Tank Reconnaissance Batt. With start of Russia campaign O.O. under Div. Commander Gruf. Steiner; from Oct. 41 leader 15. Kradschtz.Kp. Germania until dissolved in May '42. Oct.41 Iron Cross 1.Thereafter in Caucasus Rgt. Adju. of the provision Rgt. Viking until wounded Sept.42.

Promoted to O.Stuf. Aug '41, to Haupt.Stuf. 9/11/42.

After hospital stay during 1943 Chief Tank Recon. Comp. in the Aufkl.Ausb.Abtlg. (Scout Training Div.) in Ellwangen. Dec. 43 posted to III. (Germ) Tank Corps. Because of initial lack of leadership put as leader of Pi.Btl. 54 on the Narwa Front. From beginning March '44 Commander of II. Rgt.49 "De Ruyter" in the Netherland Div. From March to May heavy defence battles in front sector "Lilienwald" on the bridge head Narwa, for this awarded the Knights Cross. Bestowed 6/6/44.

Your ref.   My ref.   Date

Subject

During retreat battles from Narwa brought into action as Korps. rear guard, thereafter at focus-point runway Narwa-Reval at the 'Childrens Home"Heights"'. Here on the 27/7/44 heavily wounded, transported back on last hospital ship from Reval to Gotenhafen.

Until Oct44 Mili-hospital in Zoppot, then posted as KDR. SS Tank Reconn. Training Abt. 1 in camp Senne.

9/11/44 Promoted to SS Sturmbannfuehrer.

End of March '45 in the course of all the in the Senne Camp stationed SS tank A+E Divisions and formated SS Tank brigade Westfalen opposed the American breakthrough at bridge head Remagen. Hard counter attacs about 20km south of Paderborn until total dispersing of the detachments (battalions?). Thereafter as KDR. of a mixed tank detachment (Koenigstiger, SPW etc) of the, from the west retreating 11th Army under General Floerke. Retreat battles up to the Harz, there on 18/4/45 dissolving of the Army in the area Elbingerode.

American PoW in France (Attichy, St.Avold), then internment in Heilbronn and Darmstadt.

Thereafter in building trade until de-nazification, from 1951 as salesman, from 1952 employed as sales manager in industry.

End of 1974 fallen ill as known.

A chronological biography of Carl-Heinz Fruhauf, 1914-1974.

HEINZ MACHER

Heinz Macher was one of the most accomplished fighting soldiers of the Waffen SS. His service spanned the whole of WWII from joining the SS in April, 1939 through to his capture at Bremervörde by the British in May, 1945. Although Macher rose through the ranks he subsequently achieved high rank within the SS and also was at the centre of many historic events during the course of his career, culminating in his .appointment to Himmler's personal staff with whom he was captured.

Heinz Macher served in the RAD (Reichsarbeitdienst/State Labour Service) prior to beginning his military career on April 3rd, 1939 in the Waffen SS as a combat engineer or Pioneer. He was posted to the 2nd Company of the SS Pioneer Battalion in Dresden which was close to his home in Chemnitz. Whilst at Dresden he received his basic infantry training and qualified with the K-98 rifle, P-08 pistol, MG-34 machine gun and the flamethrower. In addition to weapons training Macher also underwent training in assault tactics and bridging operations and showed an aptitude for demolitions and explosives.

Upon completing his basic training Macher's Company was involved in the Polish campaign in September, 1939 constructing a bridge across the Weichsel River spearheading the attack on Warsaw. Macher displayed outstanding leadership qualities during the Polish campaign, and following its conclusion he was selected as an officer candidate to attend the SS Junkerschule at Bad-Tolz. The leadership course at Bad-Tolz was quite lengthy lasting from October, 1939 to August, 1940. Upon successful completion of the course at Bad-Tolz he was reassigned to the SS Junkerschule at Braunsweig. During this period he was promoted on three different occasions SS Unterscharführer on the 1st of December, 1939; SS Standartenjunker (Officer Cadet) on the 1st of August, 1940; and SS Standartenoberführer (Officer) on the 19th of March, 1941.

At the end of March, 1941 Macher rejoined his old Battalion which was now the Pioneer Battalion of the 2nd SS Panzer Division "Das Reich". Within a matter of weeks of joining "Das Reich" Macher was promoted to SS Untersturmführer on the 20th of April, 1941. Upon his promotion Macher was assigned as a Platoon Leader and was very shortly to become involved in Operation Barbarossa, the invasion of Russia. His unit had been moved by rail into an assembly area north of Lubin in eastern Poland where he was attached to a reconnaissance detachment. After conducting preliminary reconnaissance around the area of the River Bug, Macher organised and executed a successful river crossing operation on the 22nd of June, 1941. This was part of the spearhead of the invasion of Russia which began in the early hours of that day.

Heinz Macher successfully led his Platoon during the first weeks of the invasion of Russia, but was wounded in August, 1941 and was hospitalised. Macher subsequently discharged himself from the Field Hospital and returned to his unit near Jelnja. He was then given command of a Punishment Detachment of troops which he led into action around Kiev. During the battle from Priluki Macher destroyed his first tank, a Russian KV-1, singlehandedly.

As part of the XXXX Panzer Corps Macher's unit saw further action at Borodina in November, 1941. During this period his unit was attached to the Tank Regiment of the 10th Panzer DIvision. Shortly after this Macher was reassigned back to the "Das Reich" Division which was involved in the drive on Moscow and became embroiled in the bloody fighting on the outskirts of the city.

After the Russian counteroffensive in the Winter of 1941 the "Das Reich" Division was forced onto the defensive. Macher's own unit formed the rearguard in his sector, and he was given personal responsibility for mining roads and houses and destroying all available bridges to cover the retreat of the remnants of "Das Reich". Throughout this period up to May, 1942 Macher led a Company formed from elements of the Pioneer Battalion which had lost most of its officers. It was during this period between August, 1941 and May, 1942 that Macher was awarded the Iron Cross 2nd Class and the Iron Cross 1st Class. Later in 1942 he also received the Eastern Front medal for the Winter Campaign of 1941-42.

Following the withdrawal of "Das Reich" Macher attended a company grade officer training course with the 9th Army before returning to "Das Reich" which was then in the process of refitting. Macher continued to serve as Platoon Leader in the Pioneer Battalion and also attended additional training courses including a pioneer officer's training course at the army pioneer School at Angers

Following these training courses Macher was redeployed on the Eastern Front as Company Commander of Pioneer Company SS Panzer Grenadier Regiment Nr. 3 "Standarte Deutschland". He participated in the defensive battles on the Oskol, and later in the offensive operations conducted by the 2nd SS Panzer Corps in and around Krasnograd and Kharkov.

During the night of the 11th-12th of March, 1943 Macher formed an assault group from his Company and conducted a daring night attack against Soviet positions on the outskirts of Kharkov. After infiltrating the Soviet lines Macher's assault detachment took the Russian defenders completely by surprise. In fierce hand to hand fighting Macher secured a substantial bridgehead within the Soviet lines and in the process killed over 90 of the Russian defenders and captured 28 in addition to substantial quantities of small arms, mortars and anti-tank weapons.

This daring attack by Macher's assault team was accomplished without the loss of any German lives and only a handful of his men suffered minor wounds. This successful assault on the Soviet lines formed a bridgehead which enabled German armoured units to pass through Macher's position and drive deep into the enemy's rear areas. In recognition of his brilliant planning and execution of this action, Heinz Macher was awarded the Knight's Cross of the Iron Cross on the 12th of April, 1943. On the same day Macher was also awarded the Close Combat clasp in bronze which he had qualified for as a consequence of the heavy hand to hand fighting at Kharkov. One week after being awarded the Knight's Cross Macher was also promoted to SS Obersturmführer on the 20th of April, 1943.

After the successful recapture of Kharkov Macher fought at Belgorod and participated in the river crossings on the Donetz. During this period Macher reconstituted his company to an assault company and consolidated all of the flamethrowers in the regiment under his command.

In June, 1943 he attended a training course and was then assigned as a Liaison Officer with the Luftwaffe attached to Stuka Squadron 77 on the Russian Front.

In July, 1943 Macher's Company was involved in Operation Citadel (the Battle for Kursk), and his was one of its first units to break through the extensive Soviet tank traps near Beresof. Despite the local success of Macher's unit, Operation Citadel was a disaster for the German Army, and his unit was withdrawn from the area to fight once again in the vicinity of Belgorod. During an attack on the town of Stepanowske he was severely wounded in the upper left arm and was evacuated to a Field Hospital near Hohenlychen. Macher was to receive no less than 12 wounds during the course of WWII; the wound he received on this occasion was severe enough for him to be awarded the Wound Badge in gold.

After convalescing Macher rejoined his unit which was still on the Eastern Front just in time to take part in the withdrawal of the "Das Reich" Division from the Eastern Front to southern France for refitting. "Das Reich" moved to France in March, 1944, and just three months later on June 6th the Allied Landings began in Normandy. The "Das Reich" Division was ordered north to Normandy and was harried along its route by members of the French Resistance which "Das Reich" reacted to by totally destroying the small French town of Oradur sur Glane and massacring almost all of its inhabitants; although there is no evidence that Heinz Macher had any involvement in the atrocities committed by elements of regiment Der Fuhrer.

It took several weeks for the "Das Reich" Division to be deployed for action near Normandy and Macher's unit was assigned a defensive sector near the town of St. Lo. Macher's Company came under almost continual aerial bombardment from the Allied tactical airforce and was subjected to continuous attacks in which Macher's Company repulsed 38 different assaults and conducted an almost equal number of counterattacks. On the 7th of August, 1944 Macher was awarded the German Cross in gold for his tenacious defence and personal bravery, and less than two weeks later on the 19th of August he was awarded the Oakleaves to the Knight's Cross making him the 554th recipient of the award. This award was for Macher's actions during the battle for Mortain where he took command of the 3rd Company of Panzer Grenadier Regiment Nr. 3.

Macher was critically wounded towards the end of the Normandy campaign, and close to death he was evacuated with the remnants of the German 7th Army as it fled through the rapidly closing Falaise Gap.

Macher recovered from his wounds which he had received in Normandy, and on the 1st of October, 1944 he was summoned to Hitler's headquarters and their received the Close Combat Clasp in gold. This award does no appear in Macher's SS Personnel File which officially ends with the award of the Oakleaves of the Knight's Cross in August, 1944.

On the 9th of November, 1944 Macher was promoted to SS-Hauptsturmführer, again this and a subsequent promotion do not appear on Macher's SS personnel file which ended with his promotion to SS-Obersturmführer on the 20th of April, 1943.

In January, 1945 SS-Hauptsturmführer Macher was assigned as a Staff Officer at Army Group Weiches which he was only attached to for a short time before being transferred to Pommerania where he was assigned to the 2nd Division under General Bleckwendt.

It was at this time that Macher began to suffer the effects of the accumulated wounds he had incurred during the course of the war. He was transferred to WASAG (Westfälisch Anhaltischen Springstoff AG) situated in Wittemberg. WASAG was a company involved in the manufacture of explosives, and Macher worked with a Dr. von Hott on research and development projects including improving the explosive content and effect of hand grenades and anti-tank mines. This involved work on a new and revolutionary form of plastic explosive, Nipolit whose explosive qualities were up to ten times more powerful than any conventional explosive then in use with the German Army. Macher was selected for this duty not only because of his wounds which severely restricted his frontline capability but also because of his background in anti-tank and demolition work as the commander of a Pioneer company.

As the war drew to a close Macher was summoned to Himmler's headquarters near Stettin on the 30th of March, 1945 whereupon Himmler personally ordered him to proceed to Wewelsburg and to destroy the Castle there. The Allied advance was getting perilously close to Wewelsburg and Himmler did not want the Castle and its contents to fall into their hands. There had been neither the time nor the means to retrieve the many artifacts stored at Wewelsburg Castle due to the speed of the Allied advance. Consequently Macher was ordered to destroy the Castle along with its contents.

To carry out this mission for Himmler, Macher chose a detachment of 15 combat engineers to accompany him to Wewelsburg. On arriving at the Castle Macher and his team planted explosives and incendiary devices in and around the Castle as well as the adjacent headquarters building: all of which were blown up and extensively damaged although not completely destroyed.

Upon completing this mission Macher returned to Himmler's headquarters where he was immediately promoted to Stürmbannführer by Himmler personally. This promotion like the previous one was not documented in Macher's SS Personnel File.

Heinz Macher remained as a part of Himmler's headquarters staff for the last few weeks of the war: finally moving to Himmler's Field Command Post at Flensburg in Northern Germany.

The final and most bizarre chapter of Heinz Macher's amazing wartime career culminated in his capture by the British in May, 1945 when along with SS Obersturmbannführer Werner Grothman, Macher was accompanying Heinrich Himmler who was then disguised as an Army Sergeant. They must have been a strange looking trio, with two SS Officers, Macher and Grothman, acting as aides (to an Army Sergeant) - which surprisingly did not raise any suspicions with their British captors who were not aware of Himmler's true identity, and who remained ignorant of the fact that they had captured the head of the SS. When it finally dawned on them who they had captured, Himmler committed suicide during interrogation.

The career of Heinz Macher and his fortuitous appearance at several significant points during and at the end of WWII are all the more amazing when one realises that he joined the SS in 1939 at the age of 19 as an ordinary SS-Mann, rose through the ranks to become a Stürmbannführer whilst along the way accumulating virtually every high award Germany could bestow upon a soldier, and finally ended the war at Himmler's side still only aged 25. Heinz Macher is alive today and resides with his family in Germany.

A Studio portrait photograph of Hauptsturmführer Heinz Macher. He is wearing on his tunic the following awards: **Knight's Cross of the Iron Cross with Oakleaves, German Cross in Gold, Close Combat Clasp in Gold, Iron Cross 1st Class,** and **Silver Wound Badge.** On his right upper sleeve Macher also has the **Tank Destruction Award.**

Macher in his Staff Car shortly after suffering a wound in combat to his left arm, Normandy 1944.

Macher with family and friends while on convalescence leave recovering from wounds received during the Normandy campaign.

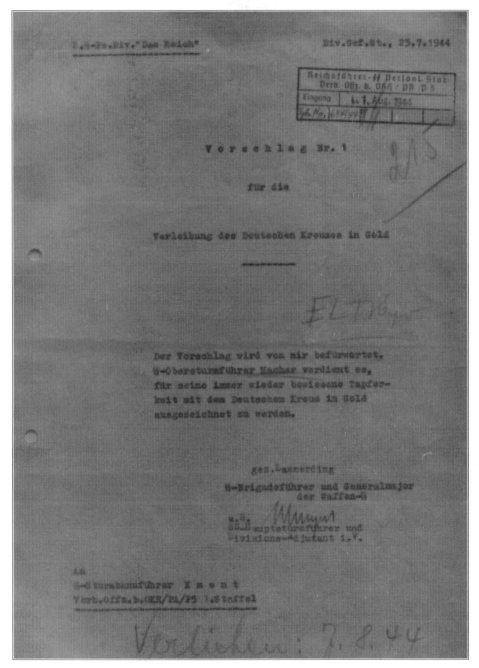

An endorsement for the German Cross in Gold to SS-Obersturmführer Heinz Macher. He was nominated for this bravery award on 23rd of July 1944 whilst in action in Normandy serving with 2nd SS-Panzer Division "Das Reich". The stamp at the top righthand of the document indicates that the award has been approved by Reichsführer-SS on 1st of August 1944. At the foot of the page is the typed approval of the OKH (Army High Command) with a pencilled award date of 7th of August 1944.

IDEOLOGICAL & PROPAGANDA PUBLICATIONS

A veritable mountain of ideological literature was produced during the tenure of the Third Reich 1933-1945. The consistent theme of all this literature was directed towards illustrating the superiority of the Germanic Aryan Race compared to foreign ethnic groups such as Slavs, Negroes, Orientals and especially Jews. To this end the SS-Mann was frequently portrayed as an exemplary specimen to the superior Aryan Being.

The following pages document only a tiny sample of the ideological material which was published at the instigation of the Nazi Party in this era. Generally the propaganda fell into three distinct categories:
1. **the undisguised, blatantly racist;**
2. **the pseudo-scientific,**
3. **the subtle type which led the reader to draw their own but inevitable conclusion.**

Within these three categories there were numerous subdivisions which sought to appeal to a specific social group or class. Also there were publications which used this material as a means of recruiting members to a specific organisation such as the SS. When studying the subject of Nazi ideological publications it becomes evident that the content became more blatant and vociferous with each passing year.

A further sinister aspect of the publication of much of this material was that ultimately it became self-fulfiling. The early examples of anti-Jewish literature eventually became so refined that exterminating the race would seem a natural progression.

The pseudo-scientific approach to ideological propaganda was used most detrimentally against those mentally and physically disabled, the "Sub-normal" members of society classed as "Untermensch" (Subhumans), not only in Germany but also later in Occupied Territories. By the use of graphs and projections these Pseudo-scientific publications grouped together photographs of "Untermensch" along with demographic charts to illustrate that if this class of people were not kept in check they would soon outnumber Aryan stock and ultimately pollute the world.

The SS featured quite prominently in most of this type of material. Members of the SS were regularly portrayed as the ultimate Aryan Being in terms of: racial purity, Aryan characteristics, fitness and beauty and were held up as a paragon model for all Germans to emulate.

The theme of the ideal German mother and child was also used extensively throughout this type of publication and was inevitably used to draw comparisons between the German mother and less favoured ethnic groups. Another reason for portraying the ideal German wife and mother was to reinforce the theme of racial purity: whereby the pure Aryan blood should not be polluted through interacial marriage and procreation.

A great deal of time and expense was expended on trying to establish the Germans descent from ancient Nordic cultures. To this end numerous archeological expeditions were financed, not only in Germany but worldwide. Innumerable article were published during the 1930's often by quite reputable scientists and archeologists propounding the ascent of the Aryan Race from its ancient origins to the pinnacle of National Socialist Germany. A much documented subject, principally financed by the Reichsführer-SS Heinrich Himmler, was the Externsteine (the German equivalent of Stonehenge), which was an ancient Saxon archeological site near modern day Paderborn, Germany which ultimately became enshrined in SS mythology.

Much of what was written during the Third Reich, and even contained in Hitler's MEINE KAMPF, was by no means new or revolutionary ideology: a great deal of the substance of the ideological concepts of the Third Reich had been borrowed from much earlier writings dating back to the 19th Century when Charles Darwin (1809-1882) published his ORIGIN OF SPECIES (1858) with its main theme of natural selection in Nature and the concept of the survival of the fittest, followed by a later book DESCENT OF MAN (1871) which contained the same evolutionary principles but applied to human origins. This fuelled other writers and philosophers such as the German philosopher Friedrich Nietzsche (1844-1900) who expounded the theory of the racial "Superman". Later in the 19th Century an English anti-Semitic writer, Houston Stewart Chamberlain (1855-1927), who became a naturalised German citizen in 1916 and married Wagner's daughter Eva, also wrote at length about the superiority of the Nordic Race, principally in his book DIE GRUNDLAGEN DES NEUNZEHNTEN JAHRHUNDERTS/THE MYTH OF THE 19TH CENTURY (1899) which profoundly influenced many people in the early part of the 20th Century including Adolf Hitler and was extensively drawn upon in formulating Nazi ideology. Indeed many other prominent writers including Cecil Rhodes (1853-1902), the English explorer and conqueror of much of Africa, wrote at the beginning of this century that he believed the world would ultimately by ruled by the Nordic Anglo-Saxon peoples of America, Britain and Germany. The significant difference between these earlier outbursts of racial superiority and Nazi ideology was that for the first time in1933 a whole State adopted what had previously merely been a philosophical theory as a cornerstone of State Policy which would ultimately have its effect on most of the civilised world.

Seht Euch die Menschen an ...!

So sieht eine deutsche Mutter aus — so eine artfremde.

Es ist nicht alles gleich, was Menschenantlitz trägt! Deshalb wählen wir unsere Frauen, die Mütter unserer Kinder, nach unseren strengen nationalsozialistischen Auslesegrundsätzen!

Herausgeber O.T.-Schulungsdienst, Sonderführer Curt Hetzer, Berlin-Charl 13, Avus Nordschleife
Für den Inhalt verantwortlich: Kreisleiter Franz Buchner, Starnberg/Oby.
Photo : Angelika v. Braun

März 1942

Blatt 136

Seht Euch die Menschen an ... !

Wer wird nicht beim Anblick dieser Gesichter empfinden, was wir mit germanisch-deutschen Menschen meinen. Sie sind Ausdruck unserer Seele.

Herausgeber O.T.-Schulungsdienst, Sonderführer Curt Hetzer, Berlin-Chorl.13, Avus Nordschleife
Für den Inhalt verantwortlich: Kreisleiter Franz Buchner, Starnberg/Oby.
Photo: Bild-Archiv des Reichsnährstandes

Februar 1942   Blatt 127

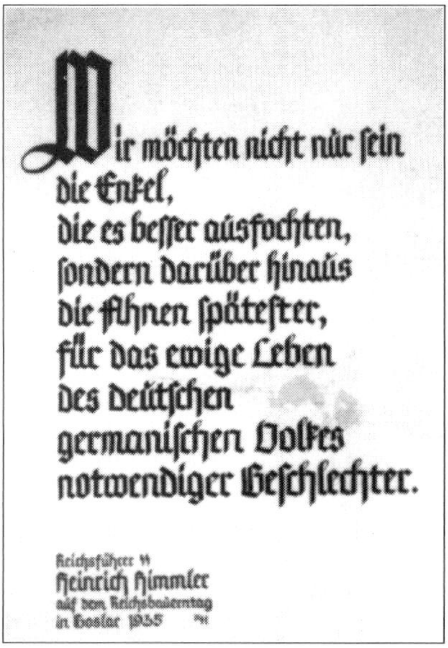
Wir möchten nicht nur sein
die Enkel,
die es besser ausfochten,
sondern darüber hinaus
die Ahnen spätester,
für das ewige Leben
des deutschen
germanischen Volkes
notwendiger Geschlechter.

Reichsführer SS
Heinrich Himmler
auf dem Reichsbauerntag
in Goslar 1935

Inside backcover - sieg des weffen sieg des kinds.

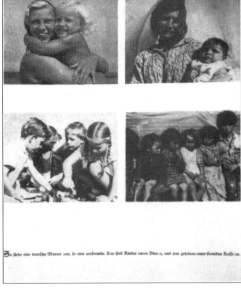

ob Landwerker, ob dieses holländische Käsermädchen ob
jenes normegische Bauernpaar oder Fischer der Nordseeküste — bei al
der gleiche Ausdruck germanisch deutschen Wesens.

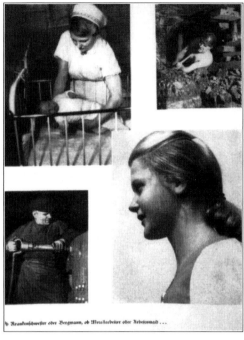

ob Krankenschwester oder Bergmann, ob Metallarbeiter oder Arbeitsmaid ...

De Erkenntnis, daß das nordische Blut das im Volkskörper überwiegende, das Gesicht
des Volkes prägende, den Volkscharakter bestimmende und die Herzen verbindende ist, sie
beweist Allgemeinart des Volkes.
Überall, an der See und in den Bergen, am Rhein, der Donau und der Memel, in allen
Gauen des Reiches ...

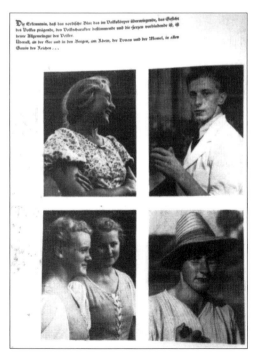

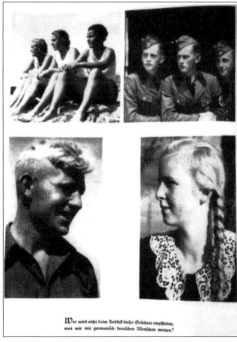

Wer wird nicht beim Anblick dieser Gesichter empfinden,
was wir mit germanisch-deutschen Menschen meinen?

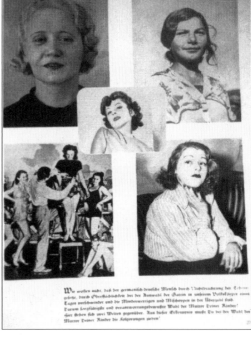

und in allen germanischen Ländern — sie prägen es diese Völker vom deßkindern, Norwegern, Dänen und Schweden — reist von diesen nordisch bestimmten, germanisch-deutsch Mensch entgegen.

(Holländer Oldenburg — Norwegerin und Dänin von der Hamburger RfA Lagerung Schwede Larßen.)

Wir wissen um die Reinheit des Blutes und sind stolz darauf . . .

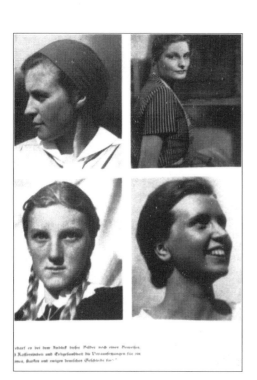

sharf es bei dem Anblick dieser Völker nach einem Menschen. 3 Rassereinheit und Erbgesundheit die Voraussetzungen für ein imes, starkes und einiges deutsches Geschlecht sin

SS RECRUITING PAMPHLET

The type of recruiting pamphlet illustrated here was circulated widely throughout Germany and the Occupied Countries and was produced in all the major European languages in order to attract foreign volunteers for the Waffen-SS. The pamphlet contains information about the structure of the Waffen-SS, and on the inside cover gives the criteria required for any prospective volunteer. The pamphlet also carries numerous pictures of the Waffen-SS in action.

Front cover of the Waffen-SS recruiting pamphlet.

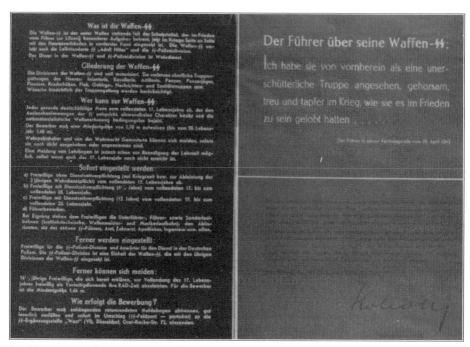

Inside cover of the Waffen-SS recruiting pamphlet.

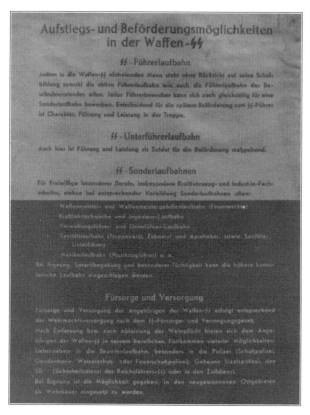

Title page of the Waffen-SS recruiting pamphlet.

Centre pages showing the Waffen-SS in action.

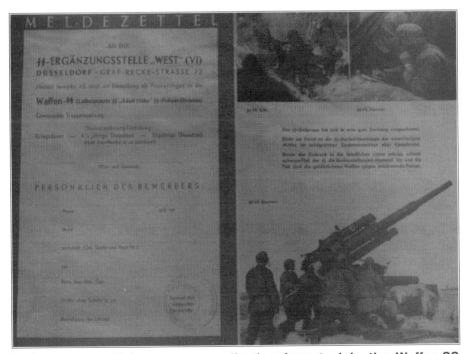

Inside pages which carry an application form to join the Waffen-SS specifically the Leibstandarte SS "Adolf Hitler" or SS-Polizei Division. The application form has actually had an SS validation stamp applied to it.

PROPAGANDA ITEMS

Wartime recruiting poster for the Waffen-SS. The poster invites volunteers over the age of 17 to enlist.

Wartime Waffen-SS recruiting poster urging men to join the organisation.

Front cover of the SS' own newspaper "Das Schwarze Korps"/"The Black Corps". This issue from January, 1943 has the headline "Sie haben nichts gelernt!"/"You have learned nothing". The Front page also carries a gruesome cartoon of a Mongoloid Russian straddling a European City with a small figure of Franklin D. Roosevelt propped up on a walking stick and saying "Ich bringe euch die Freiheit!"/"I bring you freedom". This kind of comment was typical of the paper which consistently pursued the theme of communist domination of Europe.

Another page from "Das Schwarze Korps" with the headline "Fur die Waffen-SS"/"For the Waffen-SS". This section of the newspaper has news about the Waffen-SS in the Frontline, and in the top right hand corner carries a photograph of Herman Fegelein with a report about his award of the Oakleaves to the Knight's Cross for action on the Eastern Front whilst commanding SS Cavalry Division "Florian Geyer".

Another page from the January, 1943 edition of "Das Schwarze Korps" which has several photographs of the Waffen-SS in action on the Eastern Front and a short article extolling their many exploits.

SS LIEDERBUCH
(SS Songbook)

The following is a selection of pages from the "SS Leiderbuch" (SS Songbook). The songbook was published by the NSDAP Central Publishing Office in Munich. This type of material was not strictly an issue item, but was more of a personal article intended as a comfort for the SS-Mann. Also illustrated is a copy of an SS Diary which was also an optional purchase item: it carried a portrait photo of Heinrich Himmler on the inside cover. The books could be purchased at the soldier's main installation or in the rest areas. These and other associated items were all part of building esprit de corps and strengthening morale.

Front cover of the SS Songbook.

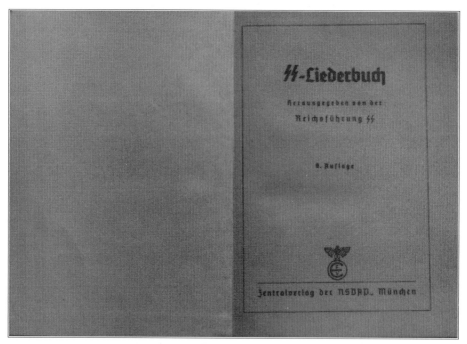

Title page of the SS Songbook.

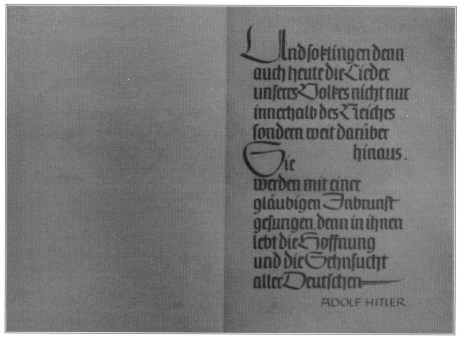

Dedication page of the SS songbook containing a greeting from Adolf Hitler in Gothic script.

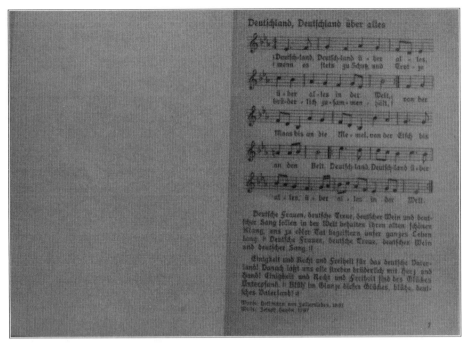

Songsheet from the SS songbook with the music and words of "Deutschland, uber alles".

Inside page of the SS Songbook with a picture of the SS Honour ring and a modified form of the SS motto "Unsere Ehre heisst Treue" (Our Honour is Loyalty).

Inside cover of the SS Diary bearing a photograph of Heinrich Himmler along with a patriotic message.

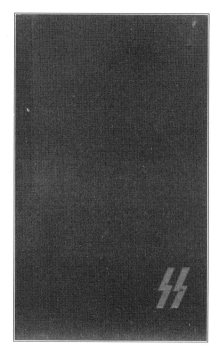

Front cover of an SS Diary.

NOMINATION & AWARD
DOCUMENTS

Any award for bravery such as the German Cross in Gold or the Knight's Cross required a nomination document explaining in detail the circumstances and actions under which an individual had performed deeds of valour meriting the award of the particular decoration.

A detailed narrative was prepared by an officer who witnessed or was involved in the action for which the award was proposed. This nomination document was then passed up through the chain of command for approval by higher authority.

The first part of the nomination document was a standard format giving personal details of the individual, followed by the action narrative. Service distinctions and prior awards to the nominee were also recorded in the initial sections of the nomination. In the case of Nomination for the German Cross in Gold one question asks if the nominee had been previously recommended for award of the Knights Cross. The purpose of this question was to ascertain if the nominee was being recommended for the German Cross in Gold as a "consolidation award" after being rejected for the award of the Knights Cross. Should the answer to this particular question be yes then the award of the German Cross in Gold would usually be rejected as this decoration could only be awarded by specific nomination and not as a "runner up prize" for the Knights Cross.

This particular nomination document was prepared by the Regimental Commander of SS-Tank Regiment "Das Reich" for SS-Oberscharführer Matthias Thurner and was submitted on 26/7/1943. At the time of his nomination for the German Cross in Gold Matthias Thurner was serving as a platoon sergeant in the anti-tank detachment of SS Panzer Division "Das Reich."

The first portion of this nomination records Thurners personal details, then carries on to recount in great detail the circumstances surrounding Thurners actions which gave rise to him being recommended for this high gallantry award.

(NOMINATION DOCUMENT FOR THE GERMAN CROSS IN GOLD)

The front page of this document bears the bold heading **Nomination Nr. 1** and is subheaded "for the awarding of the German Cross in Gold". At the foot of the document is the date 24.7.1943, and it is signed by a SS Hauptsturmfuhrer. The document is addressed to O.K.H./Pz.1.Staffel V. (German Army High Command).

SURNAME	FORENAME	BIRTHPLACE	DATE	RANK	DUTIES
Thurner	Matthias	Flachau	3.1.1916	SS-Oscha Plt. Ldr. active	antitank section "Das Reich"
Home Address: Erding, Upper Bavaria					

Service Distinctions	-Has he been mentioned in the Honour Roll of the German Army?	-Has he had been mentioned in dispatches of Army High Command?	-Military Service since 1939
Iron Cross II 5.7.40 Inf. Assault 20.4.42 Est. Fnt.Mdl 1.9.42 Iron Cross I 31.9.41 Wound Badge 20.1.42			
Tank Assault Badge no date Anschluss and Sudetenland Medal no date	NO	NO	Tank driver since 1.10.39 Plt. Ldr. since 25.2.43

Has there been a previous recommendation for the award of Knight's Cross?   NO.

Fathers profession: Forestry worker

1.) The Kradschtz. battalion was deployed for defence in the Jelnja salient in the area of Ushakowa.

SS-Oscha Thurner was positioned on the right flank of the Kradschtz. battalion defending the right flank with his 3.7cm. antitank section. At dawn on 24.7.43 the enemy attacked the village of Ushakowa in regimental strength following a heavy artillery barrage. Thurner, disregarding his own safety and showing prudent leadership, managed to halt the enemy attack inflicting great losses. After 3 hours of heavy fighting, the enemy withdrew.

2.) During the advance of the regiment SS "D" via Rusa to Istra

SS Oscha Thurner was deployed to defend the flanks with one 5cm (mot.z.) antitank gun and one 3.7 cm (mot.z.) antitank gun attached to the 3rd "D" Company, SS regiment Deutschland.

On the heights of Staraja the enemy attacked in battalion strength the right flank of regiment SS "D" with tanks and infantry.

Thurner, fighting in front of his own infantry with his 2 antitank guns, immobilised 3 "T 34" tanks and forced the others to withdraw. The enemy infantry, who had advanced to within 200m of friendly positions were repulsed after Thurner inflicted heavy losses on them using high explosive ammunition in his antitank guns.

3.) On 6.4.43 the enemy, at divisional strength moved to an area Northeast and Northwest of Nowaja-Wodolage.

SS Regiment "Deutschland" deployed on the right of the Division (SS Div Das Reich) had orders to reach Msha-sector and defend the bridgehead. SS Oscha. Thurner was attached to SS Regiment Deutschland with his 7.5cm (Mot.z) antitank platoon.

While SS Regiment "D" was in a forward assembly area. A formation of enemy tanks attacked their position. Thurner quickly engaged his section and gave pursuit destroying 3 T-34s and 2 "Mark II" tanks. He also successfully fought enemy infantry positions using High-explosive ammunition, during an attack by SS Regiment "D".

4.) During a counter attack against the Russian tank assault NW. of Gr. Lutschki within the group of Reitzenstein, SS-Oscha Thurner was ordered to deploy his antitank platoon, take over the lead and open fire from a depression onto enemy tanks north of the hill.

Thurner manouvered his tanks into the safety of the depression and at maximum effective range they managed to destroy 8 "T34" tanks within a matter of a few minutes. Thurner himself destroyed 5.

Thurner showed outstanding personal bravery and excellent leadership.

5.) On 8.7.43 the SS antitank section "Das Reich" went into action via Gressnoje-Kotschetowka against the 11th Russian Armoured Division, leaving their damaged and immobilised tanks under the command of SS-Oscha Thurner in the village of Kalinin.

At 10:30 the enemy attacked the village, (where supply units of the division were stationed), with 4 "T34" and 2 "Churchill" tanks supported by infantry.

Thurner had 2 Mark IV tanks, one with a defective fire control system, and one with a defective engine. First he gave orders to detach the machine gun and engage the enemy.

As the enemy tanks rolled into the centre of the village, Thurner manouvered the tank with the defective engine backwards and opened fire on the enemy.

Through this brave and decisive action one Churchill tank was destroyed, and the other tanks were forced to retreat. The enemy infantry was halted and denied access to the village as a result of the suppressive fire of the dismounted machine gun.

SS Obergruppenführer Hausser and SS Gruppenführer Krueger were both witnesses to this engagement.

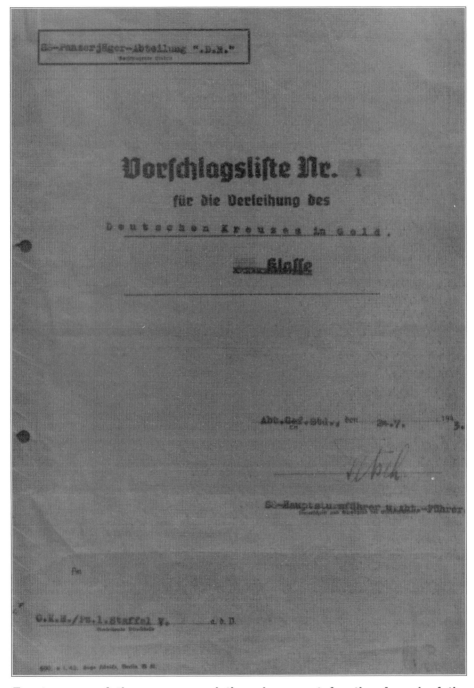

Front cover of the recommendation document for the Award of the German Cross in Gold to Matteus Thurner.

lfd. Nr.	Zuname	Vorname (Rufname)	Geburts- Ort	Geburts- Tag	Dienstgrad Dienstverh.	Truppenteil Dienststelle, Heimatanschrif
1	Thurner	Matthias,	Flachau	3.1.1916	SS-Oscha. Zugführer aktiv.	SS-Pz.Jg.Abt. "Das Reich". Erding/Obb. Krankenhausstr 13.

Näher verliehene Kriegsauszeichnungen mit Angabe der Verl.-Dakumi	Bereits genannt in Ehrenblatt des Deutschen Heeres?	Anerkennungsschreiben des O.K.M. erhalten?	Bisherige Kriegs- verwendung seit 1939?
E.K.2.Kl. 5.7.1940, Sturmabz. 20.4.1942, Ostmed.: 1.9.1942, E.K.1.Kl.:18.9.1941, Verw.Abz.:20.1.1942, Sd.Abz.f.d.Nieder- kämpfen v.Pz.Kw. Osterr.-Ung.und JKK.Med.	n e i n	n e i n	Seit 1.10.39 Geschützführer, seit 25.2.43 Zugführer.
	Hat bereits ein Vorschlag zur Verleihung des Ritterkreuzes vorgelegen?		
	n e i n		

Beruf des Vaters: Forstarbeiter.

1.) Das Kradschtz.-Btl. war im Seinja-Bogen im Raum von Ushakowa zur Ver-
teidigung eingesetzt.
SS-Oscha. Thurner mit seiner 3,7 cm Pak am rechten Flügel des K.-Btl.
eingesetzt, hatte den Auftrag, die rechte Flanke zu sichern.
Im Morgengrauen des 24.7.43 griff der Feind nach vorhergegangenem starken
Art.-Feuer in Rgt.-Stärke den Ort Ushakowa an .
Thurner mit seiner 3,7 cm Pak gelang es durch sein persönliches Draufgänge-
tum und umsichtige Führung den fdl. Angriff am rechten Flügel des K.-Btl.
zum Halten zu bringen und dem Feind starke Verluste beizufügen,
sodass sich der Feind nach 3 stündigem Feuerkampf wieder geschlagen zurück-
ziehen musste.

2.) Beim Angriff des Rgts.SS-"D" über Rusa nach Istra wurde SS-Oscha.Thurner
mit 1 Pak 5 cm (mot.Z.) und 1 Pak 3,7 cm (mot.Z.) der 3./SS-"D" zum
Flankenschutz zugeteilt.
In Höhe von Staraja griff der Feind mit Panzern und Infanterie in Btl.-
stärke die rechte Flanke des Rgt.SS-"D" an.
T. mit seine 2 Pzjg.-Kanonen vor der eigenen Inf. kämpfend, nahm zunächst
den Kampf gegen die fdl. Panzer auf, schoss dabei 3 "T34" ab und zwang
die restlichen Panzer zum Abdrehen.
Die inzwischen auf 200 m herangekommene fdl. Infanterie konnte erst
dann in Verein mit dem 3./SS-"D" abgeschlagen werden, als Thurner mit
seinen beiden Pak-Geschützen durch Sprenggranatenbeschuss dem Feind
schwerste Verluste beibrachte.

3.) Am 6.3.1943 setzte sich der Feind in Stärke einer Division mit Teilen
planmässig aus Nowaja-Todolaga in dem Raum nordostwärts und nordwestlich
ab. SS-"D" an der rechten Flanke der Division eingesetzt, hatte den
Auftrag, den Msha-Abschnitt zu erreichen und sich in den Besitz des
Brückenkopfes zu setzen.
SS-Oscha. Thurner mit seinem Pakzug 7,5 cm (mot.Z.)wurde zum Panzerschutz
dem SS-Rgt."D" unterstellt.
Schon die Bereitstellung des Rgts."SS-"D" wurde durch fdl. Panzer gestört
die Thurner mit seinen 7,5 cm Kanonen bis kurz vor die fdl. Inf.-Stellunge
verfolgte und dabei 3 "T34" und 2 "Mark II" abschoss.

Kurze Begründung und Stellungnahme des Zwischenvorgesetzten

auch während dem Angriff des Rgts. SS-"D" bekämpfte Thurner durch Sprenggranatenbeschuss wirksam fdl. Inf.-Stellungen.

Beim Gegenstoss gegen den russ. Panzerangriff Nw. Gr. Lebocki im Rahmen der gep. Gruppe von Reitzenstein hatte SS-Oscha. Thurner mit seinem mittl. Panzerzug den Befehl, an Tigerkp. angelehnt, als Spitzenzug vorzurollen und Feuerüberfall auf rollenden fdl. Panzerangriff nördlich der Höhe aus der Mulde zu eröffnen.
T., der durch Funkbefehle seine Panzer im Schutz der Mulde geschickt in gute Schussentfernungen brachte, konnte innerhalb weniger Minuten mit dem Zug 8 Panzer "T34",
mit eigenem Panzer 5 "T34" vernichten.
Bei diesem Panzerkampf hat Thurner wiederum überragende persönliche Tapferkeit und geschickte Führungsgabe gezeigt.

Am 8.7.1943 rollte die SS-Pz.Jg.Abt."L.R."unter Zurückbelassung nicht-einsatzbereiter Panzer unter Führung von SS-Oscha. Thurner in den Ort Kalinin, zum Angriff über Grossmoje-Kotschetowka gegen Vormarschstr. de
ll.rn.Div.-
Gegen 10.30 Uhr griff der Feind den von Trosseinheiten der Division besetzten Ort Kalinin mit 4 "T34" und
2 Churchill
mit aufgesessener Infanterie an.
T., der mit 2 Panzer IV, davon einer mit Kanonenschaden, der andere infolge Getriebeschaden im Ort zurückblieb, gab zu Boust den Befehl, die MG. mann bauen und die fdl. Infanterie zu bekämpfen.
die fdl. Panzer rollten als nur Ortsmitte vor, diese Gelegenheit wahrnehmend, liess T. den infolge Getriebeschaden nur rückwärts fahrenden Panzer IV so aus der Deckung fahren, dass er das Feuer gegen die fdl. Panzer eröffnen konnte.
Durch die persönliche Tapferkeit und das entschlossene Handeln Thurner wurde 1 Panzer "Churchill" abgeschossen, die restlichen Panzer zum Abdrehen gezwungen und die fdl. Inf. dem Ort ferngehalten.

SS-Obergruppenführer Hausser und SS-Gruppenführer Krüger waren Zeuge dieses Feuerkampfes.

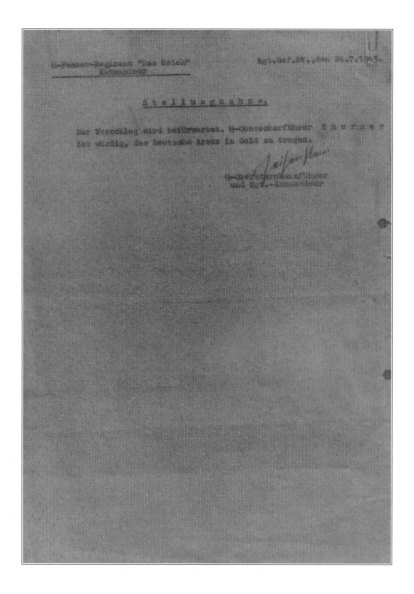

SS-Panzer Regiment "Das Reich"
Commander

26.7.1943

COMMENTS

I support this nomination. SS Oberscharführer Thurner is worthy to be a bearer of the German Cross in Gold.

SS-Obersturmbannführer
and Regiment Commander

GERMAN CROSS
IN GOLD

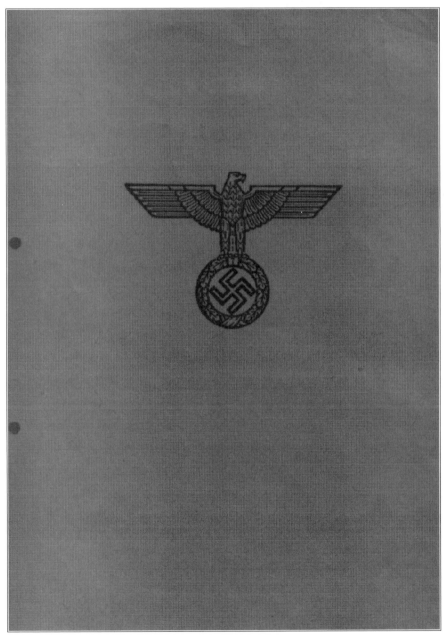

Front cover of the folder in which the official announcements for the Awards of the German Cross were sent to the relevant units.

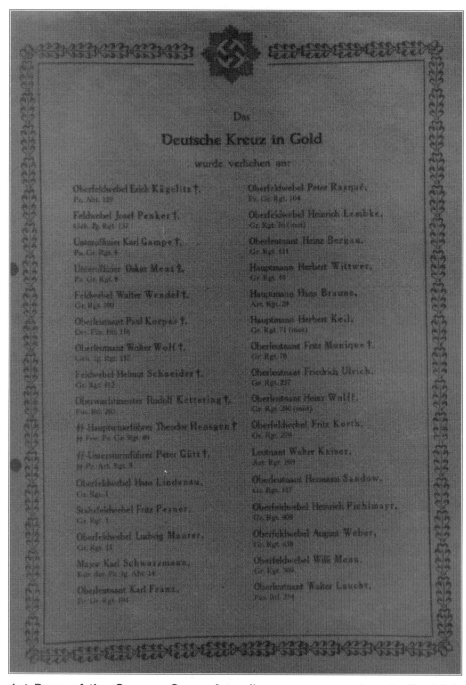

1st Page of the German Cross Award's announcement: note the high percentage of Awards to the Waffen-SS on both sheets of this announcement, disproportionate to their actual numbers in the Wehrmacht.

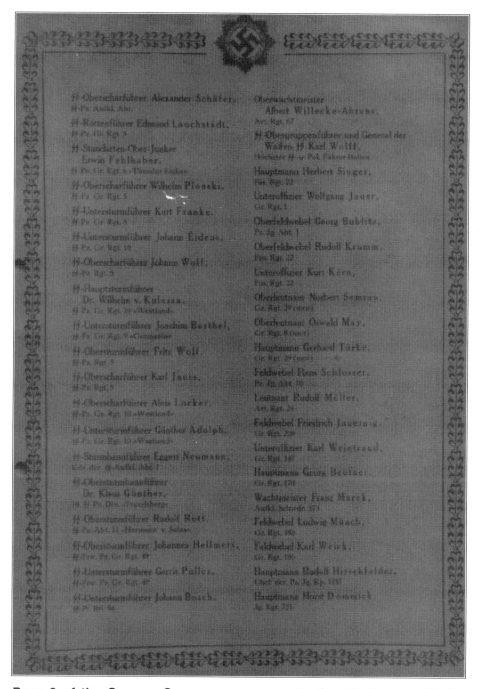

Page 2 of the German Cross announcement: of particular note is the name of SS-Obergruppenführer Karl Wolff whose name appears as the 2nd entry in column 2.

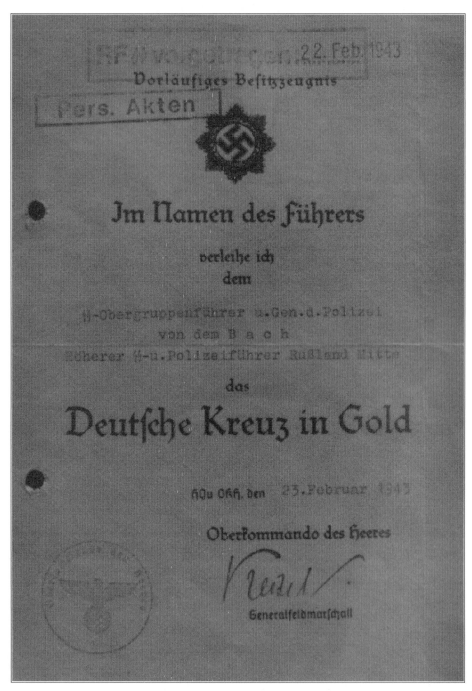

Award document for the German Cross in Gold to SS-Obergruppenführer von dem Bach-Zelewski. The Award is dated the 23rd of February, 1943. The top of the Award document carries an endorsement from the Reichsführer-SS authorising the Award, dated the 22nd of February 1943.

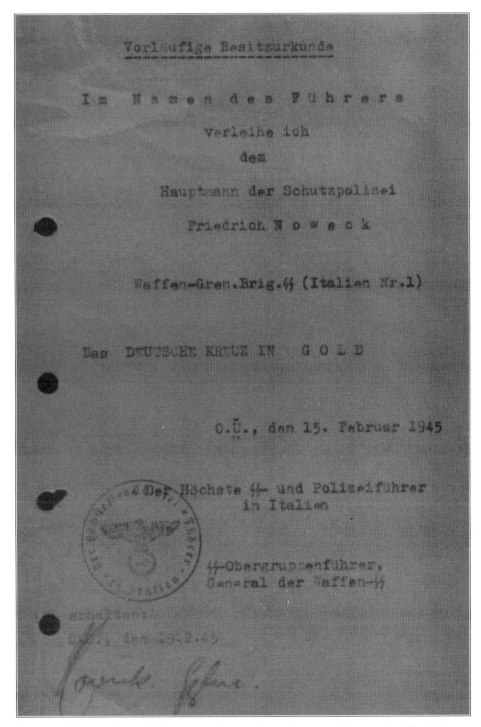

A **provisional Award document for the German Cross in Gold** to a member of the Italian Waffen-SS Grenadier Brigade (Italien Nr. 1). The date of the Award is the 15th of February, 1945.

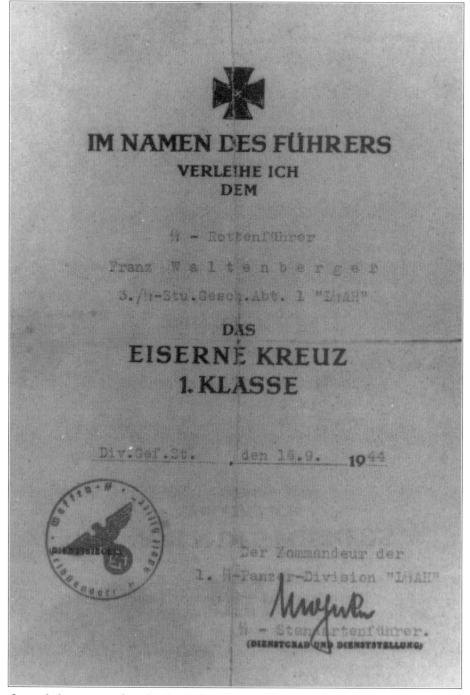

Award document for the Iron Cross 1st Class to SS-Rottenführer Franz Waltenburger, who served with the 3rd SS Assault Gun detachment of SS-Panzer-Division "LSSAH". The document is signed by SS-Standartenführer Wilhelm Muhnke.

Photograph of SS-Standartenführer (later General) Willhelm Muhnke awarding the Iron Cross 2nd Class to members of the Waffen-SS during the Normandy Campaign in July, 1944.

SS-FALLSCHIRMJAGER BATTALION 500/600

A parachute unit composed of volunteers from the SS was first put forward as an idea as early as 1936 following the creation of the Luftwaffe's first parachute regiment. In 1937 a number of volunteers from the SS-Standarte "Germania" were selected to undergo a specialist parachute training at the Luftwaffe's training school at Stendal. The SS volunteers successfully completed their training and also took part in demonstration jumps for members of the High Command. Initially these SS volunteer parachute troops were attached to the Fallschirm Regiment "Herman Goering".

The feasibility of forming an SS parachute unit failed to find any favour in Germany until 1943. This was due to the large number of Luftwaffe paratroop regiments already in existence and their excellent war record thus far in World War II. However following the audacious and successful commando raid to rescue Benito Mussolini carried out by Otto Skorzeny in 1943, the whole subject of a specialist SS airborne unit was once again revived.

In late 1943 a new SS unit, SS-Fallschirm Battalion 500, was formed and was constituted from 50% volunteers from Waffen-SS units and 50% from SS penal battalions, This latter group of men was designated as "B-Soldaten" (Probationary Troops) who were serving sentences in SS penal battalions for disciplinary rather than criminal offences. If they subsequently proved themselves in combat they could earn back their former ranks and privileges.

The unit was brought together at its new homebase at Neustrelitz and was then sent to Matarushka-Banja near Kralijevo in eastern Yugoslavia for parachute training from Luftwaffe instructors. The unit was by now almost 1,000 strong and was under command of SS-Sturmbannführer Gillhofer. During its training SS-500 had to contend with a constant struggle for valuable resources especially aircraft from which to carry out jumps and also for towing gliders. For these roles they normally used the old but reliable Ju-52 and the antiquated and not so reliable Italian Savoia Machette.

Upon completion of their training in early 1944 SS-500 Battalion was deployed to fight Yugoslavian partisans, a task which they performed quite competently earning the respect of other SS and Army units with which they served. At this time SS-500 was commanded by

SS-Haupstürmführer Rybka. In May, 1944 a plan was formulated code named Operation "Roesselsprung" to kidnap the Yugoslav partisan leader, Josef Broz Tito, at his fortress headquarters near Drvar in northwestern Yugoslavia. Tito's headquarters were regarded as impregnable because of its isolated location and also because it was guarded by more than 6,000 seasoned partisans. Capturing Tito by a coup de main would have been an enormous blow to the morale of Yugoslav partisans and could have proven crucial to the outcome of the bitter struggle being waged between the Wehrmacht and the partisans. Also there were at Tito's headquarters at Drvar a considerable number of delegates from the various Allied forces acting as representatives of their various governments and also providing military and logistic support for Tito. As an additional flourish to Operation Rosselsprung the attack was to be carried out on Tito's birthday - May, 25th, 1944.

At dawn on May 25th, 1944 SS-Fallschirmjager Battalion 500 along with members of the German Army's elite Brandenburg Division began the assault on Drvar. 654 men of SS-500 were dropped in the first wave: 314 by parachute and 340 by glider.The ensuing battle at Drvar developed into one of the most bloody conflicts of the war (even judged by the brutality of partisan warfare in Yugoslavia). The men of SS-500 fought with great courage and inflicted appaling losses on the partisans, but in the process suffered a staggering 80% casualty rate with only 200 of the SS paratroopers coming out unscathed from a total of almost 1,000 men who mounted the initial assault. After 24 hours the mission was aborted after Tito and the Allied delegation had escaped and the few remaining men of the SS-500 were facing annihilation. They were saved by the timely intervention of elements of Otto Kumm's "Prinz Eugen" Gebirgsjager Division coming to the rescue and by receiving air cover from Luftwaffe fighter-bombers.

The outcome of the battle for Drvar might have been different but for the participation of Allied Heavy Bombers operating from bases in Italy who mounted a continuous shuttle service in support of the partisans dropping thousands of tons of bombs on the lightly armed men of SS-500. The remnants of the decimated battalion now only included 15% of the original 500 B-Soldaten who were reinstated to their former ranks after proving themselves at the Battle of Drvar. Amongst the other casualties of the action were the Battalion's commanding officer SS-Haupstürmführer Rybka who was severely wounded; SS-Hauptstürmführer Obermeyer, the battalion 2nd in Command who was killed, and the battalion Adjutant SS-Oberstürmführer Mertely who was also seriously wounded.

The battalion was withdrawn from active service and reformed from new recruits under the command of SS-Haupstürmführer Milius who took over command of the battalion on June 26th, 1944. The battalion was then deployed on the Eastern Front as a "Fire Brigade" rapid deployment force and played a critical role in the Battle of the Narva Bridgehead. Following the withdrawal westwards, SS-500 fought numerous battles throughout the Baltic States and East Prussia.

In September, 1944 the unit was transferred to Austria and took up position just outside Vienna. SS-500 was then attached to SS-Sturmbannführer Otto Skorzeny who was planning an airborne operation to kidnap the Hungarian Regent Admiral Horthy from his fortress hideout in the Hungarian capital Budapest. This operation was subsequently abandoned, and Skorzeny and the men of SS-500 entered Budapest on foot. Following the occupation of the Budapest Citadel, the men of SS-500 were once again transferred to their permanent barracks at Neustrelitz where they were brought up to strength of 1,000 men once again by the addition of remnants of other Wehrmacht units. Although the unit was still designated as a Fallschirm battalion none of the new recruits received any parachute training, and indeed less than 15% of the unit's men remained who had received the previous intensive airborne training. In late 1944 the unit was redesignated as SS-Fallschirm Battalion 600.

A detachment of SS-600 was reassigned to take part in Operation "Greif" once again under the command of Otto Skorzeny. These men were to be dropped behind the American lines in the Ardennes dressed in US Army uniforms to cause the maximum amount of confusion during the initial stages of the Ardennes Offensive. A number of these men were captured by US forces and were subsequently shot as spies.

In February, 1945 the entire battalion of SS-600 joined Otto Skorzeny's combat group then fighting the Russians on the River Oder. SS-600 was assigned to defend a bridge over the Oder at Schwedt which they did successfully; however they became the victim of a horrendous mistake by an engineer officer who inadvertently allowed the bridge to be blown whilst most of the SS-600 battalion were on the wrong side of the river. Although isolated on the eastern bank of the Oder, the men of SS-600 held off massively superior numbers of Soviet troops for three days: in the process losing almost 100 dead and more than 500 wounded. Eventually the remnants of SS-600 made their way across the river Oder using anything that would float including barn doors and window shutters.

Rather than surrender to the Russians the remaining members of SS-600 made their way west towards their barracks in Mecklenburg: eventually surrendering to the US Army troops near Hagenow on May 2nd, 1945.

SS-FALLSCHIRMSCHUTZENSCHEIN
(SS Paratroopers Qualification Certificate)

This SS document was a modified form of the Luftwaffe Paratroopers Qualification Certificate, and was issued to SS members of the SS-Fallschirmjager Battalion 500/600 upon completion of their parachute training course. This document was supplementary to the other regular SS documents such as the Soldbuch and Wehrpass carried by SS personnel.

As a consequence of the hurried formation of SS-Fallschirmjager Battalion 500/600 there were no specific paratroop related SS document available for this newly formed unit. Therefore with the unit receiving all of its training from Luftwaffe personnel it was necessary to adopt existing Luftwaffe documentation for the men of SS-500/600 upon completion of their parachute training.

The individual to which this document pertains SS-Oberscharführer Walter Hummel received his parachute training from Luftwaffe instructors at their Parachute Training School at Kraljevo in Eastern Yugoslavia. Upon completion of his training in early 1944 Hummel went on to take part in Operation "Rosselsprung" (the operation to Kidnap Tito) on May 25th, 1944.

Walter Hummel carried his SS Paratrooper's document with him for many years after the end of the war, as a consequence of this some of the detail on this document is somewhat faded. However despite this ageing the SS-Fallschirmschutzenschein must rank as one of the rarest of all SS documents especially when one considers how small the SS-500/600 Battalion was. At its full strength in 1944 the unit never exceeded more than 1,000 men, and indeed by the end of World War II only some 180 men survived its subsequent actions on the Eastern Front. There are probably only a handful of genuine examples of this type of document in existence today.

SS-Fallschirmschutzenschein (SS Paratroopers Qualification Certificate) to
SS-Oberscharführer Walter Hummel. The photograph on the licence pictures
Hummel wearing his SS tunic. The certificate documents: Hummel's name,
rank, service number, date of birth and training dates. His photograph bears
two SS unit validation stamps, and his unit commanders signature.

Studio portrait of Walter Hummel taken after his qualification as an SS-Fallschirmjager in 1944. On his SS tunic he has the ribbons of the Iron Cross 2nd Class and Winter War Medal through the second button hole of the tunic. On his left breast he is wearing the Iron Cross 1st Class, Infantry Assault Badge, Silver Wound Badge and the Luftwaffe Paratrooper's Badge. It is evident from this photograph that at least some members of the SS 500/600 Battalion who were trained by the Luftwaffe at Kraljevo received the Luftwaffe Fallschirmjager Badge and <u>not</u> the Army version of the badge as has been generally stated for this particular unit in the past.

ANNIVERSARY AND DATES OF SIGNIFICANCE TO THE SS

Undoubtedly the reader cannot help but notice that the same dates reoccur repeatedly on SS Award documents, promotions, special orders, recruit induction notices, etc: in fact virtually all SS documents of any importance were dated to coincide with anniversaries of special significance to the SS or the Nazi Party.

Most of the anniversary dates used on SS documents were derived specifically from events relating to the Nazi Party's short history including Hitler's birthday and his accession to power. However the NSDAP, as the parent organisation of the SS, also adopted long standing and popular German holidays such as National Labour Day (traditionally a Socialist holiday) and incorporated them into their own celebrations calendar. A further favourite ploy with the NSDAP was to take traditional Nordic pagan festivals such as the Day of the Winter Solstice and attempt to impose it in place of the established Christian Christmas Festival.

There were also innumerable "Party Days" throughout the year which occurred as annual events to raise funds for the Nazi Party: these had started as far back as the 1920's. However these Party Days did not hold the same significance as commemorative dates. A selection of the most important SS and NSDAP commemorative dates and anniversaries are listed below:

JANUARY 30TH - HITLER'S ACCESSION TO POWER:
Hitler came to power legitimately on the 30th of January, 1933. Consequently this date became one of the most important days for all SS and Nazi Party members. After Hitler came to power, the 30th of January became a National Holiday for all the German people. A measure of the significance of this date is shown by the fact that an SS Regiment was given the date "30 JANUAR" as its official title and was worn on the cuffband of the SS members of the regiment.

FEBRUARY 24TH - NSDAP FOUNDATION DAY:
Although the NSDAP acquired its title on April 1st, 1920 the official date for celebrating this Part Day was changed to February 24th due to the fact that the early Nazis very soon realised they had founded their party on "April Fool's Day". Consequently they adopted the new Foundation Day.

MARCH 16TH - HEROES REMEMBRANCE DAY:

This had traditionally been "National Mourning Day", a day set aside for the care of German war cemeteries, however after the Nazis came to power they gave this date its new name of "Heroes Remembrance Day" and fixed the date at March 16th, where previously National Mourning day had been designated as the 5th Sunday before Easter (occurring on different dates). The Nazis also used this date to commemorate their early victories such as the remilitarisation of the Rhineland (1936) and the reintroduction of conscription (1935).

APRIL 20TH - HITLER'S BIRTHDAY:

The anniversary of Hitler's birth in 1889 was probably the highest holiday in the Nazi Party calendar, and after 1933 became a National German Holiday lavishly celebrated with ceremonies and torchlight parades when the whole of Germany was decked out in red/white/black swastika flags. Hitler's birthday was the principle occasion for SS investitures and awards in keeping with their status as the Fuhrer's personal bodyguard. It became customary on this day for Hitler to award a commemorative gift to large numbers of men in the SS.

MAY 1ST - NATIONAL LABOUR DAY:

This had been the German Socialist's and Communist's most revered day. In keeping with Hitler's plan to eliminate all communists from German political life, he also deprived them of their May Day holiday - replacing it with a more traditional holiday for the whole people and yet another opportunity to further National Socialist ideals and weaken the hold of the Communist Party. This wooing of the German working class led to the birth of a section of workers referred to by Goebbels as "beefsteak Nazis" (who were brown on the outside but red on the inside).

MOTHERING SUNDAY - 2ND SUNDAY IN MAY:

The long standing national celebration of German motherhood was another day hijacked by the Nazi Party and turned into a National Socialist ceremonial day: when German mothers were publically awarded the Mother Cross for producing children to populate Hitler's Reich. A fascimile of Hitler's signature was impressed onto the reverse side of every Cross of Honour of the German Mother.

JUNE 21ST - SUMMER SOLSTICE:

This pagan festival was lavishly celebrated by the Nazis and especially the SS who had adopted much of the Nordic culture. The occasion of the Summer Solstice was used to commemorate Nazi Party martyrs who had fallen in the furtherance of the establishment of the Party. Bonfires were lit following torchlit processions, and SS men would ritually leap across the flames of the fire in a symbolic purification ceremony.

NUREMBERG RALLY DAYS - SEPTEMBER:

In the early days of the Nazi Party there had been no set dates for their annual open-air rallies which had taken place in various months and at different locations during the 1920's, and had been held variously in January, June, August and September. However after the Nazis came to power Nuremberg became the fixed venue for the Party's annual national convention. The Nuremberg Rallies became spectacular events organised and staged managed by Albert Speer and were usually held over a four day period from August 31st - September 3rd.

HARVEST FESTIVAL - OCTOBER:

Another pagan festival given prominence by the Nazis: Celebrated as a form of thanksgiving to Mother Earth for the fruits of the harvest. This festival was used by the Party to draw the farming community of Germany to its bosom.

NOVEMBER 9TH - ANNIVERSARY OF THE MUNICH PUTSCH:

Along with Hitler's birthday this was the most sacred day in the calendar of the Nazi Party and the SS when the "Martyrs" of the November 8-9, 1923 Beerhall Putsch were revered by Hitler an the Party. Each year the attempted coup by Hitler and his early followers was reinacted on the streets of Munich, and culminated in a torchlit vigil at the Feldherrnhall where a number of the original marchers had been shot during their abortive attempt to seize power. The Feldherrnhalle Monument was the focal point of all the Nazi celebrations of this event.

WINTER SOLSTICS - DECEMBER:

This ancient pagan festival was reintroduced nationally by the Nazis in a subtle attempt to supplant the traditional Christian celebrations of Christmas. They built around this festival a vast amount of folklore using ancient pagan symbols such as the burning of the yule log etc. This festival became an important and integral part of SS folklore with the rituals being formalised to the extent of having a 70 page booklet published, "The SS Celebrations of Life", devoted to instructing the SS man and his family in the correct ways to celebrate the Winter Solstice festival.

SS-DIENSTALTERLISTE
AND THE TOTENKOPFRING
(SS Service Rank and Seniority List)

The SS-Dienstalterliste had its origins in the earlier office rank lists (Rang-Liste der Koniglich Preussischen Armee) of the Prussian and later German Army. The SS with its obsession for documentation and detail refined the concept of an officer's rank list and enlarged the scope of its content to incorporate information about SS officers not found in any other military or paramilitary rank list.

The rank lists produced by the SS in the early years were quite rudimentary merely listing the individual's: name, rank, seniority and Party Number etc. However as the ranks of the SS swelled in the early to mid-1930's the content of the SS-Dienstalterliste also grew, not only in the number of entries but also in the additional details attributed to each officer listed. Also as new Awards and distinctions became available to members of the SS such as the Honour Sword, Totenkopfring and Sport's Badge there was more information readily available to be compiled and duly entered on the Dienstalterliste.

When the entries in the Dienstaterliste are studied carefully they surrender to the researcher a vast amount of information pertaining to the individuals who appear on its pages. The most comprehensively documented editions of the SS-Dienstalterliste are those which appeared in the five year period between 1938-1942. Prior to these dates the smaller number of officers on the SS Roll, the sparcity of Awards and the fact that many officer's careers had not yet blossomed meant that most of the information was at best rudimentary and often quite mundane: this was due to the fact that most of the awards which appeared on the early Dienstalterliste related to service in world War I usually by the much older officers. Jumping forward to post-1942 provisions for some entries started being omitted whilst others such as the Sword and Ring were amalgated within a single entry column.

Taking the 1938 Dienstalterliste as an example of one of the more comprehensive lists, one finds a wealth of information not only about the Awards but also their importance in the eyes of the SS. The Golden Party Badge took precedence over all other Awards including Gallantry Awards such as the Iron Cross. These military Awards won in world War I were entered immediately after the Gold Party Badge. These badge and medals appeared on the list immediately following the individual's name.

The next section of the 1938 list is probably the most interesting for it contains five separate entry columns which document the following items from left to right: the SS Honour Sword, SA Sport's Badge, Reich Sport's Badge, and Lebensborn. The symbols and entry positions of the first four items are self-explanatory and quite easy to identify and follow. However the fifth and final entry column is the most intriguing of all the entry details and requires some elaboration.

"Lebensborn" literally means "Spring of Life" - a euphemism for an SS breeding program instituted in the mid-1930's to further the procreation of pure Aryan children sired by SS officers mated with selected young women of good and proven Aryan stock. There was no long term emotional commitment or involvement between the two prospective parents. The SS officer after being selected was granted special leave to attend a Lebensborn clinic where he spent an enjoyable and hopefully fruitful few days with his assigned partner. The Lebensborn children born from this clinical mating would eventually number tens of thousands: the ultimate goal being to produce a race of "supermen" who would populate the "Thousand Year Reich".

Following the birth of a child when an SS officer had successfully mated in the Lebensborn program an entry would be made in the appropriate Lebensborn column of the SS-Dienstalterliste. The entry was in the form of a Nordic symbol (Y) which was the ancient birth sign. As will be noted on the specimen page of the 1938 Dienstalterliste, SS-Standartenführers would appear to have been not only enthusiastic participants in the Lebensborn program but also outstandingly successful!

The Totenkopfring held a special significance to members of the SS. Due to the strict criteria attached to the awarding of the Ring it acquired a mystic and exclusivity which went far beyond its being just a piece of decorative SS jewellry. The ring's status as an Award was reflected by the fact that it appeared as a separate and specific honour in the SS-Dienstalterliste.

In the 1935 Dienstalterliste, the award of the Totenkopfring appeared after the name of the recipient; however by 1938 the Ring had been elevated to a separate column next to the recipients name; also the Ring depicted in the 1938 list was somewhat more decorative than earlier and later war time entries in the Dienstalterliste. In these later lists, such as that for 1944, the Totenkopfring although still appearing in a separate column is now depicted once again as a plain circle. Also the column which had previously been reserved exclusively for the Ring now contained entries giving details of individuals who had been awarded the SS Sword. Where the award of the Ring and the Sword coincided for the same individual, the depiction of the Sword hilt appeared within the circle representing the Ring.

It is quite evident from studying the Dienstalterliste that the criteria for the award of the Totenkopfring was strictly adhered to.

This is born out by the fact that many high ranking and often quite famous SS commanders did not receive the Totenkopfring because they failed to qualify either by late entry into the SS or because their SS number was too high: Oberführer Dr. Oskar Derlewanger is a case in point. Similarly there are instances of individuals up to the rank of Gruppenführer who did not receive the Totenkopfring - once again for the reasons previously stated and also because they either held only honourary SS rank or had transferred from the Army to the Waffen-SS too late in the war to meet the service time requirements of the Ring's award criteria. Therefore it is not always safe to assume that because a particular member of the SS held high rank or was well decorated that they were necessarily eligible for award of the SS-Totenkopfring.

When studying different annual editions of the Dienstalterliste some anamolies do occur: the most common being where an individual is credited with being awarded the Ring in one Dienstalterliste and the record of the award no appearing in later editions. This was due to the strict stipulation that any officer convicted of certain serious offenses could be stripped of the SS-Totenkopfring either for a specific period of time or even permanently. The withdrawal of the Totenkopfring honour appeared as either a blank space or a short horizontal dash in the appropriate column next to the individual's name.

Lfd. Nr.	Name	Dienststellung	Partei-Nr.			SS-Nr.

SS=Standartenführer:

Lfd. Nr.	Name	Dienststellung	Partei-Nr.			SS-Nr.
122	Bed Johann, O	Stab Oa. Südwest	6 911	—	—	179
123	Berni Frih, O	10. Sta.	23 270	—	—	178
124	Delp Hermann, ⚡ O	⚡-Hauptamt	99 503	—	—	1 253
125	Dr. Brand Kurt	z. b. V. Oa. Nordwest	182 777	—	—	3 870
126	Hinsch Hans, O	z. b. V. Oa. Nord	156 425	—	—	1 745
127	Herbert Willi, O, M.d.R.	F. 36. Sta.	43 222	—	—	1 031
128	Weitermann Willi, ⚡ O	⚡-Hauptamt	12 194	—	—	296
129	Reinhardt Ludwig, O	F. 63. Sta.	67 869	—	—	13 926
130	Schmelcher Willi, O, Pe.Vr., M.d.R.	F. 10. Sta.	90 783	—	—	2 648
131	Dr. Denler Hans, O	Stab RF ⚡	—	515 008	—	19 467
132	Dr. Müller Friedrich, O	Stab Oa. Nord	320 586	—	—	14 722
133	Baueus Hans, O	z. b. V. RF ⚡	—	843 258	—	16 471
134	Maier Johann, ⚡ O	Stab Oa. West	122 119	—	—	2 292
135	Ludwig Kurt, O, M.d.R.	F. 57. Sta.	17 225	—	—	1 397
136	Dr. Weber Friedrich	Ehrenf. z. 6. Sta.	—	1 310 670	—	—
137	Dr. Diels Rudolf, Reg.Pr.	Ehrenf. z. Oa. West	—	—	—	187 116
138	Schuster Karl, O	Stab Oa. Nordwest	328 622	—	—	6 236
139	Ortlepp Walter, St.Rat, Pe.Vr., M.d.R.	S=D Hauptamt	66 836	—	—	11 319
140	Ihle Wilhelm, O	F. 32. Sta.	67 958	—	—	2 036
141	Müller Erhard, O	F. 69. Sta.	19 100	—	—	70
142	Röder Wilhelm, ⚡	z. b. V. RF ⚡	469 137	—	—	119 493
143	Zahn Konrad, M.d.R.	z. b. V. Oa. Südwest	245 481	—	—	1 858
144	Bod Karl, O	F. Ab. XXVIII	411 630	—	—	8 569
145	Friedrich Max, O	⚡-Hauptamt	268 665	—	—	6 149
146	Herwig Karl, O	F. 53. Sta.	97 428	—	—	5 447
147	Krause Heinrich, O	F. 26. Sta.	138 994	—	—	2 358
148	Jahnke Fritz	F. 3. R. Sta.	—	753 227	—	14 725
149	Velz Horst, O	F. 82. Sta.	63 081	—	—	12 211
150	Weber Josef, ⚡ ⚡ O	⚡-Hauptamt	103 010	—	—	1 319
151	Loritz Hans, O	F.R.L. Esterwegen	298 668	—	—	4 165
152	Poggenauer Leonhard, ⚡ O	⚡-Hauptamt	229 707	—	—	3 017
153	Stein Walter, O	Stab Oa. Ost	255 956	—	—	12 780
154	Fischer Franz, O	F. 3. Sta.	112 226	—	—	2 874
155	Beutel Lothar, O	S=D Hauptamt	135 238	—	—	2 422
156	Schraufstetter Gottfried, ⚡ O	Stab Oa. Süd	—	530 796	—	12 027
157	Jeppe Wilhelm, O	Stab Oa. Nordost	21 936	—	—	679
158	Bröling Karl, O	Stab Oa. West	214 769	—	—	3 059
159	Heiz Georg, O	F. 62. Sta.	333 628	—	—	4 436
160	Schulz Robert, O, M.d.R.	S=D Hauptamt	3 654	—	—	392
161	Müller Alfred, ⚡ ⚡ O	F. 34. Sta.	—	1 274 660	—	3 128
162	Wystrach Hans, O	Stab Oa. Südost	2 249	—	—	6 011
163	Scholz Herbert	z. b. V. Oa. Ost	—	505 786	—	70 300
164	Hausamen Fritz, O	Stab Oa. Südost	308 914	—	—	8 583
165	Hofmann Otto, O	F. Ab. XV	145 729	—	—	7 646
166	Meyer Fritz, ⚡	F. 23. Sta.	33 146	—	—	3 196
167	Frey Kurt, ⚡ O	z. b. V. Oa. Süd	29 148	—	—	1 688
168	Streckenbach Bruno, O	S=D Hauptamt	489 972	—	—	14 713
169	Dr. Edhardt Georg, O	F. 14. Sta.	146 717	—	—	43 197

The SS-Standartenführer Page from the 1935 SS-Dienstalterliste. Note the award of the Totenkopf Ring is indicated by a circle next to the recipient's name.

SS-Standartenführer:

Lfde. Nr.	Name, Vorname	Dienststellung	Partei-Nr. 1–1,8 Mill.	Partei-Nr. über 1,8 Mill.	SS-Nr.	Geburts- datum
335	Dolp Hermann	Stab SS-Hauptamt	99 503	—	1 293	12. 9. 89
336	Brinkmann Paul	b. Stab Ab. XVII	139 161	—	3 415	31. 7. 91
337	Montag Fritz	b. Stab Ab. XXXIII	55 027	—	27 558	14.11.96
338	Hinsch Hans	b. Stab Oa. Nordwest	156 426	—	4 745	21. 3.01
339	Einspenner Richard	Stammabt. 9	139 226	—	12 817	25. 9.91
340	Schier Berthold	b. Stab Ab. III	561 185	—	13 835	29.11.87
341	Herbert Willy	J. 58. Sta.	43 222	—	1 031	28. 5.04
342	Dr. Müller Friedrich-Wilhelm	Oa. Arzt Nordwest	355 586	—	14 722	26. 1.97
343	Maier Johann	Stammabt. 1	122 119	—	2 292	21. 5.89
344	Diels Rudolf, Reg.Dr.	b. Stab Ab. IV	—	3 955 308	187 116	16.12.00
345	Jhle Wilhelm	J. Ab. XXXIV	67 958	—	2 036	23.10.89
346	Dr. Trummler Hans	SD-Hauptamt	73 599	—	254 581	24.10.00
347	Gumps Max	Stammabt. 79	787 049	—	29 515	4.12.91
348	Reck Wilhelm	b. Stab SS-Hauptamt	88 632	—	1 422	19. 8.88
349	Zahn Konrad	Stammabt. 32	245 481	—	1 868	6. 4.91
350	Gnade Albert	b. Stab Ab. IV	2 798	—	13 983	25. 1.86
351	Hertwig Karl	J. 53. Sta.	97 428	—	5 447	25. 7.95
352	Krause Heinrich	J. 47. Sta.	138 994	—	2 358	7. 7.07
353	Pelz Horst	b. Stab Ab. VII	63 081	—	12 211	3. 7.95
354	Weber Josef	J. Sch. Braunschweig	103 010	—	1 319	11. 7.83
355	Heiß Georg	Stammabt. 62	333 628	—	4 436	18. 5.95
356	Frhr. von Reitzenstein Friedrich	Stammabt. 34	89 052	—	1 643	29.11.88
357	Müller Alfred	b. Stab Oa. Süd	1 274 660	—	3 128	16. 3.01
358	Dr. Scholz Herbert	SD-Hauptamt	1 207 857	—	70 360	29. 1.06
359	Dr. Hausamen Fritz	Stammabt. 62	308 914	—	8 583	7. 4.86
360	Schulz Robert, M.d.R.	b. Stab Oa. Nord	3 654	—	392	28. 7.00
361	Meyer Fritz	Stab Ab. VI	33 146	—	3 196	26. 4.00
362	von Woedtke Alexander	Jnsp.Stammabt.Nord	294 710	—	11 629	2. 9.89
363	Schwarzkopff Reinhart	Stammabt. 45	390 899	—	6 016	6. 5.95
364	Maurice Emil, M.d.R.	b. Stab Ab. I	39	—	2	19. 1.97
365	Reich Otto	J. 4. SS-T. St. Ostmark	289 356	—	9 948	5.12.91
366	Mozel Heinz	J. 80. Sta.	25 502	—	2 954	10. 9.01
367	Magnus Axel	b. Stab SS-Hauptamt	—	5 389 265	175 036	26.11.92
368	Wagner Robert	Stab Oa. Nord	145 301	—	1 672	7. 4.02
369	Schwahn Erich	b. Stab SS-Hauptamt	—	4 831 190	236 410	26. 6.77
370	Friderici Arthur	Stammabt. 69	26 484	—	8 010	27. 5.00
371	Schulz von Dratzig Rudolf	SD-Hauptamt	162 436	—	12 332	15. 7.97
372	Dr. Mohr Eugen	b. Stab Ab. XXVI	475 090	—	28 788	22. 6.96
373	Schön Willy	Stammabt. 7	18 360	—	182	2. 3.94
374	Dr. Großmann Erich	J. San. Abt. XXVI	720 199	—	27 786	30. 1.02
375	Dr. Teitge Heinrich	Oa. Arzt Ost	320 080	—	5 736	16. 7.00
376	Dr. Wendler Richard	SD-Hauptamt	93 116	—	36 050	22. 1.98
377	Dietrich Hans, M.d.R.	b. Stab SS-Hauptamt	8 454	—	3 397	19. 9.98

The SS-Standartenfuhrer Page from the 1938 SS-Dienstalterliste. Note that award of the Ring is now recorded in a seperate column but using the same symbol as in previous lists.

ﬀ-Gruppenführer:

Lfde. Nr.	Name, Vorname		Dienststellung	Partei-Nr.	ﬀ-Nr.	Geburts-datum	Führer- bzw. Offz.-Dienstgrad bei der Waffen-ﬀ, Wehr-macht, Polizei	Gruppen-führer
98	*Rodenbücher Alfred, ✠ I M. d. R.		b. ﬀ-Pers. Hauptamt	413 447	8 229	29. 9. 00	Korv. Kpt. d. R.	9. 9. 34
99	Frhr. von Holzchuher Wilhelm, ● ✠ II ● ● ● Reg. Pr. a. D.		b. Stab Oa. Main	75 001	314 975	2. 9. 93	Lt. a. D.	9. 9. 34
100	Kaul Curt, ● ✠ I ● ● ● 圖 ● II M. d. R.		ﬀ-Pers. Hauptamt, z. Zt. W. ﬀ	244 964	3 392	5. 10. 90	Gen. Lt. d. P.	30. 1. 37
101	Hennicke Paul, ● ✠ I ● 圖 ● I St. Rat, M. d. R.		kdrt. ﬀ-Hauptamt	34 492	1 332	31. 1. 83	Gen. Lt. d. P.	30. 1. 38
102	Willikens Werner, ● ✠ I ● ● ● 圖 ✠ I St. Sek., St. Rat, M. d. R.		b. RuS-Hauptamt	3 353	56 180	8. 2. 93	Hptm. z. V.	30. 1. 38
103	Reischle Hermann Dr., ● ✠ I ● ● ● ✠ II M. d. R.		b. ﬀ-Pers. Hauptamt	474 435	101 350	22. 9. 98	Hptm. d. R.	11. 9. 38
104	Sporrenberg Jakob, ● ✠ II ● I M. d. R.		Stab Oa. Nord	25 585	5 809	16. 9. 02	Gen. Lt. d. P.	1. 1. 40
105	von Bomhard Adolf, ✠ I ● ● ● ● I		Hauptamt O. P., Gen. Insp. Pol. Sch.	3 933 982	292 711	6. 1. 91	Gen. Lt. d. P.	9. 11. 40
106	Riege Paul, ✠ I ● ● ● I		b. Stab Oa. Südost	2 658 727	323 872	27. 4. 88	Gen. Lt. d. P. a. D.	9. 11. 40
107	Bracht Werner, ✠ I ● ● I		Stab RF ﬀ	2 579 550	310 476	5. 2. 88	Lt. d. R. a. D.	20. 4. 41
108	Turner Harald Dr., ✠ I ● ● 圖 ● I St. Rat		Stab RF ﬀ	181 533	34 799	8. 10. 91	m. d. U. d. Gen. Lt. W. ﬀ	27. 9. 41
109	Streckenbach Bruno, ● ● ● ✠ I ● I		Kdr. 19. W. Gr. Div. ﬀ	489 972	14 713	7. 2. 02	Gen. Lt. d. P. u. W. ﬀ	9. 11. 41
110	Müller Heinrich, ✠ I ● ● ● 玊 ● I		RSl-Hauptamt, Chef Amt IV	4 583 199	107 043	28. 4. 00	Gen. Lt. d. P.	9. 11. 41
111	Schreyer Georg, ✠ I ● ● ● 圖 ● I ●		b. Stab Oa. Spree	766 705	327 419	16. 7. 84	Gen. Lt. d. P. a. D.	9. 11. 41
112	Jedicke Georg, ✠ I ● ● ● I		b. Stab Oa. Ostland	846 948	323 869	26. 3. 87	Gen. Lt. d. P. a. D.	12. 12. 41
113	von Oelhafen Otto, ✠ I ● ● ● ● I		b. Stab Oa. Böhmen-Mähren	4 736 616	327 493	8. 6. 86	Gen. Lt. d. P. a. D.	12. 12. 41
114	Meyszner August, ● ● ● ✠ I ● I M. d. R.		Hauptamt O. P., Gen. Insp. Gend.	6 119 650	263 406	3. 8. 86	Gen. Lt. d. P.	1. 1. 42
115	Meinberg Wilhelm, ● ✠ II ● ✠ I St. Rat		Stab RF ﬀ	218 582	99 436	1. 3. 98	—	30. 1. 42
116	Johst Johannes, ✠ I St. Rat		Stab RF ﬀ	1 352 876	274 576	8. 7. 90	—	30. 1. 42
117	von Mackensen Hans-Georg Dr., ✠ II ● ● ✠ I Bot.		Stab RF ﬀ	3 653 634	289 239	26. 1. 83	Hptm. d. R. a. D.	30. 1. 42
118	Jung Rudolf Prof., ● ✠ I G. L. e. h., M. d. R.		b. Stab Oa. Fulda-Werra	85	276 690	16. 4. 82	—	16. 4. 42
119	Petri Leo, ✠ I ● ● ● I		ﬀ-Führg. H. A., Chef Amt I	590 193	209 076	20. 10. 76	Gen. Lt. W. ﬀ	30. 4. 42
120	Hilgenfeldt Erich, ● ✠ I ● ✠ I M. d. R.		Stab RF ﬀ	143 642	289 225	2. 7. 97	Hptm. d. R.	30. 4. 42
121	Becker Herbert, ✠ I ● ●		Stab RF ﬀ	3 144 750	310 477	13. 3. 87	Gen. Lt. d. P. a. D.	20. 4. 42
122	Korsemann Gerret, ● ✠ I ● ● II		Stab RF ﬀ, z. Zt. W. ﬀ	47 735	314 170	8. 6. 95	Gen. Lt. d. P.	1. 7. 42
123	Freyberg Alfred, ● ✠ II ● ✠ I Mi. Pr. a. D., M. d. R.		b. Stab Oa. Elbe	5 830	113 650	12. 7. 92	Lt. d. R.	12. 7. 42
124	Ahrens Georg, ● ✠ I ● ● ● I St. Sek., St. Rat		b. Stab Oa. Nordsee	403 019	36 226	29. 4. 96	Hptm. d. R.	9. 11. 42
125	Globocnik Odilo, ● ✠ I ● I ●		Höh. ﬀ-Pol. F.	443 939	292 776	21. 4. 04	Gen. Lt. d. P.	9. 11. 42

SS-Gruppenführer Page from the <u>1944</u> SS-Dienstalterliste. Note that the Ring now appears in a single column with the SS Sword inside the Ring circle where appropriate.

Abbreviations

Abkürzungen

Ab. = ff-Abschnitt	H. R. Sch. = Hauptreitschule	-PE- = -Prinz Eugen-
Abt. = Abteilung	Hstuf. = ff-Hauptsturmführer	Pers. Hauptamt = Personalhauptamt
a. D. = außer Dienst	-HW- = -Horst Wessel-	Pers. Stab RF ff = Hauptamt Persönlicher Stab Reichsführer-ff
A. Korps = Armee-Korps	H. W. L. = Hauptwirtschaftslager	Pi. Sch. = Pionierschule
Amtsgr. = Amtsgruppe	Inf. = Infanterie	Po. D. = Polizeidirektor
Art. = Artillerie	Insp. = Inspekteur	Po. Pr. = Polizeipräsident
Art. Sch. = Artillerieschule	Inst. Abt. = Instandsetzungsabteilung	Pol. = Polizei
Ass. Arzt = Assistenzarzt	Int. = Intendant	Pol. Gebietsf. = Polizeigebietsführer mit den Rechten eines ff-Pol. F.
Aufkl. Abt. = Aufklärungsabteilung	Jg. Rgt. = Jägerregiment	Pz. Gr. = Panzergrenadier
Ausb. = Ausbildungs-	J. Sch. = Junkerschule	Pz. Jg. = Panzerjäger
b. = Führer beim Stab (Hauptamt)	K. = Kraftfahrsturm	Pz. Korps = Panzerkorps
BdO = Befehlshaber der Ordnungspolizei	-K- = -Kama-	Reg. Pr. = Regierungspräsident
BdSich P. u. SD = Befehlshaber der Sicherheitspolizei und des Sicherheitsdienstes	K. Admiral = Konteradmiral	RF ff = Reichsführer-ff
	Kav. = Kavallerie	Rgt. = Regiment
BdW. ff = Befehlshaber der Waffen-ff	-KE- = -Kurt Eggers-	Rittm. = Rittmeister
Bot. = Botschafter	Kdo. = Kommando	R. K. = Reichskommissar
Brig. = Brigade	Kdr. = Kommandeur	R. Mi. = Reichsminister
Btl. = Bataillon	kdrt. = kommandiert	R. L. = Reichsleiter
char. = charakterisierter	Kdt. = Kommandant	RSD = Reichssicherheitsdienst
-D- = -Deutschland-	Kdtr. = Kommandantur	RSi-Hauptamt = Reichssicherheitshauptamt
-DF- = -Der Führer-	K. L. = Konzentrationslager	R. St. = Reichsstatthalter
Div. = Division	Kom. Gen. = Kommandierender General	R. Sta. = Reiterstandarte
-Dm- = -Danmark-	Korv. Kpt. = Korvettenkapitän	RuS-Hauptamt = Rasse- und Siedlungshauptamt
d. P. = der Polizei	Kpt. = Kapitän	
-DR- = -Das Reich-	Kradsch. = Kradschützen	Sch. = Schule
d. R. = der Reserve	Kroat. = Kroatien	Schp. = Schutzpolizei
D. St. = Dienststelle	K. Sch. = Kraftfahrschule	-Sk- = -Skanderbeg-
E. = Ersatz	K. T. Lehranst. = Kraftfahrtechnische Lehranstalt	Sta. = ff-Standarte
Einsatzgr. = Einsatzgruppe		Stabsf. = Stabsführer
Estn. = Estnische	K. T. Vers. Abt. = Kraftfahrtechnische Versuchsabteilung	Staf. = ff-Standartenführer
F. = Führer		Stammabt. = Stammabteilung Bezirk
-F- = -Frundsberg-	L. = Leiter	stellv. = stellvertretender
-FG- = -Florian Geyer-	-L- = -Leibstandarte-	St. Kdt. = Standortkommandant
Freg. Kpt. = Fregattenkapitän	-Lm- = -Langemarck-	St. Mi. = Staatsminister
Frw. = Freiwilligen	Laz. = Lazarett	St. Rat = Staatsrat
Frhr. = Freiherr	Leg. = Legion	St. Sek. = Staatssekretär
F. Schp. = Feuerschutzpolizei	Lett. = Lettische	Stubaf. = ff-Sturmbannführer
Führg. H. A. = Führungshauptamt	L. Hptm. = Landeshauptmann	Stu. G. = Sturmgeschütz
-G- = -Germania-	L. Rat = Landrat	St. Verw. = Standortverwaltung
Gal. = Galizische	-LffAH- = -Leibstandarte-ff Adolf Hitler-	-T- = -Totenkopf-
Geb. Div. = Gebirgsdivision		T. N. = Technische Nothilfe
Gen. = General	Lt. = Leutnant	Tr. Üb. Pl. = Truppenübungsplatz
Gend. = der Gendarmerie	Maj. = Major	u. = und
Gen. Lt. = Generalleutnant	M. d. R. = Mitglied des Großdeutschen Reichstags	Uf. Sch. = Unterführerschule
Gen. Maj. = Generalmajor		U. St. Sek. = Unterstaatssekretär
Gen. Obst. = Generaloberst	m. d. U. d. = mit der Uniform des	Ustuf. = ff-Untersturmführer
Ges. = Gesandter	ML Pr. = Ministerpräsident	V. Admiral = Vizeadmiral
G. K. = Generalkommissar	-N- = -Nord-	Verw. D. = Verwaltungsdienste
G. L. = Gauleiter	Na. Abt. = Nachrichtenabteilung	Verw. Sch. = Verwaltungsschule
Gouv. = Gouverneur	Nachsch. = Nachschub	Vet. = Veterinär
Gr. = Grenadier	Na. Sch. = Nachrichtenschule	VomL = Volksdeutsche Mittelstelle
-GvB- = -Götz von Berlichingen-	Ndl. = Niederlande	-W- = -Wiking-
-H- = -Hohenstaufen-	-Nl- = -Nordland-	W. E. = Weltanschauliche Erziehung
-Ha- = -Handchar-	Oa. = ff-Oberabschnitt	WH = Wehrmacht Heer
H. A. = Hauptamt	O. B. = Oberbefehlshaber	-Wl- = -Westland-
Hauptamt R. K. F. = Reichskommissar für die Festigung deutschen Volkstums-Stabshauptamt	Oberf. = ff-Oberführer	W. = Waffen
	Oblt. = Oberleutnant	W. T. Lehranst. = Waffentechnische Lehranstalt
-HJ- = -Hitlerjugend	Obst. = Oberst	W.-V. Hauptamt = Wirtschafts-Verwaltungshauptamt
Höh. (Höchst.) ff-Pol. F. = Höherer (Höchster) ff- und Polizeiführer	Obstarzt. = Oberstarzt	z. b. V. = zur besonderen Verwendung
	Obstlt. = Oberstleutnant	z. D. = zur Disposition
Hptm. = Hauptmann	Obstvet. = Oberstveterinär	z. V. = zur Verfügung
	O. P. = Ordnungspolizei	z. Zt. = zur Zeit
	O. Pr. = Oberpräsident	
	O. Stabsarzt = Oberstabsarzt	
	Ostubaf. = ff-Obersturmbannführer	
	Ostuf. = ff-Obersturmführer	

Page of abbreviated SS terms used in the SS-Dienstalterliste.

Nur für den Dienstgebrauch!

Dienstaltersliste

der

Schutzstaffel

der NSDAP.

(SS-Oberst-Gruppenführer — SS-Standartenführer)

Stand vom 9. November 1944

Herausgegeben vom SS-Personalhauptamt

Berlin 1944
Gedruckt in der Reichsdruckerei

Title page of the 1944 SS-Dienstalterliste. The entries in this list cover the SS ranks from SS-Standartenführer to SS-Oberst-Gruppenführer and is headed with Heinrich Himmler's name as Reichsführer-SS.

Dienstalterliste

der

Schutzstaffel

der N.S.D.A.P.

Stand vom 1. Juli 1935

Bearbeitet von der Personalkanzlei
des Reichsführers-SS

Berlin 1935
Gedruckt in der Reichsdruckerei

Title page of the 1935 SS-Dienstalterliste. The entries in this list cover the SS ranks from SS-Untersturmführer to SS-Obergruppenführer and is headed with Heinrich Himmler's name as Reichsführer-SS.

SS=Führer zur Verfügung

lfd. Nr.	Name	Dienststellung	Partei-Nr.			SS-Nr.
			1 Serie	Zweite Serie	über 1 Million	
1	Himmler Heinrich, ⚡ O., R.L., St.Rat, M.d.R.	Reichsführer SS	14 303	—	—	168
2	Heß Rudolf, ⚡ O., N.Mi., R.L., M.d.R.		16	—	—	—

SS=Obergruppenführer:

3	Schwarz Franz Xaver, ⚡ O., R.L., M.d.R.	z. b. V. RFSS	6			38 500
4	Dietrich Josef, ⚡ O., St.Rat, M.d.R.	F.-Da. Ost	89 015	—	—	1 177
5	Weitzel Fritz, O., St.Rat, Pr.Pr., M.d.R.	F.-Da. West	18 833	—	—	408
6	Daluege Kurt, O., St.Rat, M.d.R.	z. b. V. RFSS	31 981	—	—	1 119
7	Darré Walter, O., R.Mi., R.L., M.d.R	Chef R. u. S. Hauptamt	248 256	—	—	6 882
8	Buch Walter, ⊝O., R.L., M.d.R.	z. b. V. RFSS	7 733	—	—	81 353
9	von Woyrsch Udo, O., St.Rat, M.d.R.	z. b. V. RFSS	162 349	—	—	3 689
10	Krüger Wilhelm, St.Rat, M.d.R.	z. St. ohne Verwendung	171 199	—	—	6 123

SS=Gruppenführer:

11	Erbprinz zu Waldeck und Pyrmont Josias, O., M.d.R.	F.-Da. Rhein	160 025	—	—	2 139
12	Amann Max, ⊝O., R.L., M.d.R.	z. b. V. RFSS	3	—	—	53 143
13	Frhr. von Eberstein Karl, O., Reg.Pr., M.d.R.	F.-Da. Mitte	15 067	—	—	1 386
14	Jeckeln Friedrich, O., M.d.R.	F.-Da. Nordwest	163 348	—	—	4 367
15	Bouhler Philipp, ⚡ O., R.L., M.d.R.	z. b. V. RFSS	12	—	—	54 932
16	Wittje Kurt, O., M.d.R.	z. b. V. RFSS	256 189	—	—	5 870
17	Schmauser Ernst, O., M.d.R.	F.-Da. Süd	215 704	—	—	3 359
18	Lorenz Werner, O., St.Rat, M.d.R.	F.-Da. Nord	317 994	—	—	6 636
19	Dr. Dietrich Otto, O., R.L., M.d.R.	Ehrenf. z. Da. Süd	126 727	—	—	101 349
20	Forster Albert, O., G.L., M.d.R.	Ehrenf. z. 36. Sta.	1 924	—	—	158
21	Rube Wilhelm, G.L., St.Rat, O.Pr., M.d.R	Ehrenf. z. 27. Sta.	71 682	—	—	114 771
22	Grimm Wilhelm, O., R.L., M.d.R.	Ehrenf. z. Da. Süd	10 134	—	—	199 823
23	Kaufmann Karl, R.St., G.L., M.d.R.	Ehrenf. z. 28. Sta.	32 667	—	—	119 495
24	Hildebrandt Friedrich, R.St., G.L., M.d.R.	Ehrenf. z. 22. Sta.	3 653	—	—	128 802
25	Fichler Karl, O., R.L., M.d.R.	Ehrenf. z. Da. Süd	37	—	—	91 724
26	Lorper Wilhelm, ⚡, R.St., G.L., M.d.R.	Ehrenf. z. 21. Sta.	6 980	—	—	142 592
27	Klagges Dietrich, M.d.R.	z. b. V. Da. Nordwest	7 646	—	—	154 006
28	Heißmeyer August, O., M.d.R.	Chef SS-Hauptamt	21 573	—	—	4 370
29	Körner Paul, O., St.Set., M.d.R.	z. b. V. Da. Ost		714 328	—	23 076
30	Prützmann Hans, O., M.d.R.	F.-Da. Südwest	142 290	—	—	3 002
31	Heydrich Reinhardt, O., St.Rat	Chef S-D Hauptamt	—	544 916	—	10 120
32	von dem Bach Zelewski Erich, O., M.d.R.	F.-Da. Nordost	489 101	—	—	9 831
33	Eicke Theodor, O.	Inspekteur K.L.	114 901	—	—	2 921
34	Nebenbücher Alfred, O.	F.-Hilfswerk	413 447	—	—	8 229
35	Frhr. von Holzschuher Wilhelm, Reg.Pr	z. b. V. RFSS	75 001	—	—	214 975
36	Murr Wilhelm, R.St., G.L., M.d.R.	Ehrenf. z. Da. Südwest	12 873	—	—	147 545
37	Wahl Karl, G.L., Reg.P., M.d.R.	Ehrenf. z. Da. Süd	9 803	—	—	228 007
38	Sandel Fritz, ⚡, R.St., G.L., M.d.R.	Ehrenf. z. Da. Mitte	1 395	—	—	254 800
39	Redieß Wilhelm, O., M.d.R.	F.-Da. Südost	2 839	—	—	25 574

The **1935** SS-Dienstalterliste showing recipient's of the Totenkopf Ring starting with Heinrich Himmler and Rudolf Hess and descending through SS-Obergruppenführer and SS-Gruppenführer.

PERSONNEL DOCUMENTS OF THE SS

Lfde. Nr.	Name	Dienststellung	Partei-Nr.			SS-Nr.

SS=Brigadeführer:

| 4412 | Henze Max, O, M.d.R. | z. B. Oa. Ost | 80 481 | — | — | 1 167 |
| 4413 | Willikens Werner, St.Sef., M.d.R. | z. B.R.u.S.Hauptamt | 3 355 | — | — | 56 180 |

SS=Oberführer:

4414	Zigler Alfred	z. B. Oa. Süd	—	1 075 131	—	29 546
4415	Zeermann Otto, O	z. B. Oa. Ost	271 267	—	—	3 901
4416	Sattler Karl, O, M.d.R.	z. B.SS	241 933	—	—	19 474

SS=Standartenführer:

4417	Helwig Hans, O	z. B. Oa. Südwest	55 875	—	—	1 725
4418	Brinkmann Paul, O	z. B. 30. Sta.	139 161	—	—	3 415
4419	Montag Fritz	z. B. Ab. XV	57 027	—	—	27 558
4420	Einspenner Richard	z. B. Ab. XIII	139 226	—	—	12 817
4421	Schier Berthold	z. B. Ab. III	—	561 185	—	13 835
4422	Schwarz Franz, O	z. B. Ab. XXX	—	530 627	—	15 776
4423	Humps Max, O	z. B. Oa. Südwest	—	787 049	—	29 515
4424	Reck Wilhelm, O	z. B. Ab. III	88 632	—	—	1 422
4425	Gnade Albert, O	z. B. Ab. IV	2 798	—	—	13 983
4426	Frhr. v. Reitzenstein Friedrich, O	z. B. Oa. Süd	89 052	—	—	1 643
4427	Frhr. v. Thüngen Hilolf, O	z. B. Oa. Süd	173 397	—	—	1 928
4428	Mozel Heinz	z. B. Oa. Nord	26 502	—	—	2 954
4429	Deuschl Hans	z. B. Ab. XV	147 015	—	—	8 894
4430	Schwahn Erich	z. B.SS	—	—	—	236 410
4431	Friederici Arthur, O	z. B. Ab. XXV	26 484	—	—	8 010
4432	Schulz von Drahig Rudolf, O	z. B. Ab. XXI	162 436	—	—	12 332
4433	von Marzewski Erich, O	z. B. SS-Hauptamt	370 631	—	—	53 465
4434	Schön Willy, O	z. B. Ab. II	18 860	—	—	182

SS=Obersturmbannführer:

4435	Neufeldt Hermann, O	z. B. Ab. XXII	333 167	—	—	5 124
4436	Weberpals Karl	z. B. Ab. XIII	319 932	—	—	5 653
4437	Weber Erich, O	z. B. Ab. VI	151 565	—	—	5 169
4438	Dr. Feldmann Hermann	z. B. Oa. Südwest	335 626	—	—	4 950
4439	Zenn Kurt, O	z. B. 30. Sta.	32 688	—	—	9 526

The 1935 SS-Dienstalterliste showing recipient's of the Totenkopf Ring with the ranks of SS-Brigadefuhrer, SS-Oberführer, SS-Standartenführer and SS-Obersturmbannführer.

Lfd. Nr.	Name	Dienststellung	Partei-Nr.			SS-Nr.
4440	Wotrich Emil	z. B. Ab. XXVI	—	679 646	—	10 507
4441	Bannach Franz	z. B. Ab. XXVI	371 321	—	—	18 523
4442	Bauer Josef, O	z. B. 31. Sta.	14 834	—	—	1 195
4443	Weißfleg Wilhelm, O	z. B. Ab. XVIII	149 343	—	—	19 777
4444	Dr. Minne Hans	z. B. Ab. XV	—	558 248	—	19 259
4445	Dr. Klaule Paul, O	z. B. Ab. XXV	242 126	—	—	4 899
4446	Reich Albert, O	z. B. 15. Sta.	377 488	—	—	6 130
4447	Taenzler Hans	z. B. Oa. Ost	297 656	—	—	9 947
4448	Rogausch Friedrich, O	z. B. 77. Sta.	114 449	—	—	15 571
4449	Kleed Ernst, O	z. B. Ab. XX	328 490	—	—	20 307

SS-Sturmbannführer:

Lfd. Nr.	Name	Dienststellung	Partei-Nr.			SS-Nr.
4450	Argus Fritz, O	z. B. 41. Sta.	150 523	—	—	1 921
4451	Haiegg Wilhelm	z. B. 29. Sta.	59 413	—	—	2 278
4452	Lorenz Helmut	z. B. Ab. XVI	260 937	—	—	25 482
4453	Ziebach Josef	z. B. Ab. VI	383 292	—	—	7 612
4454	Schütten Heinrich, O	z. B. 25. Sta.	40 593	—	—	4 693
4455	Geisenhof Hans, ⚡ O	z. B. 34. Sta.	337 422	—	—	8 616
4456	Schmitt Willi, O	z. B. Ab. X	328 614	—	—	4 951
4457	Dahl Ferdinand, O	z. B. 69. Sta.	249 563	—	—	5 361
4458	Dackebusch Herbert, O	z. B. Oa. Ost	165 785	—	—	18 038
4459	Dr. Schnittert Hans, O	z. B. Ab. V	342 631	—	—	6 733
4460	Globt Fritz, O	z. B. 51. Sta.	176 639	—	—	2 948
4461	Rudel Fritz, O	z. B. Ab. II	6 905	—	—	1 002
4462	Seeger Alfred, O	z. B. Oa. Ost	231 846	—	—	2 817
4463	Lickenweg Hans, O	z. B. 71. Sta.	—	972 872	—	28 344
4464	Müller Erwin, O	z. B. Oa. Nordwest	306 903	—	—	14 677
4465	Conrau Friedrich, O	z. B. Ab. XXV	472 874	—	—	13 787
4466	Kleinschmid Martin, O	z. B. 3. Mo. Sta.	430 027	—	—	12 538
4467	Pieforski Gelig, O	z. B. Ab. XI	87 172	—	—	21 362
4468	Winkler Richard, O	z. B. Ab. XII	490 177	—	—	13 183
4469	Bartling Wilhelm	z. B. Oa. Nordwest	8 577	—	—	184
4470	Dr. Hammelsatz Karl, O	z. B. Ab. XVI	366 301	—	—	8 985
4471	Daluege Erich	z. B. 8. Sta.	11 463	—	—	30 842
4472	Dr. Grote Heinrich, O	z. B. 6. Sta.	—	1 248 830	—	44 005
4473	Dr. Kluck Helmut	z. B. 2. R. Sta.	—	719 865	—	46 084
4474	Dr. Stapfner Corbinion, O	z. B. 31. Sta.	102 164	—	—	10 214
4475	Schmidt Georg W., N.d.R.	z. B. Oa. Ost	33 660	—	—	20 548
4476	Dr. Heiter Robert, O	z. B. 67. Sta.	243 022	—	—	11 314
4477	Rad Willy, O	z. B. 64. Sta.	168 329	—	—	2 569

The <u>1935</u> SS-Dienstalterliste showing recipient's of the Totenkopf Ring which is a continuation of SS-Obersturmbannführer and SS-Sturmbannführer.

Lfd. Nr.	Name	Dienststellung	Partei-Nr.			SS-Nr.
			1 (bis 100)	Sonderr. (bis 1000)	über 1000	

SS=Hauptsturmführer:

4478	Eich Hans	z. V. Ab. XV	73 403	—	—	5 401
4479	Oesterreich Heinz, O	z. V. 18. Sta.	235 490	—	—	3 191
4480	Mahr Johann	z. V. 25. Sta.	458 481	—	—	6 408
4481	König Otto, O	z. V. Oa. West	94 424	—	—	24 068
4482	Gaut Walter	z. V. 39. Sta.	88 630	—	—	10 435
4483	Welz Matthäus, O	z. V. 29. Sta.	279 095	—	—	4 465
4484	Jörg Franz, O	z. V. 1. Sta.	259 673	—	—	8 088
4485	Dr. Stahl Wilhelm, O	z. V. 7. Sta.	302 450	—	—	10 219
4486	Dr. Foeden Ernst, O	z. V. 49. Sta.	—	789 100	—	43 968
4487	Hildebrandt Ernst	z. V. 15. Sta.	—	1 661 468	—	25 517
4488	Schubert Max, O	z. V. 3. Sta.	102 389	—	—	5 364
4489	Platt Bruno, O	z. V. 55. Sta.	380 196	—	—	8 272
4490	Geurdel Willy	z. V. 6. Sta.	—	560 667	—	13 836
4491	Harbwein Karl	z. V. Ab. X	160 263	—	—	34 496
4492	Elser Otto, O	z. V. Oa. Süd	—	754 128	—	36 914
4493	Dr. Fulke Paul	z. V. 22. Sta.	73 956	—	—	58 522
4494	Dr. Berkmann Max	z. V. 34. Sta.	—	1 117 921	—	54 967
4495	Dorn Max, O	z. V. Ab. XX	180 303	—	—	10 243
4496	Lichtenberg Melchior, O	z. V. 20. Sta.	407 720	—	—	6 724
4497	Freter Alfred, O	z. V. 25. Sta.	490 514	—	—	8 842
4498	Niggeloh Hermann, O	z. V. 69. Sta.	241 731	—	—	5 908
4499	Dr. Kölzow Hans, O	z. V. 6. Sta.	102 624	—	—	1 961
4500	Mages Hans, O	z. V. 2. Sta.	31 637	—	—	630
4501	von Kapff Karl	z. V. 1. Sta.	267 452	—	—	180 133
4502	Gable Ernst, O	z. V. 1. Sta.	78 003	—	—	1 338
4503	Jurk Walter	z. V. 3. Mo. Sta.	29 792	—	—	44 795
4504	Karl Peter, O	z. V. 54. Sta.	—	660 084	—	18 646
4505	Schaale Richard, O	z. V. 43. Sta.	428 144	—	—	9 906
4506	Pünfer Richard, O	z. V. 45. Sta.	136 289	—	—	16 212
4507	Gottwald Johannes, O	z. V. 16. Sta.	392 769	—	—	9 049
4508	Witt Michael, O	z. V. 29. Sta.	4 774	—	—	1 677
4509	Thoms Hermann, O	z. V. 28. Sta.	—	999 386	—	45 578
4510	Derg Ludwig, O	z. V. 34. Sta.	104 984	—	—	1 403
4511	Ramonat Otto, O	z. V. 60. Sta.	31 530	—	—	11 950
4512	Wiegmann August, O	z. V. 31. Sta.	97 853	—	—	3 036
4513	Dr. Greiff Karl	z. V. 6. Sta.	401 839	—	—	7 060
4514	Vaehlicke Willi, O	z. V. 30. Sta.	186 860	—	—	2 516
4515	Weyand Karl, O	z. V. 25. Sta.	27 716	—	—	2 857
4516	Kaphengst Karl, O	z. V. Oa. Süd	89 055	—	—	8 495
4517	Guglhör Michael, O	z. V. 1. Sta.	34 017	—	—	1 012
4518	Dr. Stödle Edmund	z. V. 29. Sta.	—	—	1 860 913	87 281
4519	Röhl Ludwig, O	z. V. 1. Sta.	88 024	—	—	1 239
4520	Eberer Max, O	z. V. 34. Sta.	3 986	—	—	423
4521	Flasche August, O	z. V. 19. Sta.	—	509 777	—	21 421
4522	Schäfer Otto, O	z. V. 3. Mo. Sta.	—	361 206	—	36 529
4523	Sprang Paul, O	z. V. 7. Mo. Sta.	309 642	—	—	5 417
4524	Faulhaber Walter, O	z. V. 43. Sta.	238 283	—	—	10 786
4525	Neubauer Fritz, O	z. V. 77. Sta.	—	779 889	—	27 654
4526	Pfannenschwarz Karl	z. V. Oa. Südwest	—	508 908	—	55 190
4527	Graf zu Dohna Hermann, St.Rat	z. V. 61. Sta.	—	808 228	—	102 880

The <u>1935</u> SS-Dienstalterliste showing recipient's of the Totenkopf Ring with the rank of SS-Hauptstürmführer.

Lfde. Nr.	Name	Dienststellung	Partei-Nr.			SS-Nr.	Unter-sturmführer	Ober-sturmführer	Haupt-sturm-führer
			1-500000	500001-1000000	über 1000000				
4772	Ludewig Kurt, O	z. B. 3. Mo. Sta.	84 438	--	---	41 438	20. 4. 34		
4773	Schwenn Friedrich, O	z. B. 5. Mo. Sta.		754 500	---	41 689	20. 4. 34		
4774	Schuchard Harry	z. B. 11. Mo. Sta.	--	677 561		42 291	20. 4. 34		
4775	Janik Heinrich	z. B. 17. Sta.	258 861		---	42 297	20. 4. 34		
4776	Bonnet Albert, O	z. B. 32. Sta.	481 290			42 818	20. 4. 34		
4777	Feld Adolf	z. B. 59. Sta.	--	1 235 092		44 012	20. 4. 34		
4778	Brandt Thees	z. B. 88. Sta.	--	1 438 389		44 678	20. 4. 34		
4779	Schween Ernst	z. B. 17. Sta.	407 449			44 736	20. 4. 34		
4780	Nelusa Gustav	z. B. 3. Mo. Sta.	--	573 135		46 672	20. 4. 34		
4781	Veitbold Hermann	z. B. Ab. 11	--	713 114		47 060	20. 4. 34		
4782	Fank Alfred	z. B. 22. Sta.	182 619			48 923	20. 4. 34		
4783	Kesmer Martin	z. B. 3. Mo. Sta.	--	1 179 618		50 505	20. 4. 34		
4784	Lahrmann Fritz	z. B. 3. Mo. Sta.	283 293			50 508	20. 4. 34		
4785	Milde Harald	z. B. 28. Sta.	367 412			53 615	20. 4. 34		
4786	Gerhardt Karl	z. B. 3. Mo. Sta.	--	843 490		53 771	20. 4. 34		
4787	Hofmann Max, O	z. B. Ab. IX	--	803 405		53 801	20. 4. 34		
4788	Simmermann Max	z. B. 32. Sta.	--	1 298 072		55 351	20. 4. 34		
4789	Dittrich Georg	z. B. 46. Sta.	187 193	--		59 700	20. 4. 34		
4790	Büchlers Max	z. B. Ab. V	---	882 705		64 051	20. 4. 34		
4791	Schlette Walter	z. B. 13. Sta.	47 536		--	68 000	20. 4. 34		
4792	Jahn Albert	z. Oa. Nord			1 866 572	93 259	20. 4. 34		
4793	Strauße Walter	z. B. 47. Sta.	178 138			100 337	20. 4. 34		
4794	Hermann Arthur	z. B. 48. Sta.	245 986	--		121 152	20. 4. 34		
4795	Völkner Karl	z. B. 59. Sta.	—	1 324 620	---	160 325	20. 4. 34		
4796	Mittmann Gotthard, O	z. B. 16. Sta.	--	829 409	--	51 818	28. 4. 34		
4797	Werner Alfred	z. B. 47. Sta.	—	847 772	---	24 499	5. 5. 34		
4798	Boußet Helmut	z. B. 3. Mo. Sta.	—	550 973	---	27 497	10. 5. 34		
4799	Heberer Walter	z. B. 80. Sta.	—	675 068	--	93 405	10. 5. 34		
4800	Hebderich Fritz	z. B. Ab. III	--	692 604	---	49 496	11. 5. 34		
4801	Langguth Kurt	z. B. 28. Sta.	63 496	--	---	4 748	6. 6. 34		
4802	Bauer Hans, ✠	z. B. 42. Sta.	253 004	--		53 004	7. 6. 34		
4803	Wiedmann Otto	z. B. 58. Sta.	—	871 555	---	116 033	12. 6. 34		
4804	Remmer Fritz, O	z. B. 56. Sta.	185 759	—	---	3 272	14. 6. 34		
4805	Marschke August	z. B. 39. Sta.	314 796	—	---	22 459	17. 6. 34		
4806	Stahnke Wilhelm	z. B. 39. Sta.	—	638 646	---	22 472	17. 6. 34		
4807	Dr. Fischer Hans	z. B. 67. Sta.	—	1 187 881	---	29 627	18. 6. 34		
4808	Niegisch Artur	z. B. 75. Sta.	—	541 549	---	35 009	18. 6. 34		
4809	Müller Johannes	z. B. 48. Sta.	163 596	—	---	4 430	4. 7. 34		
4810	Schwartz Albert	z. B. Ab. XXVI	228 771	—	---	6 532	4. 7. 34		
4811	Frhr. v. Reibnitz Günther	z. B. Ab. VI	412 855	—	---	66 010	4. 7. 34		
4812	Völkle Fritz	z. B. 72. Sta.	371 691	—	---	4 965	10. 7. 34		
4813	Ressing Wilhelm, O	z. B. 19. Sta.	294 089	—	---	4 075	9. 8. 34		
4814	Gemander Erich, O	z. B. 23. Sta.	92 286	—	---	6 523	29. 8. 34		
4815	Martin Erwin, O	z. B. 15. Sta.	—	—	---	48 712	24. 9. 34		
4816	Reifer Josef, O	z. B. 32. Sta.	48 715	—	---	1 581	9. 11. 34		
4817	Treiber Kurt, O	z. B. 32. Sta.	—	523 575	---	2 932	9. 11. 34		
4818	Schwartz Wilhelm	z. B. 5. Sta.	239 204	---	---	3 048	9. 11. 34		
4819	Hinke Gustav	z. B. Ab. XXVII	90 596	—	---	3 277	9. 11. 34		
4820	Ueymann Otto	z. B. 32. Sta.	392 147	—	---	4 174	9. 11. 34		
4821	Seger Georg	z. B. 3. Mo. Sta.	171 290	—	---	8 605	9. 11. 34		
4822	Wolf Paul	z. B. 54. Sta.	133 458	—	---	13 190	9. 11. 34		

The <u>1935</u> SS-Dienstalterliste which is a continuation of SS-Hauptstürmführer recipients of the Totenkopf Ring.

Lfd. Nr.	Name	Dienststellung	Partei-Nr. bis 400 000	Partei-Nr. 400 000-1 Million	Partei-Nr. über 1 Million	SS-Nr.	Untersturmführer	Obersturmführer	Hauptsturmführer
4823	Krüger Horst	z.V. 75. Sta.	385 876			14 494	9.11.34		
4824	Barth Ernst, O	z.V. 20. Sta.	217 628			22 748	9.11.34		
4825	Kühn Hermann, O	z.V. Ov. Ob	207 761			27 492	9.11.34		
4826	Rettmann Wilhelm	z.V. 7. Mo. Sta.		1 142 665		30 214	9.11.34		
4827	Friedrich Eduard	z.V. 41. Sta.		741 855		32 567	9.11.34		
4828	Römer Albert	z.V. 91. Sta.	127 517			39 405	9.11.34		
4829	Müller Friedrich	z.V. 75. Sta.		1 407 646		39 878	9.11.34		
4830	Häßler Wilhelm	z.V. 6. Sta.	474 177			48 332	9.11.34		
4831	Wolff Rudolf	z.V. 75. Sta.		1 011 017		50 854	9.11.34		
4832	Bod Christoph	z.V. 17. Sta.	6 538			53 542	9.11.34		
4833	Martschle Gerhard	z.V. Ab. 11	65 740			59 683	9.11.34		
4834	Gravenhorst Walther	z.V. Ab. XV	67 118			63 283	9.11.34		
4835	Kriebler Ernst	z.V. 45. Sta.			2 248 283	70 430	9.11.34		
4836	Arendt Emil	z.V. 7. R. Sta.				83 458	9.11.34		
4837	Peter Johann	z.V. 4. Sta.				129 293	9.11.34		
4838	Dr. Veh Eduard	z.V. Ab. XXIX		557 665		131 115	9.11.34		
4839	Ristau Lothar	z.V. 3. Mo. Sta.	316 161			212 058	9.11.34		
4840	Kaiser Hanns	z.V. Ab. IV	67 664			1 186	1. 1.35		
4841	Sievers Kurt	z.V. 51. Sta.		671 647		15 721	1. 1.35		
4842	Grams Paul	z.V. Ab. XIII	447 860			30 229-	1. 1.35		
4843	Beder Alfred	z.V. 10. Na. Sta.				169 299	19. 1.35		
4844	Wiedenmann Hans	z.V. 31. Sta.	97 958			21 654	30. 1.35		
4845	Vergande Gustav	z.V. 77. Sta.		988 721		35 377	30. 1.35		
4846	Merle Konrad, O	z.V. 43. Sta.		505 332		53 532	30. 1.35		
4847	Tank Fritz	z.V. 77. Sta.		1 267 039		57 121	30. 1.35		
4848	Puther Karl	z.V. 20. Sta.	41 360			965	18. 2.35		
4849	Werner Erich	z.V. 6. Sta.	92 727			3 690	20. 4.35		
4850	Rafchel Thomas	z.V. 43. Sta.	373 495			16 195	20. 4.35		
4851	Meyer Willy	z.V. 8. Na. Sta.		952 495		46 864	20. 4.35		
4852	Kaletfch Henry	z.V. 28. Sta.		1 056 721		50 321	20. 4.35		
4853	Buffe Otto	z.V. 80. Sta.		1 362 076		63 908	20. 4.35		
4854	Schridel Leopold	z.V. Ab. XVIII	2 574			34 116	1. 6.35		

The <u>1935</u> SS-Dienstalterliste which is a continuation of SS-Hauptstürmführer recipients of the Totenkopf Ring. Note that there are only three recipients on this page due to them being lower on the seniority scale.

SS=Obersturmführer:

Lfde. Nr.	Name	Dienststellung	Partei-Nr. 1 bis 100000	100001 bis 1000000	über 1000000	SS-Nr.	Untersturmführer	Obersturmführer	Sturmführer
4528	Bernd Willi, O	z. B. 10. Sta.	23 269	—	—	4 798	12. 2.31	9.11.33	
4529	Faust Emil, O	z. B. 5. Sta.	151 165	—	—	2 381	11. 3.31	9.11.33	
4530	Dr. Krug Werner, ⚡	z. B. 50. Sta.	174 924	—	—	3 867	21. 3.31	9.11.33	
4531	Reich Alfred, O	z. B. 13. Sta.	285 724	—	—	3 448	15. 5.31	9.11.33	
4532	Küsner Friedrich, O	z. B. 42. Sta.	410 818	—	—	10 356	13.10.31	9.11.33	
4533	Eckmann Wilhelm, O	z. B. 8. Sta.	5 774	—	—	6 505	1.12.31	9.11.33	
4534	Müller Kurt, O	z. B. Ab. III	231 793	—	—	6 369	6.12.31	9.11.33	
4535	Frommhold Emil, O	z. B. Oa. Ost	62 161	—	—	12 776	6.12.31	9.11.33	
4536	Goesien Hans, O	z. B. 39. Sta.	165 022	—	—	13 205	6.12.31	9.11.33	
4537	Hirsch Paul	z. B. 20. Sta.	—	625 446	—	5 776	21. 2.32	9.11.33	
4538	Bergmann Dietrich, O	z. B. 25. Sta.	—	527 388	—	13 040	21. 2.32	9.11.33	
4539	Kessel Fritz	z. B. 33. Sta.	454 397	—	—	6 491	24. 3.32	9.11.33	
4540	Seehaus Ludwig, O	z. B. 33. Sta.	9 154	—	—	705	2. 4.32	9.11.33	
4541	Schilfen Otto, O	z. B. 69. Sta.	249 339	—	—	4 741	2. 4.32	9.11.33	
4542	Machni Ernst, O	z. B. 78. Sta.	43 389	—	—	1 283	24. 8.32	9.11.33	
4543	Hahmann Georg, O	z. B. 78. Sta.	183 697	—	—	7 189	24. 8.32	9.11.33	
4544	Kienberger Josef	z. B. 29 Sta.	177 143	—	—	10 604	24. 8.32	9.11.33	
4545	Clausen Hans, O	z. B. Oa. Nord	398 638	—	—	17 071	24. 8 32	9.11.33	
4546	Kops Walter, O	z. B. 58. Sta.	165 786	—	—	1 840	9. 9.32	9.11.33	
4547	Elligsen Erich, O	z. B. 51. Sta.	4 210	—	—	5 888	7.10.32	9.11.33	
4548	Nell Paul, O	z. B. 25. Sta.	27 881	—	—	5 530	9.11.32	9.11.33	
4549	Goch Hermann, O	z. B. 25. Sta.	—	518 030	—	8 796	9.11.32	9.11.33	
4550	Dr. Hinrichsen Fritz	z. B. 50. Sta.	—	799 716	—	20 299	9.11.32	9.11.33	
4551	Elsner Martin, O	z. B. 86. XXIV	383 459	—	—	6 014	12.11.32	9.11.33	
4552	Otto Albert, O	z. B. 86. XXVIII	256 124	—	—	2 801	1.12.32	9.11.33	
4553	Barthelmes Rudolf	z. B. 47. Sta.	264 814	—	—	9 468	24.12.32	9.11.33	
4554	Wieland Hans	z. B. 7. Sta.	—	657 896	—	19 890	24.12.32	9.11.33	
4555	Brandes Hermann, O	z. B. 49. Sta.	99 917	—	—	2 022	30. 1.33	9.11.33	
4556	Hoppe Max, O	z. B. 86. XVIII	69 936	—	—	7 163	7. 8.33	24.12.33	
4557	Flickner Franz, O	z. B. 69. Sta.	335 427	—	—	5 040	17. 9.31	30. 1.34	
4558	Preßien Hans	z. B. 86. XVI	388 298	—	—	52 187	9.11.33	17. 2.34	
4559	Seibl Johann	z. B. 31. Sta.	188 495	—	—	5 708	30. 1.33	9. 3.34	
4560	Eichler Hubert, O	z. B. 36. Sta.	371 269	—	—	8 838	—	11. 3.34	
4561	Eickhoff Heinrich, O	z. B. Ab. IV	—	549 534	—	12 239	31. 7.33	16. 3.34	
4562	Walschle Bruno, O	z. B. 6. Sta.	250 325	—	—	12 187	9.11.33	16. 4.34	
4563	Schrettenbrunner Ludwig, ⚡O	z. B. 1. Sta.	246	—	—	40 581	31. 7.33	20 4.34	
4564	Achtzehn Kurt, O	z. B. 43. Sta.	—	604 700	—	29 913	24.12 32	28. 4.34	
4565	Schöffel Heinrich, O	z. B. 70. Sta.	140 777	—	—	5 168	24.12.32	26. 5.34	
4566	Vatermann Josef, O	z. B. 43. Sta.	356 244	—	—	16 244	24.12.32	27. 5.34	
4567	Voltolini Jesko, O	z. B. 54. Sta.	—	711 220	—	25 821	9.11.33	15. 6.34	
4568	Heukuck Franz, O	z. B. 39. Sta.	—	786 257	—	23 457	2. 3.33	17. 6.34	
4569	Just Hermann, O	z. B. 74. Sta.	156 018	—	—	12 823	12. 6.33	17. 6.34	
4570	Meier Josef, O	z. B. 74. Sta.	182 411	—	—	43 276	12. 6 33	17. 6.34	
4571	Kirberg Alfred, O	z. B. 86. XXIII	315 921	—	—	50 702	24. 3.34	1. 7.34	
4572	Hadbart Hugo, O	z. B. 16. Sta.	—	531 647	—	9 056	9.11.33	4. 7.34	
4573	Schöuknecht Georg, O	z. B. 16. Sta.	428 334	—	—	10 775	9.11.33	4. 7.34	
4574	Nitsche Otto, O	z. B. 8. Sta.	—		1 402 669	40 008	20. 4.34	4. 7.34	

The <u>1935</u> SS-Dienstalterliste showing recipient's of the Totenkopf Ring with the rank of SS-Obersturmführer.

Lfte. Nr.	Name	Dienststellung	Partei-Nr. 1—100 000	Partei-Nr. 100 001—300 000	Partei-Nr. über 1 000 000	SS-Nr.	Unter-sturmführer	Ober-sturmführer	Haupt-sturm-führer
4575	Venner Gerhard	J. B. 27. Sta.	—	—	1 975 805	63 444	20. 4. 31	4. 7. 31	
4576	Weigert Karl, O	J. B. 1. Sta.	—	1 200 995	—	47 291	20. 4. 34	12. 8. 31	
4577	John Leonhard, O	J. B. 1. Sta.	86 875	—	—	1 405	20. 4. 34	22. 8. 31	
4578	Willens Hans, O	J. B. 28. Sta.	99 587	—	—	15 710	22. 3. 31	23. 8. 31	
4579	Schrib Karl, O	J. B. Ab 1	—	1 275 219	—	39 545	24. 12. 33	25. 8. 31	
4580	Lemke Werner, O	J. B. 9 Sta	471 032	—	—	43 277	20. 4. 34	29. 8. 34	
4581	Lembrecht Hermann, O	J. B. 40. Sta.	—	647 924	—	13 913	14. 3. 32	9. 9. 34	
4582	Meier Franz, O	J. B. 35. Sta.	—	720 377	—	19 543	1. 12. 32	9. 9. 34	
4583	Gericke Otto	J. B. 14. Sta.	374 505	—	—	21 520	1. 12. 32	9. 9. 31	
4584	Ferlings Wilhelm, O	J. B. 25. Sta.	260 389	—	—	3 420	30. 1. 33	9. 9. 34	
4585	Müller Horst, O	J. B. 4. Re. Sta	200 592	—	—	43 385	30. 1. 33	9. 9. 34	
4586	Dr. Reis Hugo, O	J. B. 5. Sta.	159 194	—	—	47 594	30. 1. 33	9. 9. 34	
4587	Dr. Vilz Fritz, O	J. B. 12. Sta.	334 610	—	—	47 726	30. 1. 33	9. 9. 34	
4588	Alberts Theodor, O	J. B. 30. Sta.	223 673	—	—	3 603	20. 4. 33	9. 9. 34	
4589	Richter Willy, O	J. B. 20. Sta.	451 007	—	—	4 887	20. 4. 33	9. 9. 34	
4590	Pelz Karl, O	J. B. 43. Sta.	138 063	—	—	51 972	20. 4. 34	9. 9. 34	
4591	Reus Adolf, O	J. B. 20. Sta.	25 559	—	—	16 700	20. 4. 33	9. 11. 34	
4592	Wittner Bertold, O	J. B. Oa. Ost	181 537	—	—	39 176	12. 6. 33	9. 11. 34	
4593	Dallner Georg, O	J. B 3. Sta.	—	597 995	—	32 926	1. 8. 33	9. 11. 34	
4594	Weigelt Gottfried, O	J. B. 46. Sta.	44 931	—	—	2 780	9. 11. 33	9. 11. 34	
4595	Wieding Egon, O	J. B. 1. Sta.	318 919	—	—	14 230	9. 11. 33	9. 11. 34	
4596	Schnettgen Hans, O	J. B. 58. Sta.	—	1 107 792	—	31 324	30. 1. 34	9. 11. 34	
4597	Dr. Goerlich Max	J. B. 63. Sta.	—	884 375	—	146 717	2. 2. 31	9. 11. 34	
4598	Neumann Paul, O	J. B. 3. Sta.	6 618	—	—	8 490	20. 2. 34	9. 11. 34	
4599	Soika Josef, O	J. B. 45. Sta.	413 034	—	—	6 045	28. 2. 34	9. 11. 34	
4600	Tromm Walter, O	J. B. 81. Sta.	127 120	—	—	2 669	20. 4. 34	9. 11. 34	
4601	Grabow Hans, O	J. B. 75. Sta.	264 307	—	—	6 647	20. 4. 34	9. 11. 34	
4602	Dr. Hohenkirch Bernhard, O	J. B. Ab. XVII	345 101	—	—	106 663	24. 12. 33	1. 1. 35	
4603	Vogel Adolf, O	J. B. 8. Sta.	189 733	—	—	26 838	24. 12. 32	19. 1. 35	
4604	Pelz Bruno, O	J. B. 43. Sta.	428 543	—	—	18 409	24. 12. 32	20. 4. 35	
4605	Düser Albert, O	J. B. 56. Sta.	—	747 575	—	28 469	24. 12. 33	20. 4. 35	
4606	Globisch Alexander, O	J. B. 70. Sta.	—	989 411	—	42 463	28. 2. 34	20. 4. 35	
4607	Voigt Harald	J. B. Ab. XXIII	—	1 774 712	—	140 783	21. 3. 34	20. 4. 35	
4608	Leister Karl, O	J. B. 72 Sta	21 183	—	—	31 179	13. 4. 34	20. 4. 35	
4609	Müller Georg	J. B. 42. Sta.	124 660	—	—	12 809	10. 5. 34	20. 4. 35	
4610	Schwarz Heinrich	J. B. 32. Sta.	231 150	—	—	4 675	9. 11. 34	20. 4. 35	
4611	Mehrenpfennig Otto	J. B. 59. Sta.	110 947	—	—	41 917	9. 11. 34	20. 4. 35	
4612	Thieme Max	J. B. 3. Re. Sta.	—	562 118	—	34 986	20. 4. 34	1. 6. 35	

SS-Untersturmführer:

Lfte. Nr.	Name	Dienststellung	Partei-Nr. 1—100 000	Partei-Nr. 100 001—300 000	Partei-Nr. über 1 000 000	SS-Nr.	Unter-sturmführer	Ober-sturmführer	Haupt-sturm-führer
4613	Bosch Karl, O	J. B. 34. Sta.	199 990	—	—	3 685	18. 5. 31		
4614	Laise Erich	J. B. 65. Sta.	184 853	—	—	6 880	19. 11. 31		
4615	Lang Hans	J. B. 48. Sta.	—	650 974	—	12 950	2. 2. 32		
4616	Kraft Franz	J. B. 10. Sta.	65 350	—	—	4 915	9. 9. 32		
4617	Dornheim Wilhelm	J. B. 42. Sta.	226 482	—	—	4 857	1. 10. 32		
4618	Fischer Ernst, O	J. B. 47. Sta.	5 448	—	—	21 908	1. 12. 32		

The **1935** SS-Dienstalterliste showing a continuation of SS-Obersturmführer recipients and the start of the SS-Untersturmführer recipient's of the Totenkopf Ring.

Pfte. Nr.	Name	Dienststellung	Partei-Nr.			SS-Nr.	Unter-sturmführer	Ober-sturmführer	Haupt-sturmführer
			1 bis 5000	5000 (100000)	über 100000				
4619	Kügler Albert, O	J. B. 43. Sta.	189 617	—	—	6 511	21. 12. 32		
4620	Derra Hans, O	J. B. 36. Sta.	—	679 580	—	14 880	21. 12. 32		
4621	Taupe Max, O	J. B. 8. Sta.	—	503 555	—	18 873	21. 12. 32		
4622	Habasch Karl, O	J. B. 16. Sta.	—	673 903	—	18 807	21. 12. 32		
4623	Reffe Bernhard, O	J. B. 51. Sta.	25 810	—	—	20 363	21. 12. 32		
4624	Meißleg Karl, O	J. B. 7. Sta.	135 157	—	—	4 658	30. 4. 33		
4625	Altenbrandt Wilhelm, O	J. B. 2. Sta.	97 639	—	—	4 281	30. 4. 33		
4626	Sievers Joachim	J. B. 88. Sta.	196 350	—	—	9 010	30. 4. 33		
4627	Bachmann Anton, O	J. B. 7. Sta.	18 375	—	—	10 853	30. 4. 33		
4628	Wendler Rudolf, O	J. B. 48. Sta.	321 319	—	—	11 130	30. 4. 33		
4629	Schmidt August, O	J. B. 20. Sta.	407 726	—	—	12 228	30. 4. 33		
4630	Först Friedrich	J. B. 25. Sta.	16 221	—	—	26 129	30. 4. 33		
4631	Bauer Ludwig	J. B. 41. Sta.	—	812 826	—	31 517	30. 4. 33		
4632	Reißing Karl, O	J. B. 13. Sta.	376 272	—	—	38 080	30. 4. 33		
4633	Woestmann Gerhard	J. B. 6. Sta.	—	816 228	—	39 638	30. 4. 33		
4634	Daniel Josef, O	J. B. 23. Sta.	—	674 008	—	40 314	30. 4. 33		
4635	von Villiez Franz	J. B. 42. Sta.	—	630 193	—	12 814	12. 6. 33		
4636	Böttcher Wilhelm	J. B. 3. Mo. Sta.	—	530 865	—	13 111	12. 6. 33		
4637	Rüd Walter, O	J. B. 42. Sta.	—	1 107 863	—	36 625	12. 6. 33		
4638	Dr. Ebert Otto, O	J. B. Oo. Ost	—	1 361 071	—	48 321	12. 6. 33		
4639	Mödel Herbert	J. B. 42 Sta.	152 319	—	—	3 810	6. 7. 33		
4640	Machui Josef, O	J. B. 78 Sta.	325 589	—	—	3 325	31. 7. 33		
4641	Rendel Peter, O	J. B. 78 Sta.	325 500	—	—	4 900	31. 7. 33		
4642	Bürkle Oskar	J. B. 62 Sta.	—	1 029 780	—	49 607	31. 7. 33		
4643	Schmidt Paul, O	J. B. 3. M. Sta.	—	—	—	83 132	5. 8. 33		
4644	Seelaß Karl, O	J. B. 5. Sta.	—	1 112 027	—	36 952	22. 8. 33		
4645	Paffehl Theodor, O	J. B. 5. Mo. Sta.	392 376	—	—	6 702	3. 9. 33		
4646	Bruning Paul	J. B. Ab. III	—	550 958	—	25 726	3. 9. 33		
4647	Jödel Ernst, O	J. B. 6. Sta.	319 221	—	—	35 029	3. 9. 33		
4648	Kelling Adolf, O	J. B. 28. Sta.	94 250	—	—	50 406	3. 9. 33		
4649	Dr. Jung Fritz	J. B. 68. Sta.	—	1 002 831	—	70 304	4. 9. 33		
4650	Linne Karl, O	J. B. 30. Sta.	480 034	—	—	5 363	9. 11. 33		
4651	Langner Ernst, O	J. B. 16. Sta.	310 741	—	—	9 054	9. 11. 33		
4652	Sander Kurt	J. B. 64. Sta.	—	652 111	—	10 710	9. 11. 33		
4653	Schmidt Heinrich, O	J. B. 7. Mo. Sta.	—	704 080	—	11 847	9. 11. 33		
4654	Wehrgott Albert, O	J. B. 77. Sta.	—	644 011	—	35 359	9. 11. 33		
4655	Ditterich Otto, O	J. B. 56. Sta.	—	1 143 715	—	44 288	9. 11. 33		
4656	Komitsch Erich, O	J. B. 23. Sta.	—	1 296 957	—	45 863	9. 11. 33		
4657	Krüger Oskar	J. B. 64. Sta.	—	1 143 680	—	60 488	9. 11. 33		
4658	Hirschfeld Emil	J. B. 22. Sta.	—	—	—	72 854	9. 11. 33		
4659	Dr. Loß Karl, O	J. B. 30. Sta.	223 513	—	—	118 402	9. 11. 33		
4660	Leyde Kurt	J. B. 3. Mo. Sta.	—	997 282	—	46 670	1. 12. 33		
4661	Strang Hermann, O	J. B. 6. Mo. Sta.	380 251	—	—	21 532	21. 12. 33		
4662	Hedert Heinrich, O	J. B. 2. Sta.	—	583 304	—	24 093	21. 12. 33		
4663	Feige Arthur, O	J. B. Ab. III	410 693	—	—	43 968	24. 12. 33		
4664	Schlünfen Carl O	J. B. 21. Sta.	—	681 024	—	44 027	24. 12. 33		
4665	Kring Ernst	J. B. 50. Sta.	—	1 288 830	—	44 039	24. 12. 33		
4666	Fuhrmann Fritz	J. B. 6. Sta.	989 111	—	—	63 770	24. 12. 33		
4667	Nöhl Hans, G	J. B. 1. Sta.	3 301	—	—	39 949	1. 1. 34		
4668	Chubin Hermann, O	J. B. 62. Sta.	11 534	—	—	1 761	30. 1. 34		
4669	Sauer Paul, O	J. B. 13. Sta.	185 618	—	—	5 375	30. 1. 34		
4670	Eater Oskar, O	J. B. 62. Sta.	—	552 588	—	6 076	30. 1. 34		

The <u>1935</u> SS-Dienstalterliste showing a continuation of SS-Unterstürmführer recipients of the Totenkopf Ring.

346

Lfde. Nr.	Name	Dienststellung	Partei-Nr.			SS-Nr.	Unter-sturmführer	Ober-sturmführer	sturm-führer
			1–600 000	600 001–1 000 000	über 1 000 000				
4722	Albrecht Karl, O	J. B. 20. Sta.	185 087	—	—	2 842	20. 4. 34		
4723	Dellingrath Hans, O	J. B. 20. Sta.	106 903	—	—	2 879	20. 4. 34		
4724	Werkhausen Heinrich	J. B. 3. Mo. Sta.	231 804	—	—	3 126	20. 4. 34		
4725	Schönlein Heinz	J. B. 46. Sta.	302 421	—	—	4 730	20. 4. 34		
4726	Keller Karl	J. B. 46. Sta.	335 117	—	—	5 675	20. 4. 34		
4727	Apfel Hermann	J. B. 25. Sta.	186 236	—	—	6 905	20. 4. 34		
4728	Koch Willi, O	J. B. 69. Sta.	223 635	—	—	7 551	20. 4. 34		
4729	von Klosewski Werner, O	J. B. 39. Sta.	118 313	—	—	8 976	20. 4. 34		
4730	Schütte Herbert, O	J. B. 16. Sta.	310 765	—	—	9 081	20. 4. 34		
4731	Herz Willy, O	J. B. 33. Sta.	281 715	—	—	9 486	20. 4. 34		
4732	Bachmann Richard	J. B. 57. Sta.	—	581 304	—	10 919	20. 4. 34		
4733	Möhle Otto	J. B. 21. Sta.	98 052	—	—	10 943	20. 4. 34		
4734	Krieg Paul	J. B. 3. Mo. Sta.	62 099	—	—	12 775	20. 4. 34		
4735	von der Osten Kurt, O	J. B. 74. Sta.	200 400	—	—	12 827	20. 4. 34		
4736	Jüttner Rudolf	J. B. 46. Sta.	350 805	—	—	13 364	20. 4. 34		
4737	Wagner Emil, O	J. B. 30. Sta.	423 108	—	—	14 787	20. 4. 34		
4738	Nagel Otto, O	J. B. 5. Sta.	—	534 283	—	15 797	20. 4. 34		
4739	Stegner Ernst, O	J. B. 30. Sta.	267 231	—	—	16 766	20. 4. 34		
4740	Wüster Karl, O	30. Sta.	—	700 764	—	18 847	20. 4. 34		
4741	Hinrichs Karl	J. B. 77. Sta.	448 195	—	—	19 208	20. 4. 34		
4742	Althaus Wilhelm, O	J. B. 72. Sta.	—	891 378	—	19 327	20. 4. 34		
4743	Jeschke Heinrich	J. B. 39. Sta.	—	616 555	—	20 193	20. 4. 34		
4744	Braasch Paul	J. B. 39. Sta.	—	616 531	—	20 198	20. 4. 34		
4745	Gerhards Robert, O	J. B. 32. Sta.	—	846 485	—	20 687	20. 4. 34		
4746	Vollmer Walter	J. B. 86. Sta.	241 213	—	—	21 889	20. 4. 34		
4747	Eicker Louis, O	J. B. 47. Sta.	243 085	—	—	21 954	20. 4. 34		
4748	Kopp Friedrich, O	J. B. 19. Sta.	—	817 453	—	23 330	20. 4. 34		
4749	Endräßelker Rudolf	J. B. 7. Sta.	—	718 324	—	23 591	20. 4. 34		
4750	Vogler Heinrich	J. B. 3. Mo. Sta.	—	591 839	—	23 634	20. 4. 34		
4751	Frhr. von Reitzenstein Ludwig, O	J. B. 34. Sta.	292 837	—	—	25 361	20. 4. 34		
4752	Tauber Kurt, O	J. B. 2. Mo. Sta.	207 352	—	—	25 774	20. 4. 34		
4753	Kürsten Paul, O	J. B. 78. Sta.	402 476	—	—	26 316	20. 4. 34		
4754	Paulus Peter, O	J. B. 78. Sta.	324 229	—	—	26 346	20. 4. 34		
4755	Stoll Kurt, O	J. B. 2. Mo. Sta.	—	761 465	—	26 398	20. 4. 34		
4756	Grab Fritz, O	J. B. 79. Sta.	—	758 815	—	27 272	20. 4. 34		
4757	Heußler Paul	J. B. 63. Sta.	371 798	—	—	27 301	20. 4. 34		
4758	Christoffer Paul, O	J. B. 39. Sta.	—	881 344	—	27 670	20. 4. 34		
4759	Dr. Podbig Franz, O	J. B. 70. Sta.	189 237	—	—	29 911	20. 4. 34		
4760	Beck Alfred, O	J. B. 69. Sta.	378 967	—	—	30 345	20. 4. 34		
4761	Wid Theodor	J. B. 62. Sta.	—	575 386	—	32 589	20. 4. 34		
4762	Schmitt Heinrich, O	J. B. 30. Sta.	146 215	—	—	33 279	20. 4. 34		
4763	Wernecke Hans	J. B. 4. Sta.	—	1 019 926	—	33 522	20. 4. 34		
4764	Ruß Albert, O	J. B. 61. Sta.	234 692	—	—	34 922	20. 4. 34		
4765	Schott Tom, O	J. B. 9. Sta.	—	1 469 364	—	36 863	20. 4. 34		
4766	Freist Eduard, O	J. B. 11. Mo. Sta.	—	572 936	—	37 301	20. 4. 34		
4767	Weiß Theodor, O	J. B. 82. Sta.	—	616 202	—	38 978	20. 4. 34		
4768	Delmelite Franz, O	J. B. 69. Sta.	173 948	—	—	39 020	20. 4. 34		
4769	Heimesath Ernst, O	J. B. 49. Sta.	—	1 283 919	—	39 855	20. 4. 34		
4770	Winkler Max	J. B. 7. Sta.	380 747	—	—	39 912	20. 4. 34		
4771	Pehning Kurt	J. B. 21. Sta.	—	681 069	—	40 425	20. 4. 34		

The **1935** SS-Dienstalterliste showing a continuation of SS-Unterstürmführer recipients of the Totenkopf Ring.

Lfte. Nr.	Name	Dienststellung	Partei-Nr.			ff-Nr.	Unter-sturmführer	Ober-sturmführer	
4671	Lorenz Walter, O	z. V. 75. Sta.	280 267	—	—	20 054	30. 1. 34		
4672	Reiser Heinrich, O	z. V. 13. Sta.	—	847 100	—	21 842	30. 1. 34		
4673	Menz Richard, O	z. V. 50. Sta.	—	700 329	—	22 654	30. 1. 34		
4674	Hoener Otto	z. V. Ab. XXX	—	611 191	—	23 245	30. 1. 34		
4675	Wenig Hugo, O	z. V. 2. Sta.	318 084	—	—	26 372	30. 1. 34		
4676	Schmitt Helmut, O	z. V. 2. Sta.	—	261 328	—	28 967	30. 1. 34		
4677	Wirth Kurt	z. V. 2. Sta.	380 357	—	—	56 856	30. 1. 34		
4678	Dr. Krieger Richard	z. V. 62. Sta.	—	1 355 645	—	141 292	30. 1. 34		
4679	Cordemann Hermann	z. V. 6. Sta.	314 191	—	—	132 490	31. 1. 34		
4680	Steck Richard, ⊖	z. V. 3. Sta.	3 906	—	—	161 400	20. 2. 34		
4681	Dr. Baumann Friedrich	z. V. 3. Mo. Sta.	—	—	2 591 511	151 137	1. 3. 34		
4682	Peuck Johannes, O	z. V. 36. Sta.	469 690	—	—	8 835	11. 3. 34		
4683	Büscher Arnold, O	z. V. 28. Sta.	—	556 757	—	11 862	12. 3. 34		
4684	Pfister Heinz, O	z. V. 75. Sta.	373 222	—	—	18 751	20. 3. 34		
4685	Jähnel Georg, O	z. V. Ab. XXIII	346 889	—	—	11 154	22. 3. 34		
4686	Sauerborn Heinrich	z. V. 81. Sta.	426 818	—	—	7 688	25. 3. 34		
4687	Geiger Konrad, O	z. V. 79. Sta.	371 794	—	—	9 727	6. 4. 34		
4688	Rapp Jakob, O	z. V. 63. Sta.	—	884 490	—	24 454	6. 4. 34		
4689	Dr. Schönig Gustav	z. V. 75. Sta.	127 981	—	—	3 112	19. 4. 34		
4690	Baurteiß Willy, O	z. V. 6. Sta.	4 180	—	—	64	20. 4. 34		
4691	Kelder Johann, O	z. V. 20. Sta.	38 641	—	—	443	20. 4. 34		
4692	Hefmann Hans, O	z. V. 31. Sta.	14 084	—	—	685	20. 4. 34		
4693	Lambert Hans, O	z. V. 58. Sta.	13 483	—	—	724	20. 4. 34		
4694	Glitsch Herbert, O	z. V. 59. Sta.	2 265	—	—	857	20. 4. 34		
4695	Schmidt Ernst, O	z. V. 45. Sta.	40 975	—	—	979	20. 4. 34		
4696	Joachimsmeyer Willi, O	z. V. 20. Sta.	37 245	—	—	1 277	20. 4. 34		
4697	Schmuhl Willy, O	z. V. 47. Sta.	1 357	—	—	1 383	20. 4. 34		
4698	Gebhardt Hugo, O	z. V. 21. Sta.	56 650	—	—	1 384	20. 4. 34		
4699	Humbert Erich	z. V. 6. Sta.	38 598	—	—	1 909	20. 4. 34		
4700	Did Heinrich, O	z. V. 58. Sta.	62 635	—	—	1 624	20. 4. 34		
4701	Trübenbach Edmund, O	z. V. 14. Sta.	73 315	—	—	1 636	20. 4. 34		
4702	Schmitz Emil, O	z. V. 5. Sta.	100 313	—	—	1 847	20. 4. 34		
4703	Bretschneider Willy, O	z. V. 7. Sta.	18 364	—	—	1 862	20. 4. 34		
4704	Otto Edmund, O	z. V. 2. Sta.	18 911	—	—	1 886	20. 4. 34		
4705	Meinwurm Ewald, O	z. V. 58. Sta.	13 211	—	—	1 889	20. 4. 34		
4706	Kessing Wilhelm, O	z. V. 78. Sta.	168 685	—	—	1 998	20. 4. 34		
4707	Postulla Valentin, O	z. V. 45. Sta.	129 898	—	—	2 001	20. 4. 34		
4708	Wahl Ernst, O	z. V. 39. Sta.	176 887	—	—	2 157	20. 4. 34		
4709	Sonntag Erwin, O	z. V. 9. Sta.	41 358	—	—	2 200	20. 4. 34		
4710	Kneiß Otto, O	z. V. 56. Sta.	7 216	—	—	2 206	20. 4. 34		
4711	Umbau Helmuth, O	z. V. 56. Sta.	158 427	—	—	2 208	20. 4. 34		
4712	Laaser Hermann, O	z. V. 28. Sta.	96 999	—	—	2 238	20. 4. 34		
4713	Freund Hans, O	z. V. 35. Sta.	237 813	—	—	2 348	20. 4. 34		
4714	Holland Hermann, O	z. V. 58. Sta.	190 540	—	—	2 397	20. 4. 34		
4715	Söhn Hans, O	z. V. 20. Sta.	259 900	—	—	2 482	20. 4. 34		
4716	Kessing Hermann, O	z. V. 78. Sta.	132 414	—	—	2 543	20. 4. 34		
4717	Gosau Hans, O	z. V. 4. Sta.	73 866	—	—	2 546	20. 4. 34		
4718	Faehnkrich Felix, O	z. V. 15. Sta.	242 498	—	—	2 552	20. 4. 34		
4719	Klerk Heinrich, O	z. V. 3. Mo. Sta.	49 116	—	—	2 557	20. 4. 34		
4720	Wilhelm Eugen, O	z. V. 79. Sta.	111 763	—	—	2 582	20. 4. 34		
4721	Hoßfeld Walter, O	z. V. 3. Mo. Sta.	178 348	—	—	2 673	20. 4. 34		

The **1935** SS-Dienstalterliste showing a continuation of SS-Unterstürmführer recipients of the Totenkopf Ring.

Fragebogen

(Anlage zum Antrag auf Aufnahme in die Nationalsozialistische Deutsche Arbeiterpartei)

A

Vor- und Zuname (bei Frauen auch Mädchenname) Gerhard Frühauf

Beruf oder Art der Tätigkeit ¹): Kaufm. Lehrling im Einzelhandel

Wohnort ²): Hamburg 19   Wohnung: Ottersbeckallee   Straße/Platz Nr. 1

Geburtsort: Hamburg   Geburtsdatum: (Tag, Monat, Jahr) 12.7.18.

Staatsangehörigkeit: deutsch   Wenn staatenlos, frühere Staatsangehörigkeit : /

Sind Sie erbgesund? ja

Vor- und Zuname des Vaters: Wilhelm Aug. Chr. Frühauf

Geburtsort des Vaters: 16.8.77. Geburtsdatum des Vaters: (Tag, Monat, Jahr) Hamburg

Volkszugehörigkeit des Vaters: deutschland

Vor- und Zuname der Mutter: (Mädchenname) Maria Koch

Geburtsort der Mutter: Hamburg Geburtsdatum der Mutter: (Tag, Monat, Jahr) 12.11.83.

Volkszugehörigkeit der Mutter: deutschland

B

Familienstand: (ledig, verheiratet, verwitwet, geschieden) ledig

Vor- und Zuname des Ehegatten: (bei Frauen Mädchenname) -.- entfällt   entfällt

Geburtsort des Ehegatten: -.- Geburtszeit des Ehegatten: (Tag, Monat, Jahr)

Ist der Ehegatte frei von jüdischem oder farbigem Rasseeinschlag? -.- entfällt

Waren Sie früher mit einem nichtarischen Ehegatten verheiratet? nein -.- (entfällt)

Wodurch ist diese Ehe beendet worden? (Tod oder Scheidung) -.- entfällt

Wann? -.- Bei Scheidung, durch welches Gericht? -.- entfällt   entfällt

Sind Kinder aus dieser Ehe vorhanden? -.- entfällt   Wieviele? -.-

C

Haben Sie früher einer Freimaurerloge angehört? nein Welcher? -.- entfällt   entfällt

Tag des Eintritts? -.-   Tag des Austritts? -.- entfällt

Welches Amt und welchen Grad haben Sie in der Loge bekleidet? -.- entfällt

Haben Sie früher einer logenähnlichen Vereinigung (Odd Fellows und Druiden-Orden) oder einem entfällt

Geheimbund angehört? -.- Welcher oder welchem? -.- entfällt

Fragebogen (questionnaire). This document had to be satisfactorily filled out by anyone wishing to become a member of the NSDAP.

BIBLIOGRAPHY

THE ALLGEMEINE SS. Supreme Headquarters Allied Expeditionary Force Evaluation and Dissemination Section G-2 (Counter Intelligence Sub-Division); 1945.

ANGOLIA, JOHN R. LTC (RET). **CLOTH INSIGNIA OF THE NSDAP AND SA,** R. James Bender Publishing (San Jose, California; 1985).

ANGOLIA, JOHN R. LTC (RET). **FOR FUHRER AND FATHERLAND: VOLS. 1 AND 2,** R. James Bender Publishing (San Jose, Calif., USA; 1976 and 1978).

ANGOLIA, MAJOR JOHN R. ANGOLIA. **INSIGNIA OF THE THIRD REICH: Cloth Badges and Emblems,** Ducimus Books Ltd. (London; 1974).

ANGOLIA, JOHN R. LTC (RET). **ON THE FIELD OF HONOUR: A History of the Knight's Cross Bearers: VOLS. 1 and 2,** R. James Bender Publishing (San Jose, Calif., USA; 1980).

ANGOLIA, JOHN R LTC (RET). **SWORDS OF GERMANY 1900-1945,** R. James Bender Publishing (San Jose, Calif., USA; 1988).

BECK, PHILP. **ORADOUR: Village of the Dead,** Leo Cooper Ltd. (London; 1979).

BENDER, ROGER JAMES AND HUGH PAGE TAYLOR. **UNIFORMS ORGANIZATIONS AND HISTORY OF THE WAFFEN SS: VOLS. 1-5,** R. James Bender Publications (San Jose, California; 1969-1982).

BLUM, RALPH. **THE BOOK OF RUNES,** Eddison/Sadd Editions Ltd. (London).

BOWMAN, J. A. **THIRD REICH DAGGERS 1933-1945,** Imperial Publications (Lancaster, England; 1990).

BULLOCK, ALLAN. **HITLER: A STUDY IN TYRANNY,** The Hamlyn Publishing Group Ltd. (London; 1952).

CALIC, EDOUARD. **REINARD HEYDRICH,** Military Heritage Press (New York; 1982).

CHRONOLOGY OF THE SECOND WORLD WAR, Royal Institute of International Affairs, Oxford University Press (Great Britain; 1947).

COOPER MATTHEW. **THE GERMAN ARMY 1933-1945: Its Political and Military Failure,** Macdonald and Jane's (London; 1978).

COWDERY, RAY. **NAZI PARA-MILITARY ORGANIZATIONS AND THEIR BADGES,** Northstar Commemoratives, Inc. (Minneapolis, USA; 1985).

CRAIG, WILLIAM. **ENEMY AT THE GATES: The Battle for Stalingrad,** E.P. Dutton & Co. (London; 1973).

DEMETER, KARL. **THE GERMAN OFFICER-CORPS IN SOCIETY AND STATE 1650-1945,** Weidenfield and Nicolson Ltd. (London; 1965).

EISENHOWER, DWIGHT D. **CRUSADE IN EUROPE,** William Heinemann Ltd. (London; 1948).

ERTEL, HEINZ AND RICHARD SCHULZE-KOSSENS. **EUROPAISCHE FREIWILLIGE IM BILD,** Munin-Verlag (Osnabruck, Germany; 1986).

FOSTEN D.S.V. AND R.J. MARRION. **WAFFEN SS,** Almark Publications (England; 1971).

DIE GESTALTUND DER FESTE IN JAHRES UND LEBENSLAUF IN DER SS FAMILIE. Volkischer Verlag GMBH Druckerei (Wuppertal, Germany).

GRIEPENKERL, MAJOR-GENERAL. **LETTERS ON APPLIED TACTICS: TWENTY-FIVE TACTICAL EXERCISES DEALING WITH THE OPERATIONS OF SMALL DETACHED FORCES OF THE THREE ARMS**, (Translated from the 7th German edition by Karl von Donat), Hugh Rees, Ltd. (London; 1912).

HASTINGS, MAX. **DAS REICH: Resistance and the March of the 2nd SS Panzer Division through France, June 1944**, Michael Joseph Ltd. (London; 1981).

HAUSNER, GIDEON. **JUSTICE IN JERUSALEM: The Trial of Adolf Eichmann**, Thomas Nelson and Sons Ltd. (London; 1966).

HOESS, RUDOLF. **COMMANDANT OF AUSCHWITZ: The Autobiography of Rudolf Hoess**, Weidenfield and Nicolson (London; 1951).

HOHNE, HEINZ. **THE ORDER OF THE DEATH'S HEAD: The story of Hitler's SS**, (Translated from the German by Richard Barry from the title DER ORDEN UNTER DEM TOTENKOPF, Martin Secker & Warburg Ltd. 1969) Morrison & Gibb Ltd. (London; 1980).

KUNZMANN AND MILIUS. **FALLSCHIRMJAGER DER WAFFEN-SS IM BILD**, Munin Verlag (Osnabruck, Germany; 1986).

KRAUS, OTA AND KULKA, ERICH. **THE DEATH FACTORY: Document of Auschwitz**, Pergamon Press (London; 1966).

KEILIG, WOLF. **DAS DEUTSCHE HEER 1939-1945**, Oberkommando des Heeres, Podzun-Verlag (Bad Nauheim, Germany; 1945).

KITCHEN, MARTIN. **A MILITARY HISTORY OF GERMANY**, Weidenfield and Nicolson (London; 1975).

KLEINFELD, GERALD R. AND LEWIS A. TAMBS. **HITLER'S SPANISH LEGION: The Blue Division in Russia**, Southern Illinois University Press (USA; 1979).

LEHMANN, RUDOLF. **THE LEIBSTANDARTE: VOLS. 1 AND 2**, JJ Fedorowitz Publishing Co (Winnepeg, Canada; 1987 and 1989).

LITTLEJOHN, DAVID. **FOREIGN LEGIONS OF THE THIRD REICH: VOLS. 1 - 4**, R. James Bender Publishing (San Jose, Calif., USA; 1979).

LITTLEJOHN, DAVID. **HITLER YOUTH**, Agincourt Press (USA, 1988).

LITTLEJOHN AND DODKINS, **ORDERS, DECORATIONS, MEDALS AND BADGES OF THE THIRD REICH: VOLS. 1 AND 2**, R James Bender Publishing (San Jose, CA., USA; 1968).

MANN, GOLO. **THE HISTORY OF GERMANY SINCE 1789**, Chatto and Windus (London; 1984).

MANVELL, ROGER AND HEINRICH FRAENKEL. **HEINRICH HIMMLER**, William Heinemann Ltd. (London; 1965).

MILNER, L. **POLITICAL LEADERS OF THE NSDAP**, Almark Publications (England; 1972).

MICHAM, SAMUEL W. **HITLER'S LEGIONS: German Army Order of Battle World War II**, Leo Cooper in assoc. with Secker & Warburg (England; 1985).

MOLLO, ANDREW. **UNIFORMS OF THE SS: VOLS. 1-7**, Historial Research Unit (London; 1967-1976).

MUSMANNO, (Justice) MICHAEL A. **THE EICHMANN KOMMANDOS**, Peter Davies Ltd. (Altrincham, England; 1961).

PASSMORE, MICHAEL J. **SS PORCELAIN ALLACH**, T L O Publications

(England; 1972).

PADZWELL, KLAUS D. **DER TOTENKOPFRING**, (Germany; 1986).

REIDER, FREDERIC. **THE ORDER OF THE SS**: A Pictorial History, W. Foulsham & Co. Ltd. (England; 1981).

REITLINGER, GERALD. **THE FINAL SOLUTION: The attempt to Exterminate the Jews of Europe 1939-1945**, Vallentine, Mitchell & Co. Ltd, (London; 1953).

REITLINGER, GERALD. **THE SS: Alibi of a Nation 1922-1945**, Arms and Armour Press (London; 1981).

RUSSELL, STUART AND JOST W. SCHNIDER. **HEINRICH HIMMLER BURG: BILDCHRONIK DER SS SCHULE HAUS WEWELSBURG 1934-1945**, Verlag Heitz & Hoffkes (Essen, Germany; 1989).

SALAZAR, ALFRED. **THE NSDAP**, Imperial Publications (Lancaster, England; 1990).

SCHNEIDER, JOST W. **THEIR HONOUR WAS LOYALTY**, R. James Bender Publishing (San Jose, Calif., USA; 1977).

SCHULZE-KOSSENS, RICHARD. **MILITARISCHER FUHRERNACHWUCHS DER WAFFEN-SS: Die Junkerschulen**, Munin Verlag (Osnabruck, Germany; 1982).

SHIRER, WILLIAM L. **THE RISE AND FALL OF THE THIRD REICH**, Simon & Schuster (New York: 1960).

SNYDER, DR. LOUIS L. **ENCYCLOPEDIA OF THE THIRD REICH**, Blandford (London: 1976).

TAYLOR, A J P. **THE COURSE OF GERMAN HISTORY**, Hamish Hamilton (London; 1945).

TENENBAUM, JOSEPH. **RACE AND REICH: The Story of an Epoch**, Twayne Publishers (New York; 1956).

TOLAND, JOHN. **ADOLF HITLER**, Doubleday & Co., Inc. (New York; 1977).

TREVOR-ROPER, H.R, **THE BORMAN LETTER**, Weidenfield and Nicolson (London; 1954).

THE TRIAL OF GERMAN MAJOR WAR CRIMINALS: Proceedings of the International Military Tribual Sitting at Nurenburg Germany Volumes 1-22. Taken from the official transcript under the authority of HM Attorney-General by his Majesty's Stationery Office (London; 1947).

WEIDINGER, OTTO. **DAS REICH VOL I 1934-1939: 2nd SS Panzer Division Das Reich**, J J Fedorowicz Publishing (Winnepeg, Canada; 1990).

WENN ALLE BRUDER SCHWEIGEN (WHEN ALL OUR BROTHERS ARE SILENT): Published by the Association of Soldiers of the Former Waffen-SS, Munin Verlag (Osnabruck, Germany; 1973).

WHEELER-BENNETT, JOHN W. **THE NEMESIS OF POWER: The German Army in Politics 1918-1945**, Macmillan & Co. Ltd. (New York; 1953).

WILLIAMSON, GORDON. **THE IRON CROSS: A History 1813-1957**, Blandford Press (England; 1984).

WILMOT, CHESTER. **THE STRUGGLE FOR EUROPE**, Collins (London; 1952).

WYKES, ALAN. **HIMMLER**, Pan Ballantine (New York; 1971).